THE RACE FOR THE ÁRAS

The Author

Tom Reddy is a public relations consultant, former Cabinet Advisor, senior journalist with Independent Newspapers, screenwriter and author of the bestselling *Murder Will Out* and *The Murder File*.

THE RACE FOR THE ÁRAS

TOM REDDY

Gill & Macmillan

Gill & Macmillan
Hume Avenue, Park West, Dublin 12
with associated companies throughout the world
www.gillmacmillan.ie

© Tom Reddy 2012
978 0 7171 5343 5

Typography design by Make Communication
Print origination by Síofra Murphy
Printed in the UK by MPG Books Ltd, Cornwall

This book is typeset in Minion 11/13.5 pt.

The paper used in this book comes from the wood pulp
of managed forests. For every tree felled, at least one
tree is planted, thereby renewing natural resources.

A CIP catalogue record for this book is available from
the British Library.

5 4 3 2 1

CONTENTS

ACKNOWLEDGEMENTS

This book is dedicated to Erin and Austin for giving me all their support and valuable time to write this account.

I wish to pay tribute to the media. They acted in the public interest by asking the questions the electorate needed to have answered from the people who wanted to personify Ireland and our national identity over the next seven years.

Equally, I want to pay tribute to every candidate who aspired to be our ninth President, and to their families, friends and supporters.

Regardless of their political ideology, each candidate and would-be candidate held a vision about how they could improve and represent our country. They deserve credit in a time of great scepticism about politics, and about actors in public life, for their idealism and commitment.

My thanks, also, to everyone associated with the presidential electoral process and with the campaigns who spoke to me, both on and off the record.

Finally, thanks to Fergal Tobin of Gill & Macmillan for recognising the merit of publishing this account of the most fractious, dirty, entertaining and unpredictable election in the history of the state.

Chapter 1 ～

| THE RACE

In the dead heat of Beirut a team of armed Irish soldiers, wearing the sky-blue berets of the United Nations, waited in a jeep outside the international airport for the courier to arrive from Dublin.

Dressed anonymously in civilian clothing, the courier had flown on connecting commercial flights from the Defence Forces Human Resources Department in Newbridge, Co. Kildare, to the Middle East carrying a bundle of five hundred envelopes, each containing a ballot paper.

The courier had kept the precious parcel of papers in carry-on hand luggage, rather than risk putting them in the hold, where they might be sent on to the wrong destination. From Beirut his escort drove him south over dusty roads to the UNIFIL base in Tibnin, Lebanon, where 450 Irish soldiers were on peacekeeping duties, each one empowered to vote for the next supreme commander of the Defence Forces.

The same courier would visit other Irish missions in the region to deliver voting papers and then collect the sealed ballots. At the same time another eight couriers from Defence Forces Headquarters would travel to other far-flung corners of the globe to ensure that the constitutional right of Irish soldiers to vote would be fulfilled.

The other places the couriers travelled to included Kosovo, Uganda, Western Sahara, Côte d'Ivoire and Democratic Republic of Congo. An armed escort also met the courier when he arrived in Afghanistan, another extremely dangerous overseas post.

In September each year members of the Defence Forces must fill out form RFC so that they can receive a postal vote. As the presidential election loomed, the Defence Forces Human Resources Office liaised with each constituency returning officer to collect a postal vote for every soldier serving overseas. These ballot papers were forwarded to the Human Resources Office in Mobhí Road in Glasnevin, where they were sorted by country and allocated to the different couriers.

Because there is no postal service in some of the countries in which Irish soldiers serve with the United Nations, the Department of Defence sought quotes from two transnational courier services for delivering and collecting ballots from around the world. However, neither company could provide a service in Bihanga in Uganda or in Democratic Republic of Congo unless they sent individual couriers. However, the quote for a commercial courier was far in excess of the cost of sending a team of their own Defence Forces couriers from Ireland.

While the country would vote on 27 October, soldiers on overseas missions, to accommodate airline schedules, voted as soon as they were given their ballot paper.

In Lebanon, the largest overseas Irish mission, the courier based himself in the village of Tibnin, where he distributed more than four hundred postal votes. He then collected the marked ballot papers and flew back to Dublin, having built time in to his schedule for flight delays or other unforeseen circumstances.

The couriers kept their bundles of votes on their laps during each flight. Once through Customs they would post the hundreds of votes in the postbox in Terminal 1, or in the main concourse in Terminal 2, entrusting the votes that had travelled thousands of miles into the care of An Post, which would deliver them to returning officers in every constituency in the country.

————

In the blizzard of official forms issued by the state every year, the innocuously named PR1 is very exclusive and, were it available, would be a collector's item. It is used to record the results of the count in each constituency for the presidential election, and each one is issued exclusively to the local returning officers in each of the forty-three constituencies. It is designed to ensure authenticity in recording and reporting the official result from every presidential poll taken throughout the country.

The officials who conduct the counts would enter the poll figures on form PR1, and the contents would be verified by the local returning officer, who, once satisfied, then signed the form.

For the first count in 2011 some forms would be faxed, and for the first time the others would be scanned and emailed to the national count centre, established in the Old Printing Works in the Lower Yard of Dublin Castle.

Four fax machines, a bank of land lines and computers set up with spreadsheets were at the nerve centre of the national count. As explained by Barry Ryan of the Office of the Presidential Returning Officer, to ensure accuracy, and to counter any possible security breach, the results, faxed or emailed, were confirmed with the local returning officers by phone.

The count centre was in a room beside the press and reception centre, which was draped tastefully in curtains with four banks of work stations. There were a number of mini-stages for television cameras and press photographers. Around the windowless room, the size of half a football pitch, plasma screens hung from the walls displaying results of every count as they arrived from each constituency.

The 2011 election was only the second time that votes would be counted in the constituency in which they were cast and then collated at a national count centre. The new system was established in 1997, but there was no poll in 2004, as the incumbent, Mary McAleese, was returned without contest.

At the previous presidential election, in 1990, ballot boxes filled with the country's votes were driven to the RDS show hall in Ballsbridge, which was established as the national count centre, with corrals for each constituency count centre, sorting boxes, storage areas, central stages and a press centre. But in 1993 legislation was introduced that decentralised the counting, capitalising on the long experience and the expertise of each constituency in conducting organised counts for local and national elections.

The polling of 27 October 2011 had its own logistical characteristics. The presidential election—the contest for the post of guardian of the Constitution of Ireland—would be voted on at the same time as two proposed constitutional amendments, one relating to providing extra powers of investigation to politicians, the other to allowing judges' pay to be regulated in line with other public officials. In the Dublin West constituency a by-election would also be held to fill the seat of the late Brian Lenihan (junior) of Fianna Fáil.

The count centres throughout the country would open at 9 a.m. The first task of the teams of approximately forty counters supervised by local returning officers in each constituency was to sort the three different papers: the two referendums for constitutional amendments (blue for the Oireachtas inquiries referendum and green for the judges' pay referendum) and the white paper for the presidential poll, which had colour photographs of each of the seven candidates.

For tallymen—the dedicated party supporters who would volunteer a day and a night, and a promise for the following days if needed—this initial sorting process was slow, something that allowed them extra time to observe and estimate first and sometimes second preferences. In a general election a skilled tallyman, particularly in provincial areas, would almost be able to identify each vote as it was turned out onto the table. That level of detail—necessary in a general election for political parties to be able to identify weak and strong areas, turned votes and new votes—was unnecessary in a presidential election. This was a straightforward race, so only number 1s would be important if there was a landslide. However, preferences would be vital in deciding the outcome if candidates were grouping together with similar poll figures.

The presidential poll is the simplest and fastest to count of all elections. More than 3.1 million people were eligible to vote in the 2011 presidential election. The ballot papers would be sorted according to first preferences and the result sent by the local returning officer on form PR1 to the national count centre.

The presidential returning officer compiles all the figures and calculates the quota a candidate must reach to be elected. With only one position to fill, the quota is 50 per cent of the valid votes plus one. If a candidate receives a number of votes equal to or greater than the quota, they will be declared elected. However, if no candidate reaches the quota on the first count, the presidential returning officer will direct the local returning officers to eliminate the candidate with the lowest number of national first-preference votes. Those ballot papers are then scrutinised and the next available preferences on those papers are allocated to the remaining candidates, and this is followed by a second count.

If at the end of any count the sum of the votes of two or more of the lowest candidates is less than those of the next-highest continuing candidate, the returning officer must exclude those two or more candidates. However, this provision takes effect only if the multiple exclusion does not affect a candidate's chances of achieving more than a quarter of the quota, which would allow them to recoup their election expenses.

The Electoral (Amendment) Act (2011) limits expenditure by a candidate for the presidential election to €750,000. However, the clock on election expenditure starts ticking only after the Minister for the Environment makes the Presidential Election Order. Candidates who enter the field early are free to expend any sums of money or assets they have or have garnered before the minister's order is put into effect.

An election agent appointed by the candidate, or the candidate themselves, must account for all spending on the campaign and must provide a statement of those expenses to the Standards in Public Office Commission. A copy of this statement is then laid before each house of the Oireachtas, formally putting the information in the public domain.

The same legislation allows for candidates who receive more than a quarter of the quota to apply for reimbursement of their expenses of up to €200,000, funded by the taxpayer.

While it is unlikely that all the preferences of an eliminated candidate will transfer to one candidate, the presidential returning officer will always consider the possibility that a candidate might reach (or exceed) a quarter of the quota. As explained by Barry Ryan, if there is a possibility that a candidate might qualify to receive campaign expenses, they may well merit a separate count rather than be included in a block elimination.

Candidates are also entitled to be represented at each count centre—a real possibility for a political party nominee but less likely for an independent candidate without a national organisation. These agents are also empowered to ask for a recount of the ballot papers in their local count centre. At the national level a candidate or their agent can ask for a national recount. However, they may seek this only once during the counting process.

A further appeal, to dispute the result of the election, is available by way of petition to the High Court, presented by the Director of Public Prosecutions on behalf of a candidate or an election agent. The High Court, having considered the case, could order that the votes be recounted, or the poll taken again, in any constituency, or could declare the election void. In such a case a new election would have to be held. The High Court's decision is final, subject only to appeal to the Supreme Court on a question of law.

———

Once elected to office, the President has very few powers. Though some are significant, they may be used only rarely.

The office of President was established by the Constitution of Ireland in 1937. The President takes precedence over all other persons in the state, and exercises powers and functions conferred by the Constitution and by law.

The main function of the President is to scrutinise legislation. After consultation with the Council of State, the President may decide to refer a bill that has been passed by both houses of the Oireachtas to the Supreme Court for a decision on its constitutionality. However, if a majority of the Seanad, and at least a third of the Dáil, form a petition, the President, following consultation with the Council of State, may decline to sign a bill until the will of the people has been ascertained by referendum or general election.

Other tasks that fall to the President, rarely but significantly, are the appointment of the Taoiseach on the nomination of the Dáil, the appointment of the other members of the Government on the nomination of the Taoiseach with the previous approval of the Dáil, and the acceptance of the resignation or termination of the appointment of a member of the Government on the advice of the Taoiseach.

The President can summon or dissolve the Dáil on the advice of the Taoiseach but may refuse to dissolve it on the advice of a Taoiseach who has ceased to retain the support of a majority in the Dáil. In addition, the President can exercise the right of pardon, has the power to remit punishment imposed by a court of criminal jurisdiction and, following consultation with the Council of State, can communicate with the houses of the Oireachtas on a matter of national or public importance or address a message to the people.

While the President holds the highest office in the land, and is not answerable to either house of the Oireachtas or to any court, a safeguard is built in to the Constitution that provides a procedure for impeaching the President for stated misbehaviour.

The two previous holders of the office, Mary Robinson and Mary McAleese, stretched the influence and significance of the office by publicly associating it with their presidential themes. Mary Robinson had dramatically drawn to the attention of the world the plight of people in famine-ravaged Somalia and later to the victims of the Rwandan genocide. The work of Mary McAleese and that of her husband, Martin, in fostering North-South relations during her tenure reflected her original campaign theme of building bridges.

Governments have had every day of their tenure recorded and analysed by the media as they enjoyed or coped with controversy. Presidents, as non-political entities, have for the most part avoided controversy; but when controversy hit, it hit hard, at the office and the office-holder. The television presenter Pat Kenny would later say that media scrutiny of candidates was justified, as it would draw attention to, inform about or provide an insight into how a presidential candidate might react in the face of intense political pressure.

Controversies, some of national import, marked some of the occupants of the Áras. Dr Douglas Hyde, the country's first President and the first poet in the Park, was expelled from the GAA for attending a rugby match in his official capacity. His funeral service in St Patrick's Cathedral, Dublin, was not attended by members of the coalition Government, because of the edict of the Archbishop of Dublin, John Charles McQuaid, forbidding any Catholic attendance at a Protestant service. Instead, ministers sat sanctimoniously and ostentatiously in their cars outside the cathedral as his soul was commended to God.

The mild-mannered Erskine Childers contested the 1973 election and won the race despite the Fine Gael candidate being the favourite, having been a keen contender in the previous election against Éamon de Valera. However, there was tension between his office and the Government led by Liam Cosgrave after they rejected his proposal to establish a think-tank in the Áras—a proposal that was probably before its time.

After the untimely death in office of Childers, Fianna Fáil proposed Cearbhall Ó Dálaigh, a former Chief Justice, as its candidate. There was no opposition to his candidacy. The news editor of the *Irish Independent*, Don Lavery, recalled what was supposed to be a routine 'marking' or 'job' for him as a young reporter on the *Westmeath Examiner* at Columb Barracks, Mullingar, on Monday 18 October 1976. Loyalist bombs had caused mass murder in Dublin and Monaghan, and the IRA had murdered the British ambassador and a garda in a booby-trap bomb. The Government responded by proposing to give the Gardaí more powers in an Emergency Powers Bill. President Ó Dálaigh referred the proposed law to the Supreme Court, angering some members of the Government. The Minister for Defence, Paddy Donegan, who was formally opening a canteen in Columb Barracks, didn't deliver the speech he had brought with him.

> He stood up, and threw it down on the table in front of me. Looking at me, he said: 'I'll give you some news for the press.'
>
> I took down his remarks in shorthand as he criticised Ó Dálaigh for sending the bill to the Supreme Court. Asking why he had not sent other aspects of anti-IRA laws to the court, Donegan said: 'In my opinion he is a thundering disgrace.'
>
> A friend, an Army officer, kicked me on the shin in case I had missed the importance of the remark. I hadn't. Donegan had insulted the Supreme Commander of the Defence Forces in a room full of commissioned officers. The words used were 'thundering disgrace'—not 'f**ing disgrace' or any other phrase. Donegan was not drunk. He had been quite definite in what he wanted to say.

Lavery's report caused a political storm. Ó Dálaigh demanded the minister's resignation. Donegan offered it, but the Taoiseach, Liam Cosgrave, refused to accept it, so Ó Dálaigh resigned, becoming the only President to resign in office. The bill was subsequently found to be constitutional.

Paddy Hillery from Co. Clare, vice-president of the European Commission and a former Fianna Fáil TD and firebrand with a quiet humour, was pressured by the party leader, Jack Lynch, into accepting the role of President without a contest. He accepted; on taking up a second term he remarked that it was his reward for 'good behaviour' and effectually 'doubled' his sentence in the Park. It was a position he had never wanted, but his steely determination and low-key approach reasserted the authority of the office.

———

On Thursday 10 November 2011, the eve of the inauguration of her successor, President McAleese carried out her last official function in Dublin. Months earlier she had responded to a letter from the Society of St Vincent de Paul asking her to formally open a renovated block of long-term accommodation units for homeless men. The renovation cost €800,000 and was financed in full by the society. It provides permanent accommodation and support for eighteen people whose physical or mental health means that they cannot live independently.

According to Larry Toumey and Tommy O'Reilly, speaking at the Back Lane Hostel in the Liberties of Dublin, 'we invited her, but she named the day. She pointed out that it would be her last engagement, and she wanted it to be here.' At the event, where there was music and poetry, the President said, 'This place is evidence that love exists.' After unveiling the plaque she spoke to the small media posse, recording her last formal engagement. Was it a sad day? 'If you give me two seconds, I'll be in floods of tears, but I don't want to do that in public!'

She went on to pay tribute to the team who had worked with her over the years in the Áras. She was asked if she had any advice for the next President. 'Oh, just to enjoy it,' she replied. 'Enjoy being President. I woke up every morning full of joy. I loved every day on the job.'

That morning's *Irish Independent* editorialised under the headline 'McAleese leaves a remarkable legacy.'

The outstanding achievement of the McAleese presidency has been the improvement in North-South and British-Irish relations. Northern Ireland is now experiencing by far the most stable and peaceful period in its history while, after almost 90 years of independence, British-Irish relations have finally matured.

While many others can also claim some of the credit for these developments, there is little doubt that President McAleese and her husband Martin played a key role. Throughout her presidency the two of them have worked tirelessly to build bridges between North and South. The seeds planted by the couple will continue to bear fruit for generations to come.

In the *Irish Times* the political correspondent Deaglán de Bréadún provided analysis, saying that President McAleese defied easy categorisation.

. . . Her arrival in the Áras was seen by some commentators as the end of liberalism in Ireland, given the new head of State's conservative record on divorce, contraception and abortion. But she supported the

decriminalisation of homosexuality and caused a major shake-up in the
Catholic Church when she took Communion at a Church of Ireland service
in Dublin's Christ Church Cathedral.

There are few politicians anywhere who could spend 14 years in office
and end up more popular than when they started. The difference between
McAleese and the others is that she is richly endowed with emotional
intelligence . . .

It is too early to say what her place in history will be, but she will
certainly have one.

With only a few days of her Presidency left, McAleese invited the President-
elect and his family to the Áras for lunch (black sole and lemon soufflé with
Phoenix Park raspberries) and a tour of the building, including a visit to the
family quarters, which ended with a private discussion between the President
and her successor.

Perhaps Miriam Lord, who had just won the inaugural National
Newspapers of Ireland Award for her political reporting, on the same page in
the *Irish Times* summed up the country's warmth and great love for President
McAleese. As Lord waited with other journalists for the first citizen to usher in
the President-in-waiting and other guests,

nobody said a word. The atmosphere was hushed and a tad tense. Then a
door opened and the woman of the House came bustling from a side room
with a cheery, 'Good morning to you all!'

She wore an elegant crimson suit, but nobody would have been
surprised had Mary McAleese emerged wiping floury hands on a floral
apron. We imagined a Victoria sponge cake cooling on a wire rack in
readiness for the visitors.

Everyone relaxed. If you're an Irish President come into the parlour.
There's a welcome there for you . . .

Chapter 2 ∿

| THE RUNNERS

'I had to be absolutely whiter than white,' said Senator David Norris, talking about his sex life in Ireland.

My private life and my sexual life were lived in Israel, and here I was a nun. So, I'm used to it. I had people throwing themselves at me because I was the little tin god in the gay community here; it was nothing to do with my looks, it was that I was the champion [of gay rights].

In cold print, the 65-year-old was laying bare his sex life. It was a portent of the type of media scrutiny all candidates would go through. But only Norris was quizzed about his sex life.

Almost two years before polling in the presidential election, potential candidates and the political parties would start flying kites about who might and might not run for the Park. In political circles it was generally accepted that the party grandees Bertie Ahern, Michael D. Higgins and John Bruton were likely candidates. The name of the Fine Gael MEP Mairead McGuinness had popped up in speculation in the media alongside the former Fianna Fáil minister Mary O'Rourke and the independent senator David Norris.

Over the next year political parties and individual candidates would lick their finger, hold it up to the prevailing political wind and see if it was a fair or foul wind blowing in their direction, without committing themselves and risking the ridicule of rejection.

Months before serious political heavy-hitters began to emerge for the race, a sports columnist in the *Irish Times* would suggest Ted Walsh—the former amateur jockey and Cheltenham winner and now a trainer and television race commentator—as a good tenant for the Áras. Walsh had trained Papillon to win the Grand National in 2000 and Commanche Court to win the Irish Grand National, both horses piloted by his son Ruby. Worthy candidates would be proposed throughout the campaign, some serious, some humorous, all offering the Áras as a reward for some service. According to the *Irish Times* article,

> the Walsh clan are what this island is all about. If you heard them with Marian Finucane [on her radio chat show] on Saturday you'd have cheered. The Áras doesn't need another lawyer. God knows, the world doesn't need another lawyer in it. The Áras needs the Walsh dynasty. Just hand over a couple of hundred acres of the Park for training the horses and let Ted get on with life as usual, but have him introduced everywhere as the President of Ireland. That would be a country you'd want to come and visit, wouldn't it?

In April 2010 Fergus Finlay, the former Labour Party spin doctor and *chef de cabinet* to the Tánaiste, Dick Spring, in the coalition Government with Fianna Fáil (1993–7), went public about his presidential aspirations. He told Sam Smyth of the *Irish Independent*: 'I'd be very tempted to have a go at something like that. My gut says "yes," but I'm not 100 per cent sure how to express that eloquently.' Finlay, a strategist in Mary Robinson's election campaign, added: 'I would like the presidential election to be about the values we hold and where we would like our country to go.'

Finlay's appearance as a possible candidate just days before the Labour Party's annual conference provided delegates with another name to conjure with for the Áras. Finlay had a high media profile, with columns in the *Evening Herald* and the *Examiner* and a diary on RTE's 'Drivetime' programme. Apart from his role as CEO of Barnardo's he was also chairperson of Volunteering Ireland and the Dolphin House Redevelopment Board and served as a former chairperson of Special Olympics, Ireland. If selected as a candidate he would have a strong appeal among the disadvantaged, NGO, voluntary and caring professions and their families.

The newspaper report added fuel to the fire of speculation about who would be running for the Presidency. The Labour Party leader, Eamon Gilmore, confirmed that the party's National Executive had discussed running a presidential candidate—but they hadn't yet considered any candidate.

According to the former diplomat and journalist Eamon Delaney in that weekend's *Sunday Independent,* the most surprising development must be Fergus Finlay throwing his well thumbed hat into the ring as the Labour choice, given that Michael D. Higgins had already expressed an interest. Neither has made any thrusting commitment, of course, but have merely 'indicated that they would consider a candidacy if invited.' How noble of them.

Providing context for the emergence of a flurry of candidates, he continued:

Another FF contender, Senator Mary White, does not have the same electoral form [as Brian Crowley MEP], but she is a plucky personality and the appeal of the presidential contest is that previous electoral form, or lack of it, is not a prerequisite. Mary O'Rourke has also been spoken of, perhaps providing just the kind of soothing mammy that we need in these times of stress.

Finlay's emergence is a big surprise and cannot have pleased Michael D. He has the support of some of the Labour old guard, including Dick Spring. But Finlay's 'offer' to run is also a surprise given his abrasiveness . . . He would not shy away from picking a fight with the government of the day, even if it included Labour. It is also hard to see him mastering the glad handing necessary to get elected, but then the same was said of Mary Robinson . . .

Among the other independents interested is senator David Norris, who would be an inspired choice: cerebral and spirited, with original things to say about life and society. At least that's my opinion: I don't know how he'd go down in Hackballscross.

As far back as March 2010 John Lee of the *Irish Mail on Sunday* reported on the 'battle royal' that was about to take place after John Bruton emerged as firm favourite to be the Fine Gael candidate. There were no comments about the speculation from Bruton, who allowed the rumour to run unhindered by denial. 'The matter has been discussed and I think that John Bruton would make an excellent President,' said Lucinda Creighton, the Dublin South-East TD who would go on to become Minister for European Affairs. Damien English, a Fine Gael TD from Co. Meath, also voiced his support, saying that Bruton was highly regarded internationally and that 'he would be a fabulous candidate.' One Dublin TD was quoted as saying, 'John is hugely underrated here, but he is widely respected in the international community.'

The report suggested that the speculation about and emergence of Bruton would scupper any chance for Mairead McGuinness MEP, also from Co. Meath.

Media speculation at the time suggested that another likely candidate would be Michael D. Higgins of the Labour Party, and that Fianna Fáil would be looking at the long-time aspirant and top Munster vote-catcher Brian Crowley MEP and the three-time general election winner and former Taoiseach Bertie Ahern.

Bruton had been appointed vice-president of the party in 2009, when another former leader, Alan Dukes, stood aside when he was appointed the public interest director of the failed Anglo Irish Bank by the Fianna Fáil-Green Government. Ironically it was a poor performance in the 1990 presidential election for Fine Gael's candidate, Austin Currie (who finished third), that propelled Bruton unchallenged into the leadership of Fine Gael after Alan Dukes was forced to resign.

As chairman of the International Financial Services Centre, Bruton had issued a number of significant statements on the country's economic status, including a populist attack on the European Central Bank for failing to act as financial crisis engulfed the country. He also issued a statement defending religious education—himself a former pupil of the exclusive Clongowes Wood College. Inevitably, this sudden flurry of media activity was viewed by politicians and those who commented on them as an attempt to raise his profile as the party began considering potential candidates.

Bruton (62), was first elected to the Dáil for Meath in 1969 and held the seat until 2004, when he was appointed the first EU ambassador to the United States for five years. A former vice-president of the European People's Party, he comes from a wealthy farming background in Dunboyne.

As potential candidates emerged or faded during the following eighteen months, it became clearer that this campaign was going to be different from every other race for the Áras.

David Norris, photographed as he perched on a library step-ladder, gave a telling interview to Jason O'Toole of the *Mail on Sunday* in the same month, revealing his intention to run for the Park. Norris, a Joycean scholar, was dressed in his trademark pinstripe suit, striped tie and highly polished brogues. He said he had been approached by 'at least two' of the political parties to sound out whether he would run for them, but he said he would do so only if he could retain his independent status. Admitting that he'd like a nomination from members of the Oireachtas, he said he wouldn't rule out a nomination from Sinn Féin.

Outgoing, gregarious, outrageous in speech and manner, Norris was always willing to play up for press photographers. He seemed invariably jolly and was held in warm regard by the media for his willingness to provide provocative comment.

In May 2010 he told the *Irish Mail on Sunday* about his break-up with his long-term lover, Ezra Yizhak Nawi, an Israeli Jew, who he met in a gay bar in Dublin in the 1970s. 'I thought I was going to suffocate from the misery,' he said. Norris finally broke with him after having turned a blind eye to his partner's promiscuous behaviour and after a succession of break-ups and make-ups.

> Jewish people are very practical. And sex is just an appetite, like food, and, as far as Ezra was concerned, if I wasn't there to make him lunch he'd have a sandwich! So, there were always these 23-year-old Palestinian football players hanging around. One of them moved in, so I moved out.
>
> As far as I was concerned, it was a totally monogamous relationship. I was the little starry eyed Irish romantic. I thought it was the same with Ezra.

Norris had just publicly declared his intention to seek a nomination for Áras an Uachtaráin, preferably from the Labour Party.

The *Mail on Sunday* was a missed opportunity to clear up some of his forgotten and ambiguous past, long before electors focused on the candidates. It could have cleared the decks, allowing him to prepare for a tough political campaign that would microscopically examine his past and his past pronouncements.

On tv3 in August he spoke frankly with the host, Ursula Halligan.

> I am not a 'queer'. Young people want to use that word? Fine. Not me. I will be a fairy, not a queer. And I will not be addressed as one.

He described the Catholic Church as the greatest source of homophobia in the country, saying that gay love was still outlawed. Halligan suggested that he didn't have the support either of Oireachtas members or of county councils for getting onto the ticket. He responded in typical cheery fashion: 'Aha, well, watch this space!'

He also spoke about how he had found his mother dead in her bed, and he revealed that he had his own gravestone prepared for a cemetery in Co. Laois where his great-grandfathers are buried. 'I lay down on it to see what it was like,' he said. 'Lovely!'

Norris had also discussed his homosexuality, in some detail, with Ryan Tubridy on 'The Late Late Show' a short time before.

> I haven't been wildly promiscuous. I've had about three serious relationships, and I love every single one of them, particularly Ezra, my plumber. I always say to him when the witching hour comes, 'Now, honey, off you go, guest quarters.' We have a loving relationship, but it's not intimate in that sense.

His frank comments were to prompt questions. Why did he feel the need to go into such detail? He was the most famous gay person in the country, and probably in Irish history, after Oscar Wilde. So why should his bedroom habits become part of the national discourse about the Presidency? Who would ever have prompted a discussion about the bedroom habits of the present or former incumbents?

The columnist Jennifer O'Connell in the *Sunday Business Post* perhaps put her finger on the pulse of the issue.

Tubridy would probably have fallen off his chair if a straight male candidate for the presidency had started talking about how many sexual partners he'd had. He'd certainly have collapsed in a puddle if one of the Marys had felt the need to share such intimacies . . . He [Norris] is a savvy political operator. He understood instinctively that, however much he might wish it wasn't still the case, his homosexuality would very likely be an issue for some people, so it was better to just get it out there.

She concluded the article: 'Norris for the Áras? Yes, please.'

Perhaps it was an issue that was an overriding concern for Norris. He was, after all, as well known for campaigning for gay rights as he was for being a Joycean scholar, a Trinity College lecturer and senator. But a soft-focus appearance on the country's biggest television programme and in a Sunday newspaper interview splashed over two pages should have been enough to put a character point, and not presumably a presidential campaign issue, in the public domain. It should have been definitive and have drawn a line under the issue. But loquaciousness and a willingness to engage with the media were personality traits that would lead his campaign into trouble again and again.

In August 2010 Norris was photographed in his house, which he had bought thirty-two years earlier, in North Great George's Street, Dublin. Gradually he had lovingly restored the four-storey Georgian townhouse, and he showed the 'Life' supplement of the *Sunday Independent* around its expensively renovated and furnished interior.

He told Mary O'Sullivan that he hadn't thought about running for the Áras until a newspaper reporter rang him, asked him his intention and told him about a web site with 879 people offering their support.

I didn't come up with the idea myself, but I would certainly do my best to deserve it and to fulfil it in the best possible way. In the piece the journalist published, he said the odds on me were 50 to one. I thought 'good odds' and went down two days later to Paddy Power where I found I was 20 to one. Now I'm five to two and there are nearly 27,000 on the combined web sites in favour of me.

The odds of his winning a nomination were stacked against him, he claimed, and he appealed to the political parties to take the whip off county councils, 'out of decency,' so that he could seek a nomination.

> Virtually anyone else being elected would not be news internationally. My election would be a global news item. I would be the first head of state to be openly gay. People have known I'm gay for 40 years; they've had time to get over it. On the other hand every channel in North America would cover it and I'm a sufficiently wily old bird to deal with the questions, park them and sell Ireland like no one's business.

Like Jennifer O'Connell before her, Mary O'Sullivan was charmed by Norris. 'This man is made to be President. Vote number one David Norris,' she concluded her article.

On the same day the news pages of the *Sunday Tribune* carried a picture of the current affairs presenter of RTE's 'Prime Time', Miriam O'Callaghan, and reported her as a possible candidate for a nomination by the political parties. Her brother Jim, a barrister, is a Fianna Fáil Dublin city councillor. However, she is politically non-aligned. She said she had not been approached by

> any political party in relation to the upcoming presidential election. You are just one of quite a number of people who have contacted me in the past few weeks on this issue; a number of radio stations also called. At the moment I am just busy focusing on my job, my charity work and my family.

The *Tribune* also reported that Brian Crowley MEP was seen as the most likely Fianna Fáil candidate, while Michael D. Higgins or Fergus Finlay were likely Labour Party contenders. The sitting MEPs Mairead McGuinness and Seán Kelly, a former GAA official, were being mooted as possible Fine Gael candidates. Among the likely independent field, Senator David Norris, Seán O'Callaghan and the chairperson of the Special Olympics, Mary Davis, were 'seen as credible options.'

The following afternoon Finlay was in Dublin city centre attending a meeting. He returned to his car to find that the passenger window had been smashed and the contents of the car stolen. As he tidied up, his mobile phone began hopping as text after text came in congratulating him on being elected President of Ireland! According to Finlay, at first I thought I was the victim of some elaborate practical joke. But it transpired that Joe Duffy's 'Liveline' programme had just finished conducting a poll. After about ten thousand people had phoned in to the programme and eight or nine distinguished people had been eliminated, the show's listeners had decided that I should be given the responsibility.

In fact the programme had received 16,000 text messages offering their preferences for possible candidates, including Bertie Ahern, John Bruton, Brian Crowley, Fergus Finlay, Michael D. Higgins, David Norris, Feargal Quinn and the Ombudsman, Emily O'Reilly.

Finlay's party colleague, Higgins, bucked the trend, surviving the round-by-round cull as politicians were eliminated first. O'Reilly and Finlay went through to the final run-off, where Finlay triumphed by five hundred votes. He didn't specifically reveal his intentions, but he said that

the great thing about yesterday's poll (apart from the winner, naturally) is that it will encourage more and more people to take part in the debate. At the end, the important thing is not who you vote for—it is to get out, get involved, and start demanding change.

On 9 September he wrote a half-page article for the *Herald* with the headline 'President of Ireland? Yeah, I've decided to go for it. Here's why.' This headline (which he didn't write) may have seemed casual or flippant, but his intention was clear, firmly focused on winning the nomination and the Áras. He wrote of the decade of wealth the country had enjoyed, but he questioned its legacy. Society was still damaged by divisions and inequality, there had been political failures and a banking crisis, and after a decade of wealth all that seemed to be left was public anger, frustration and 'crumbling schools and overcrowded hospitals.'

The election is a good bit away for sure. But the time has come for us all to start discussing and debating what the presidency could and should mean to the people of Ireland, and how we can use it to start charting a new direction for ourselves.

That's the main reason I've decided to put myself forward for a nomination within my own party, the Labour Party. I know it's really early. But I think there's a great opportunity now for an open and vigorous debate about the issues involved. I'd love to see a debate about the values that should inform our entire approach—the message we should take to the people, and how we should set about winning this crucial election with a professional and committed campaign.

In light of everything that has happened in the last few years in Ireland, it has never been more important that the people be given a real choice about what kind of spirit should inform our politics in the years ahead.

That weekend's *Sunday Independent* published the results of an opinion poll by Quantum Research featuring three declared candidates and five speculative candidates. It would give comfort to Finlay.

Norris topped the poll, with 28 per cent, a figure he was to hover around in future polls; Finlay, who had declared only a few days earlier, took a creditable 20 per cent; Higgins polled 11 per cent; Davis and McGuinness 9 per cent; Ahern 7 per cent; and Mary O'Rourke 6 per cent.

In the middle of October, President Mary McAleese honoured five people who between them had given 105 years of voluntary service to the Gaisce Awards when she presented them with an inaugural Dr Patrick Hillery Medal. This award was introduced to honour people who had given twenty-one years of service, and it marked the twenty-fifth anniversary of the foundation of the youth awards. It commemorates its founder and former President of Ireland. President McAleese explained its genesis: 'Dr Hillery set up the Gaisce awards at a time when Ireland was in the throes of a very deep recession, but rather than bow to it he saw this as a challenge to build a bridge to a certain kind of future.'

On the same day in Brussels, Mary Davis was meeting the president of the European Council, Herman van Rompuy, to greet the arrival of the 'Flame of Hope' en route to the start of the European Special Olympics in Poland at the weekend. Davis acknowledged to reporters covering the event that she had been approached by supporters encouraging her to put her name forward for the Presidency. She explained:

> Life is hectic for me at the moment. Yes, a lot of people have approached me that would have worked with me in the past . . . Obviously when I organised the games in 2003 with thirty thousand volunteers, many of whom stay in touch and are all texting me, encouraging me all the way . . . but we'll see. I'm busy at the moment.

The European correspondent of the *Irish Times*, Arthur Beasley, filled in some background, reporting that she had been mooted as a possible Labour Party candidate six years ago but ruled herself out. 'When it was put to her that she was not ruling herself out now, she said: "I never rule myself out of anything . . . I'm just a go-getter through and through."'

Davis would later say that, as she travelled around the country in her Special Olympics role, dozens and dozens of people had urged her to go forward for the Presidency. 'It hadn't occurred to me up until then,' she recalled. However, she took time to think and to consult an informal kitchen cabinet of advisers about the consequences of a bid, what was required to be a candidate, who would make up her campaign team, how to raise finance, what the job required and, most importantly of all, whether it was feasible for an independent to take on the a political party nominee.

A few days later the former Fine Gael leader and Taoiseach John Bruton was interviewed on RTE's 'Drivetime' radio programme by Mary Wilson. He addressed the issue of motive.

> There is too much tendency in Ireland to look for other motives behind what people are doing, to say, 'Oh, he's saying this because he wants that.' I am saying what I am saying because I believe it, not because I want anything.

Asked specifically about the Presidency, Bruton said:

> You don't rule out anything of that nature . . . That is not really what I am interested in. I am interested in being an active servant of the country, helping it through its immediate problems by whatever little bit of advice I can offer, and helping people to see things in proportion . . . not talking about personal ambitions.

In the coming months the economic crisis, the general election and the succession of political dilemmas in the Government were centre stage. Meanwhile, out of the public eye, candidates were organising their campaigns with a view to covering both options in the face of a looming general election: would they opt to seek a nomination either from councillors or from what the opinion polls were predicting would be a radically reconstituted Dáil and Seanad?

Chapter 3 〜

| PULLED UP

Joe Duffy's 'Liveline' phone-in programme about topical issues often caused controversies and set the following day's headlines, which ensured that it was consistently in the country's five most-listened-to radio programmes. On Monday 30 May 2011 Helen Lucy Burke, a former restaurant critic and contributor to the current affairs magazine *Magill*, rang Joe Duffy to talk about a topic of the day and the need to remind people of headlines generated nine years earlier.

She had interviewed David Norris in 2002 for *Magill*, and she wanted listeners to know that she thought Norris was not a suitable candidate for the Presidency. She quoted from the article, both from Norris's words and from her own comments. Norris, she said, was in favour of 'free-range sexuality', and she went on to describe his views as 'startling', 'evil' and 'astounding.' She also alluded to a holiday he had taken in Thailand. It was a political bombshell.

Norris issued a statement to the Duffy programme trying to put the *Magill* interview in context.

During the course of a comprehensive conversation, Miss Burke and I engaged in an academic discussion about classical Greece and sexual activity in a historical context; it was a hypothetical, intellectual conversation which should not have been seen as a considered representation of my view ... The references to sexual activity were what was emphasised and subsequently picked up and taken out of context in other media outlets . . . The presentation of references to sexuality in the article attributed to me were misleading. I did not ever and would not approve of the finished article as it appeared.

John Waters, however, consultant editor of *Magill* at the time, contradicted him and insisted a few days later that Senator Norris had been given two opportunities by Burke to reconsider his comments before publication. Norris had asked for a few minor amendments and then 'pronounced himself happy for his views to go into print.'

Duffy asked Burke why she had decided to resurrect the article so many years later. He also interviewed the journalist Joe Jackson on the programme, who defended Norris, citing an interview he had conducted with Norris years before. He challenged Burke, saying she was quoting her own opinions, and said he'd be happy to review the tape of the interview for veracity.

The following morning Norris went on 'Today with Pat Kenny' to try to repair some of the damage. 'This was an academic discussion over dinner; we were tossing around ideas,' he told the audience. He made it clear that he abhorred paedophilia, and said that Burke's reference to his 'holiday' in Thailand had been 'left hanging' when in fact he was visiting the country to investigate sexual exploitation on behalf of the United Nations. 'The thing I regret most was allowing myself to be interviewed by a restaurant critic,' he said, admitting that the incident had provided a 'steep learning curve'.

On Twitter the restaurant critic Tom Doorley tweeted: 'I personally know and like both David Norris and Helen Lucy Burke. But I think David Norris would be both a better babysitter and president.' The *Irish Mail on Sunday* republished the *Magill* article the following weekend, saying that Norris 'clearly set out a string of highly controversial views on sex, paedophilia, the age of consent, incest and abuse.'

Burke said that Norris told her he objected to 'state interference' in people's sex lives, recording his initially cautious comments as follows:

I believe very strongly in people being allowed to make any choices they like, within very wide limits . . . But I also believe that once you make those choices, you should take responsibility for them . . . I wouldn't draw the line for other people. I would hope that we could produce a society in which people would be inclined to draw lines for themselves . . . There's a lot of nonsense about paedophilia. I can say this because I haven't the slightest interest in children, or in people who are considerably younger than me. I cannot understand how anybody could find children of either sex the slightest bit attractive sexually. To me, what is attractive about people is the fact that they display the signs of sexual maturity. But pre-pubescent children who lack any identifying characteristics of sexual maturity, I cannot understand why anybody would find them sexually appropriate.

On the other hand—yes, they do find them so. But in terms of classic paedophilia, as practised by the Greeks, for example, where it is an older man introducing a younger man or boy to adult life, I think there can be something said for it.

Now again, this is not something that appeals to me, although when I was younger it would most certainly have appealed to me in the sense that I would have greatly relished the prospect of an older, attractive, mature man taking me under this wing, lovingly introducing me to sexual realities, and treating me with affection and teaching me about life—yes, I think that would be lovely; I would have enjoyed that.

The conversation moved on to talk about public attitudes to paedophilia.

I think there is complete and utter hysteria about this subject, and there is also confusion between homosexuality and paedophilia on the one hand and between paedophilia and pederasty on the other.

Norris also attacked the media, criticising them by saying that,

for example, the gutter press in England and Ireland fanned the flames of this kind of thing, and they dehumanised people, called them evil beasts, perverts and all this kind of thing . . .

Of course there is a whole spectrum. In my opinion, the teacher, or Christian Brother, who puts his hand into a boy's pocket during a history lesson, that is one end of the spectrum. But then there is another. There is the person who attacks children of either sex, rapes them, brutalises them and then murders them. But the way things are presented here it's almost as if they were all exactly the same and I don't think they are.

And I have to tell you this—I think that the children in some instances are more damaged by the condemnation than the actual experience.

In her article for *Magill*, Burke said that Senator Norris 'did not appear to endorse any minimum age, or endorse my protest that a child was not capable of informed consent,' quoting him as saying that 'the law in this sphere should take into account consent rather than age.' The *Mail* commented:

When asked about incest, he seemed to have no objections in principle. As Miss Burke explained: 'He hesitated, and conceded that in the case of girls a case could be made for a ban, as a possible resulting pregnancy might be genetically undesirable.'

In the same edition John Waters (now a columnist with the *Irish Times* and the *Mail on Sunday*) crystallised the issue. In his full-page essay he wrote: 'Sorry

David, this is not about your sexuality. It's about your stance on sex abuse.'
Norris's comments about being introduced to sexual behaviour by older men
was, according to Waters, unexceptionable in itself.

> It becomes more ominous, however, when connected to other remarks in
> the interview. For example, in one passage, David Norris appears to be
> saying that sexually abused children might suffer more from the exposure
> and 'condemnation' of their abuser than from the abuse itself.
>
> Taken in the round, his comments amounted to at least an insinuation
> that this society is excessively hung up about paedophilia and that there are
> other, more laid back but perhaps more appropriate options for societies in
> perceiving and dealing with the issue.
>
> The media response to all this has, in general, been of a piece with the
> treatment of recent controversies involving the poet Cathal Ó Searcaigh
> and film director Roman Polanski. In both cases the defining question
> appeared to be not the action of these individuals but that they were being
> challenged at all.
>
> Three years ago David Norris joined with sundry 'artists' and media
> people to defend Ó Searcaigh following the showing of a shocking
> documentary that raised serious questions about his relations with teenage
> boys in Nepal. In a letter to the *Irish Times*, Norris described that controversy
> as a 'witch hunt' and questioned the motives of the filmmaker. Is there,
> perchance, a pattern here?
>
> The point about the Norris interview is that, taken as a whole, it did indeed
> trivialise what are, in this and other civilised societies, grave criminal offences.
> The big question now for this society is not whether or not we will have a gay
> president but whether or not we are serious in our distaste for paedophilia.

Waters's opinion would prove to be the central logic and argument for anyone
engaging in the debate about Norris's fitness to run for office.

In a society that had been dominated by the Catholic Church for decades,
and that had recently begun coming to terms with the sexual and physical
abuse that had been meted out to children in its care and with the systematic
cover-up of abuse by priests, Norris's apparently questionable attitudes to
paedophilia provoked outrage.

That same weekend Eoghan Harris, a former political appointment to the
Seanad, gave Norris his public imprimatur, having sat beside him in the Seanad,
where he witnessed how he had spoken about child sex abuse with genuine grief.
Fourteen years earlier Harris had provided perhaps the most memorable
sound-bite when he railed against the candidature of Mary McAleese, labelling
her a 'tribal time bomb'. As he wrote:

So let me break a story that is staring you in the face. Isn't there something slightly sick about a society which approaches former terrorists with appeasing smiles, hand outstretched to shake hands which have spilled blood, but is ready to round on a good man like David Norris who has never spilled a drop of Irish blood or even hurt the proverbial fly?

On the opinion pages of the *Sunday Times* the columnist Brenda Power revealed that Helen Lucy Burke was herself the subject of appalling abuse the previous week, when Twitter had come alive with comments directed at her age and sex, saying she was an 'attention-seeking bag lady' and a 'vicious little old woman.' According to Power,

> it would be a truly sorry day for this democracy, and a poor look out for the quality of presidential candidate we can expect, if Norris is hounded out of running for the Park over some designedly provocative comments he made ten years ago.

Norris was putting his best side out for the *Sunday World*, saying that he remained confident and that he had received countless messages of good will and a warm reception in Limerick and Clonmel, where he had been canvassing.

> When things are taken out of context—I know myself it looked bloody awful. But it depends on how the Irish people perceive me, and I can't second-guess them. Time will tell.

In the *Sunday Independent*, Jody Corcoran wrote that it was a 'sad truth' that attacks on Norris were sparked by his homosexuality.

> It is only because Norris is a homosexual that the media feel free to ask him about matters related to sexuality; but because other prospective candidates are not homosexual, the media has not, and will not, ask them about such deeply personal matters . . . When the issue of sexuality is coupled with politics, as we know, it can be lethal, so lethal as to possibly now derail the Norris campaign for the presidency.
> And that would be a great shame because, of all of the candidates, Norris is so far the most interesting and, potentially, the best to do what can be a difficult job.

The following Wednesday, 15 June, Norris convened a meeting of his election team for six o'clock. Thirteen people turned up at his campaign headquarters,

beside Davy Byrne's pub in Duke Street, including his campaign manager, Liam McCabe, and director of communications, Jane Cregan, who was on leave of absence from her post as events manager at Iarnród Éireann. The meeting was prompted by a phone call from the *Daily Mail*, who had contacted Norris to say they were going to rerun an interview he had given to them a year earlier. 'David Norris with the team made a decision to deal with every issue as comprehensively as possible, to get out there and set the record straight,' Cregan recalled.

Norris launched a media blitz to counter the *Mail*'s interview. That morning, at 2 a.m., Norris's web site was updated with a question-and-answer document addressing the contentious points raised in the interview and with a list of media interviews arranged.

The first interview was on 'Morning Ireland' and sought to elicit Norris's views on paedophilia and pederasty. He struggled to explain his case in simple, non-academic terms for a still-sleepy breakfast audience. He referred to the *Symposium* of Plato, a seven-part philosophical discussion on love, including homosexuality, until the presenter, Áine Lawlor, cut across him with a telling comment that would be repeated in later commentaries: 'But you are not running for election in Ancient Greece: you are running for election in modern Ireland.' The *Irish Times* would sum it up:

> On the face of it, Norris seemed to be saying he did not believe in an age of consent; that prostitution and drugs should be legalised, and that pederasty, as practised by the ancient Greeks, was acceptable. He also defended Cathal Ó Searcaigh against some of the allegations surrounding his contacts with young men in Nepal.

Norris would admit later that 'Thursday had been a difficult day for me and my supporters.' He still claimed the support of three hundred campaign volunteers, but political observers would question the belief of his director of communications that time was on Norris's side and that he would be able to turn the campaign around.

Norris would tell the *Irish Times* that he had engaged in an academic discussion on sexual relations between older men and younger men and boys arising from classical Greek literature.

> I made a distinction between paedophilia and pederasty, which is a totally different thing. To the average person it would not make any difference, I suppose, but to me it did because I knew what I was talking about. That got mixed up and stayed mixed up.

I abhor with every fibre of my being the idea of interference with children, sexual abuse, physical abuse and emotional abuse. My record on that speaks for itself.

As the latest resurrected article was republished, Norris appealed directly to his electorate, scrambling to regain ground.

So I stand on my deeds. I don't think that responsible people like councillors, who have a lot of responsibilities in their local area, or my fellow TDs and Senators, would actually feel it appropriate to judge me on a couple of sensationalised headlines. I don't think they would judge me on that . . .

The great thing for me is my conscience is clear. I know I have done nothing wrong. I know I have not injured anybody. I know I have passionately stood up for the rights of the abused.

He had been speaking to the recipients of the Fingal Centre awards at the Tailors' Hall, near Christ Church, another diverse event on the campaign trail. He explained that, from 14 March, when he formally launched his campaign,

I have behaved like a president and I am behaving more like a president all the time. And I feel I am being drawn towards and growing into the job. What I am asking now is that the councillors and my fellow members of the Oireachtas give me the opportunity to let the people decide.

On Sunday 19 June, as the Labour Party met to elect its nominee, the *Sunday Independent* published its opinion poll commissioned from Quantum Research. Support for Norris had not diminished with the *Magill* controversy. He topped the poll, with 30 per cent support, more than twice that of Pat Cox, his nearest rival. Cox—a former TD, MEP and president of the European Parliament—and Finlay were at 13 per cent each. Michael D. Higgins and Gay Mitchell scored 11 per cent, while Mairead McGuinness won 9 per cent, Mary Davis 7, Seán Gallagher 4 and Kathleen O'Meara 2.

While Norris still had not secured the necessary twenty Oireachtas nominations, the independent Dublin TD Finian McGrath urged support for Norris.

The absence from the field of the most popular candidate amongst the public would seriously tarnish the credibility of the highest constitutional office in the land. My position at the moment is that the winner of a campaign that does not include Mr Norris would have a flawed mandate.

The following Thursday an *Irish Independent*/Millard Brown Lansdowne opinion poll showed that Norris was still the public's favourite, with a 21 per cent rating—a drop in approval but a heartening result after all the controversy he had endured. But he still had not secured a nomination.

Higgins scored 19 per cent (the same percentage that the Labour Party achieved in a national approval ratings), while Mairead McGuinness was ahead of her party colleagues as Avril Doyle joined the race and was assessed by voters. McGuinness achieved 10 per cent and Cox 7 per cent, with Doyle picking up 3 per cent and Mitchell 2 per cent. Among the independents, Gallagher was leading, with 6 per cent, while Davis was on 4 per cent and O'Dowd on 3 per cent.

On a separate question—which of the Fine Gael candidates would be best positioned to win the Presidency—McGuinness came out on top, with 26 per cent, while Cox won 19, Mitchell 14 and Doyle 9.

A few days later, on the 24th, the *Sunday Independent* published the result of another opinion poll, showing Norris at 42 per cent, Mitchell trailing him at 21, Higgins at 16, Davis at 11 and Gallagher at 10.

In the same paper Miriam O'Callaghan, presenter of RTE's 'Frontline' programme, again dismissed rumours that she had been approached and was considering running for the Park. 'It's a story that just won't go away,' she complained.

> This started last year. It's quite extraordinary, but if people think I'm going to jump out of the bushes at the last minute and make a dash for the Park they are wrong. I will not be running for the Presidency this year. If I do you can come back and haunt me.

On Wednesday 20 July, despite still not having a nomination from four local authorities or the support of twenty Oireachtas members, Norris remained the voters' favourite to win the race for the Áras. That morning's *Irish Times*/Ipsos MRBI opinion poll showed him scoring 25 per cent. Mitchell came a close second, at 21 per cent, Higgins at 18, Gallagher 13, Davis 12 and the undeclared candidate Éamon Ó Cuív 11.

The pollsters also asked voters to rate the qualities they considered most important in the next President. A total of 38 per cent said that a candidate who could represent the country well was the most important. Honesty and reputation came second, with 17 per cent, while 9 per cent opted for personality. Ominously for a candidate who was a TD, senator or MEP, the poll had only 3 per cent believing that a candidate's political experience was the most important factor.

The opinion poll also showed that Norris was attracting cross-party support, with his strongest support coming from people in the 35–49 age group.

Mitchell's support was strongest in Dublin and weakest in Connacht-Ulster, which was the opposite of Ó Cuív, who could only muster 4 per cent support in the capital. However, Mitchell was winning the support of only half of Fine Gael voters—a cause for real concern for head office. Higgins was strongest in Munster and Connacht-Ulster but, like Mitchell, was getting the support of less than half the declared voters. Davis and Gallagher had an even spread of support among all classes and age groups, but Davis was sweeping up more Fianna Fáil votes than Gallagher.

———

Within hours Norris was going to find his political support and his hopes for the Áras rapidly slipping away. On Friday 29 July the Norris campaign came crashing to the ground as his director of communications, Jane Cregan, and director of elections, Derek Murphy, resigned, feeling let down by Norris after he had failed to disclose a plea for clemency that he had written for his former lover.

In the blogosphere and on the net, the conviction in Israel of Norris's former lover, Ezra Yizhak Nawi, in 1997 for having sex with a fifteen-year-old Palestinian boy—statutory rape—in 1992 was resurrected. Norris had provided Nawi with a character reference and had written a substantial letter pleading for clemency on Seanad Éireann notepaper.

There was a storm of comment in the social media, and its significance was not lost on the savvy 'Team Norris'. They had put a lot of effort into building an online campaign for Norris, with a regularly updated and lively web site and with constant conversations on Facebook, where he had thirty thousand fans and twenty thousand Twitter followers. The following day another 'Team Norris' member, the youth organiser Orla Foley, resigned from the campaign.

In an effort to limit the damage, Norris gave the *Sunday Independent* a copy of the letter he had written fourteen years earlier. He also provided a copy of a character reference he had written for Nawi, which he signed 'Senator David Norris, Bureau Member, Irish Foreign Affairs Committee'. The story, and an exclusive interview with Norris, was splashed over five pages in the 31 July edition.

Norris's lengthy letter, on Seanad notepaper, was written to the judges of the Israeli High Court and pleaded for mercy for his former lover, who he had known for the previous twenty-three years. According to Norris, the letter was given to Nawi's lawyers to use as they felt appropriate, and it suggested that they could forward it to the court if they felt it appropriate. In the letter he said:

I was elected to my parliamentary position ten years ago for the first time and have been re-elected on several occasions since. At the recent election held last month I received the highest vote ever recorded for the Senate, being elected on the first count, and have been widely mentioned as a possible presidential candidate in the forthcoming elections for the Presidency of Ireland.

The lengthy and detailed 'humble plea' asked for a non-custodial sentence for his 'close and personal friend', who he had first met in December 1975. Listing mitigating factors, he said Nawi had 'unwisely pleaded guilty' and had been the victim of a violent and abusive father. He also questioned the behaviour of the police, claiming that the arrest 'took place in a curious and troubling manner.' The circumstances were deeply worrying, he said. 'Mr Yizhak was lured into a carefully prepared trap.' Norris volunteered to inform the court about Nawi's character and about the legal system and its similarities to Irish law.

However my most urgent plea would not be on technical grounds, which at the end of the day I feel diffident in attempting to argue before this distinguished court. The strongest argument is ad misericordiam [for mercy].

Secure in the knowledge that Mr Yizhak will not offend again in the same way, that he is prepared to make financial compensations available to the young man involved, that lasting and perhaps permanent damage will be done to his psychological and material welfare by being imprisoned, by virtue of the fact that there is a possibility that he may attempt suicide in prison, by virtue of the fact that his elderly mother's principal support and reassurance will be removed, I earnestly beg that the court may see the possibility of securing justice not by sending him to prison but by imposing a non-custodial sentence.

Interviewed by John Drennan, Norris made an implicit admission that he had made a major political error. Of Nawi's conviction he said:

Some people will think it should have cropped up immediately. But I had compartmentalised it away. It was a shocking and painful experience . . . I anticipated there would be attacks. I trawled back ten years and we anticipated that would be enough.

According to Drennan,

the senator's subsequent admission that 'nobody knew this was coming. I never alerted people but it was so long ago and so hurtful' goes a long way to explaining why two of his top campaign team resigned so abruptly . . . Norris, who has been publicly critical of the treatment of Palestine by Israel, refrained from commenting on suggestions that he had been stitched up. But he did say: 'There is something sinister about it all. It has all the appearance of a stitch up, but I'm too close to the situation.'

In a compelling story, Norris said that when the full truth emerged he was shattered. 'But when you see someone drowning and their head surfaces, you don't push it back under. You pull them ashore and you confront them with what they have done.' He said the furore and 'the secret internet campaign' that sparked it was 'guilt by association. I am not Ezra. I have never lived his lifestyle. I loved him. But it has been many people's fate to love people who have defects.' But he said he intended to continue his campaign. 'I'm not hiding behind shadows. I have to take it on the chin and reassure people all over the country that I'm the same person I was last week.'

However, Norris's worst fears were being realised. Political support was wavering, maybe even slipping away from his candidacy. Two senators, Prof. John Crown and Mary Louise O'Donnell, publicly called on him to issue a statement clarifying the controversy. Later Senator Jillian van Turnhout, who withdrew her support for Norris, would post on her Facebook page about the 'constant barrage' of calls and emails, 'some abusive and it now feels like harassment'.

————

Meanwhile a different letter was dropping through letterboxes around the country. The Fianna Fáil MEP Brian Crowley had written to every party TD, senator and MEP asserting that the party was capable of conducting a successful campaign with him as candidate. 'I believe I have the character and competence to communicate that spirit which defines our country, our people and our history,' he said. He referred to previous conversations he had had about the office with Micheál Martin and to his agreement with him not to make any public statement until the party decided its strategy on whether to run a candidate. 'However, we are now in the run-up to decision time in early September and many of you have asked me to reconfirm my position, which is the reason for this correspondence.'

Crowley (47), from Bandon, Co. Cork, the son of the former West Cork TD and senator Flor Crowley, was paralysed from the waist down at the age of sixteen after he fell off a roof on which he had been playing rugby with friends. He always had an interest in music and in politics, often travelling to meetings with his father. He volunteered as a late-night DJ on the WKLR pirate station with the programme 'Brian Rogers and the 25th Century', earning him the nickname 'Buck' for a long time.

Albert Reynolds, the Taoiseach of the day, made him one of his Seanad nominees in 1993, saying,

> When I had the opportunity to search around for people for the Senate I thought about him, because he could fulfil so many roles in the Seanad. Here was a guy in the prime of his youth who had met with this adversity, and while many people might be inclined to lie back or write off their future life, he got a new injection of life. I thought he would be a glorious example to the youth of the country and to those with disability.

Crowley was first elected to the European Parliament in 1994 and was a consistent poll-topper, being returned at every election. A hard constituency worker, he remained hugely popular, and supporters believed that he had charisma and cross-party appeal and that he had a distance from the toxicity associated with members of the Fianna Fáil Government.

Meanwhile there was increasing speculation that Dana (Rosemary Scallon) and the distinguished artist Robert Ballagh might enter the race. Ballagh (68), a lifelong socialist and republican, had taken soundings about running a broad left-wing programme in opposition to economic cut-backs and the bank bail-out. He had discussions with Gerry Adams, president of Sinn Féin, Richard Boyd Barrett of the People Before Profit Alliance and the leader of the Socialist Party, Joe Higgins.

The entrepreneur and chairman of Aer Árann, Pádraig Ó Céidigh, also announced that he was considering standing as an independent, having been approached by a number of business and community leaders. 'I have a clear vision of the Irish as a people and our unique qualities,' he said.

In the coming days, political endorsements for Norris began slipping away as three independent TDs withdrew their pledge to support his nomination just days after the *Sunday Independent* published the clemency plea. Most significantly, Finian McGrath, the Dublin TD who had co-ordinated Norris's Oireachtas nomination bid, withdrew his support, saying that 'children and the Presidency have to come first'.

The Waterford TD John Halligan also announced that he was withdrawing his support, as did the Donegal South-West TD Thomas Pringle. Deputy Halligan felt it was a great error of judgment on his part to write the letter to the Israeli authorities appealing for leniency for Ezra Yitzhak Nawi. The office of the president must be beyond reproach and so, after consulting with my supporters, I have decided it would be inappropriate of me to support his bid for nomination.

The online news site www.thejournal.ie conducted an opinion poll that attracted almost a thousand voters. Three out of four said the revelations about Nawi would damage Norris's bid. On Eamon Dunphy's Sunday chat show on Newstalk radio the former presidential hopeful Fergus Finlay called on Norris to resign from the race, and to consider his position in the Seanad.

Clearly this is a smoking gun. It does mean that any further defence of David is impossible. He really needs to get out of being a candidate and reflect long and hard on his own future. He is probably hurt, wounded, baffled. He probably thinks the world is out to get him.

Meanwhile the independent Dublin TD Maureen O'Sullivan voiced her support for Norris, saying he should be allowed to be judged by the electorate. 'He was looking at mitigating circumstances regarding the sentence. He has been targeted in a particularly nasty way, right from the beginning.'

The August public holiday edition of the *Irish Daily Star* was unequivocal in its insistence that Norris was wrong and that he should resign from the campaign, and consider his position in the Seanad.

It is wrong and it also shows a sad absence of an open and explicit regard for the young victim in this case. Most worryingly was Norris's claim that the judge in the trial was 'factually incorrect' in saying 'there was absolutely no difference' between the case against Mr Yizhak and a similar case involving heterosexuals.

The politicians who are standing by Norris, despite this latest controversy, should also have a long rethink. Do they really want to be associated with someone who tried to plead clemency for a man convicted of statutory rape?

The *Daily Mail* reminded readers of an interview by Jason O'Toole published in the paper the previous year. In it Norris said that his relationship with Nawi had continued longer than was suggested as the controversy broke, and that he did not believe in an age of consent.

Norris was due to be the guest presenter on that night's episode of Vincent Browne's political chat show, but as the media clamour grew too loud he pulled out.

Norris had phoned the PR consultant Paul Allen on the Saturday from a friend's home in Monkstown, Co. Dublin, where he was staying while the media were camped outside his house in North Great George's Street. They met on Sunday as Norris celebrated his sixty-seventh birthday and agreed to meet again the following day, when Allen advised him to resign. Allen later recalled: 'You cannot go any further with this, I told him.' At three in the afternoon Norris agreed to the inevitable, and the team got to work on an exit strategy.

The following day, Tuesday the 2nd, the media were summoned to a press conference to be hosted by Norris outside his home. Norris, Allen and McCabe were across the road in the home of Norris's friends, the barristers Muireann Noonan and Tony Collins. They could look through the curtains and watch the event on Norris's doorstep. The speech was completed and copies printed. Norris left his friends' house by the back door and drove around the block in his black Jaguar, pulling up outside his own house at 3 p.m. in front of the assembled throng of about fifty reporters and photographers. Then, behind a red rope, his hands sometimes trembling, his eyes glazed, the toll and strain apparent on his face, he said:

I deeply regret the most recent of all the controversies concerning my former partner of twenty-five years ago, Ezra Yizhak Nawi. The fall-out from his disgraceful behaviour has now spread to me and is in danger of contaminating others close to me, both in political and personal life.

It is essential that I act decisively now to halt this negative process. I do not regret supporting and seeking clemency for a friend, but I do regret giving the impression that I did not have sufficient compassion for the victim of Ezra's crime.

I accept that more than a decade and a half later, when I have now reviewed the issue and am not emotionally involved, when I am not afraid that Ezra might take his own life, I see that I was wrong. He served his time and never offended again.

Yes, his actions were terrible, but my motivation to write the letter was out of love and concern. I was eager to support someone who has been very important and continues to be important in my life. I have been involved in many campaigns and have written many hundreds of letters on behalf of people in every continent—persecuted Tibetan monks, East Timorese, death-row prisoners in the United States of America. It is very sad that in trying to help a person I loved dearly I made a human error.

Norris did not take any questions. He was applauded by a few onlookers as he delivered his final line, a quotation from Samuel Beckett: 'Ever tried. Ever failed.

No matter. Try Again. Fail again. Fail better.' Then, with a big smile and a final theatrical wave for the cameras, he turned and closed his door on the world.

Later that evening he confirmed that he would not be resigning from the Seanad. He then began packing for a trip to his other home in Cyprus to avoid the media glare.

Meanwhile the *Irish Times* reported that

> a number of letters written by Mr Norris on behalf of Mr Nawi have not come into the public domain. Ex-campaign workers said he wrote a number of letters appealing for clemency for Mr Nawi to a range of public figures in Israel and beyond. After they were shown the letters last Thursday, a number of Mr Norris's campaign team resigned.

There would be much speculation about the content of the letters, and demands that they be made public, but they were not released.

Always robust in protecting its reputation, the Israeli embassy in Dublin issued a statement saying that allegations that it had been involved in the publication of the letter written by Norris to the court in Israel had 'absolutely no foundation'. In a statement the embassy said, 'No such letter was or is in the possession of the Embassy; as in Ireland, the judicial system in democratic Israel is entirely separate from the Government and Ministry of Foreign Affairs.'

After Norris resigned, Harry McGee in the *Irish Times* revealed the identity of the blogger who publicised the sentencing of Nawi for statutory rape in 1997. John Connolly, who blogs under the title 'The System Works', which advances strongly pro-Israeli views, rejected any claims of conspiracy or an orchestrated smear campaign. He said his source was a regular correspondent with his blog, came from a trade union background and had once campaigned for Michael D. Higgins but was not associated with the Labour Party. The party immediately issued a denial that it or its candidate had anything to do with the Norris controversy.

Connolly's role drew scorn because of its political agenda, but it also won praise for bringing about 'the first major victory of the Irish blogosphere', according to the *Irish Independent*. According to Connolly,

> there have been a lot of conspiracy theories. I have received a lot of messages that I am smearing David Norris and am an Israeli agent. There are rumours about nonsensical things about my connections with Israeli diplomats and with Mossad [the Israeli secret service]. Nobody smeared David Norris. He did not deny anything that was put out on my blog.

Connolly, from Bandon, Co. Cork, is a graduate of Griffith Law School in Dublin and has lived in England. He confirmed that he had posted his story on the Israeli embassy's Facebook page.

Back-room campaign experts and the candidates themselves would all say that the social media had a role to play, but it was only when these were taken up and put into the mainstream electronic or print media that there was clear cause and effect. However, it was clear that they were growing in importance and in reach for political campaigns—as they would again in the 2011 presidential campaign.

———

The bookies Paddy Power updated their latest betting for the Áras. Michael D. Higgins was firm favourite at 5:6, Gay Mitchell a close second at 13:8, Mary Davis 5:1, Seán Gallagher 12:1, Brian Crowley 16:1 and Mícheál Ó Muircheartaigh and Mary Hanafin 50:1. They also opened a book on whether Fianna Fáil would run a candidate, with the betting at Yes 5:4 and No 4:7.

The outspoken *Star* columnist Terry McGeehan summed up his relief that a potential constitutional crisis had been avoided after Norris withdrew.

> There are those today who might actually feel sorry for David Norris. But this man has now been demonstrably shown to be unfit to hold high office. He has shown unbelievably bad judgement in writing these letters of support in the first place for the rapist of a child.
>
> He has shown not only bad judgement but also unforgivable arrogance and unpardonable contempt towards the people of Ireland, who up to now were innocently on course to install him in the Park. So, let's shed no tears for David Norris.
>
> Instead let's breathe a deep sigh of relief—tinged with white hot anger—that he was rumbled before he got the seal of office to represent the Irish Republic at home and on the world stage. We were fecking blessed.

The editorial of the *Irish Times* was more sober in its language but said Norris had no choice but to resign. It felt that his withdrawal should not be the end of the matter, because it was possible that Norris, as the most popular candidate in the field, would not qualify as a contender. This was unacceptable, and the Government 'should ask the proposed constitutional convention to review nomination requirements for the position, rather than confine their assessment to cutting the presidential term from seven to five years.' It also said that petitions by politicians to the courts on behalf of constituents should be banned, as well as appeals to Ministers for Justice seeking reductions in fines and penalties already imposed by the courts. It concluded: 'If Mr Norris's derailed attempts to secure a nomination result in these political flaws being addressed and repaired, he will have done democracy some service.'

The following day the *Irish Independent* revealed that Nawi had fought a five-year legal battle, involving two appeals, to avoid being jailed for the statutory rape of a boy. He was sentenced to six months in prison after a plea bargain was accepted by the Jerusalem High Court. He was jailed in November 1997 but released three months later.

Dearbhail McDonald in the *Irish Independent* repeated Israeli media reports that Nawi also had convictions for the illegal use of a weapon, for possession of drugs for personal use, for entering a closed military area and for threatening behaviour.

McCabe wrote of his experience for the *Sunday Independent*, saying that fifteen months earlier he had met Norris for coffee in Leinster House and told him he needed to build a 'national support structure' and could not be a 'marginal or issues based' candidate.

He wrote that they established twenty teams across the country, with two hundred volunteers, and at close of business had thirty thousand fans on Facebook, twenty thousand followers on Twitter, and Norris had personally addressed sixteen county and city councils. And Norris's exit? 'In my view his exit was the correct decision and was handled in a professional and dignified manner.'

Chapter 4 ~

| THE RINGER?

Government TDs and senators had been reading the opinion polls with increasing trepidation. There was no doubt that they were going to take a beating from the electorate. As time progressed, the question became not how many seats they would lose but how many seats could be saved. Fear stalked the offices of the Green Party and Fianna Fáil in Leinster House.

Fine Gael seemed unassailable—and the party leader, Enda Kenny, a racing certainty to be the next Taoiseach—and the Labour Party unbeatable in Dublin. Sinn Féin was showing well and might even beat Fianna Fáil into fourth place. Seats were going to be lost, dynasties destroyed and history changed. The question was: just how bad would it be, and how accurate were the opinion polls?

'It was like a delayed funeral,' wrote Olivia O'Leary, political analyst with 'Drivetime', assessing the election for the RTE publication *The Week in Politics: Election 2011 and the 31st Dáil*. 'The government had died a long time ago, but it still had to be buried. Ultimately, most people just wanted the government out. The cold certainty with which they delivered the verdict was breathtaking.'

On Friday 25 February the country voted.

Fine Gael won an unprecedented 76 seats, an increase of 25 seats on the 2007 election. The Labour Party increased its total to 37, up 17. Sinn Féin won 14, an increase of 10. The Socialist Party won 2, having none in the previous Dáil. Similarly the People Before Profit Alliance won 2, having had no previous representation. The number of independent TDs increased from 9 to 15.

The Green Party was wiped out. Fianna Fáil was devastated, losing 58 seats, reducing its representation to 20—a historic hammering for any party and a humiliating result for Fianna Fáil.

The changed demographics in the Oireachtas would concentrate the minds of potential presidential candidates as they weighed up seeking support from the newly constituted political parties and from a range of independents and smaller parties.

Fine Gael and the Labour Party would look to the huge public endorsement they had received and would seek to transfer that to their candidate. For Fine Gael it could be the first time to elect a party nominee to the Áras, topping its successes in the local elections and the general election; for the Labour Party it was a chance to follow on the Robinson Presidency. For Fianna Fáil it posed a hard question: would there be any support for a candidate to be elected to the highest office in the land?

The presidential race had vanished from view in the media. The October election might seem a long way off, but away from the public gaze potential candidates were conscious of the time limits for winning a nomination. There were a lot of dominoes to be put in place, and summer would be a political vacuum as the Oireachtas shut down and councillors too went on annual holidays.

To win a nomination to be on the presidential election ballot there were three routes. A potential candidate could nominate themselves, but only if they were a former President and had served only one term of office: two terms and you were disqualified. In theory Mary Robinson was in the frame for the 2011 race, but she let it be known that she was not going to contest the election. However, it does not rule her out from qualifying as a candidate in a future presidential election.

The traditional route for candidates is as political party nominees. This requires the support of twenty members of the Oireachtas—less than 10 per cent of the total number of TDs and senators. However, the political parties had a history of selecting a single candidate to represent them, nominating from their own ranks and then closing those ranks. The number of independents and small parties had never reached a critical mass or likely agreement on a representative candidate, but the 2011 general election opened that possibility for the first time.

Finally, a candidate could follow the path pioneered successfully fourteen years earlier by Dana and by Derek Nally and seek a nomination from four of the country's county or city councils.

Again, the same rules were likely to be applied by members of the major political parties, where they would be whipped in to support their own candidates, block others or abstain. A free vote would be the ideal for any non-party candidate seeking this route, but that was unlikely. If a political party had decided to nominate a party candidate it would use its parliamentary party to give the candidate that authority and then whip members to dissent or at least to abstain and exclude any other possible candidate, thereby reducing the number of candidates on the ballot paper.

Time was ticking away on the political calendar, and May was going to be a crucial month. It was an ideal time for testing the waters of public opinion and for anyone who was going to commit themselves, allowing them to make initial contacts before the summer hiatus and ideally positioning them for formal nominations in the autumn.

———

On Sunday 1 May, Nick Webb, the new business editor of the *Sunday Independent*, who had succeeded former senator Shane Ross, a newly elected independent TD, would kick-start a month of media coverage of the Presidency. He announced that the entrepreneur and 'Dragons' Den' television presenter Seán Gallagher was 'to blow open the race for the Park by standing for President.'

Gallagher was a joint founder of Smarthomes, which provided wiring and equipment for new houses. At its zenith it had a staff of seventy and a turnover of more than €10 million a year. Gallagher had left the business with the downturn in the economy and joined the hit RTE programme with Sarah Newman of Needahotel, Bobby Kerr of Insomnia, Niall O'Farrell of Black Tie and the radio show host and media trainer Gavin Duffy.

The news pages carried a brief reference to the emergence of the new candidate, saying Gallagher hadn't declared but had claimed the backing of the independent senator and former supermarket magnate Feargal Quinn.

On his web site Gallagher said he was giving serious consideration to the consistent calls, from people in business, community organisations and disability groups, 'to offer myself as an independent candidate with a clear understanding of what is needed to help rebuild our community.'

A former member of Fianna Fáil's Ard-Chomhairle and its youth wing, Ógra Fianna Fáil, Gallagher immediately began canvassing Fianna Fáil members of the Oireachtas, seeking their support to secure a nomination. He insisted that he would stand as an independent and wanted only ten Fianna Fáil nominations and would then secure ten more from independent TDs and senators so that he could maintain a 'semi-detached' arrangement with his former party.

One of those he canvassed was Séamus Kirk, a TD for Louth who, as former Ceann Comhairle, was returned automatically in the 2007 general election. But the previous election in 2002 was a completely different story. 'HQ and myself were concerned about my polling,' recalled Kirk. Shockingly, he was going to lose his seat despite his years of honest service to the constituency, according to the pollsters. Kirk recalled:

> I knew Seán. I met him regularly as a TD for the constituency and he came on board as Director of Elections. I knew him as a hugely dynamic person, a great organiser, established a strong election team, who met every week, reflected and reviewed the previous week, planned for the future and built a strong campaign. He was good with the media and certainly understood where they were coming from.

A REDC opinion poll commissioned by the *Drogheda Independent* had the Fianna Fáil minister Dermot Ahern topping the poll at 26 per cent, Arthur Morgan of Sinn Féin at 16, Mairead McGuinness of Fine Gael at 14, her party colleague and sitting TD Fergus O'Dowd at 13, and Séamus Kirk trailing at 9, fifth in a four-seat constituency.

Kevin Mulligan in the *Drogheda Independent* wrote an election analysis of the success of Kirk and his team's efforts.

> Within an hour of opening the first boxes in the count centre in the Dundalk Institute of Technology it was clear that the story of this election was going to be the staggering re-election of Séamus Kirk to the first seat. And although it took many weary hours of counting, the eventual distribution of the constituency's four seats was never going to be the cliff hanger that the pollsters and political pundits predicted.

But with Gallagher in charge, Kirk had exceeded all expectations. His seat had been considered lost, but he returned with 10,190 first-preference votes and topped the poll—exceeding the vote for his party colleague Dermot Ahern, Minister for Foreign Affairs, by 170 votes. Fianna Fáil, against expectations, had scooped up more than 42 per cent of the first-preference vote in the Wee County. As Kirk recalled in the run-up to the presidential election,

> Seán was involved with the organisation, but not hugely involved in recent years, but I think in this Presidential election he'll benefit from his Fianna Fáil association . . . I'd expect him to do pretty well, I think he could well be in the final shake-up, but it will all depend on the elimination process and where the votes go. If he can keep his first preferences above other independents and any party candidate he's in with a real chance.

———

On 9 May, Fingal County Council (north Co. Dublin) was the first council to pledge its support for a candidate. David Norris had previously written to every local authority asking to address them and seeking their support, and he was

> delighted to have received their support. It means that I am a quarter way to securing a nomination to run for the Presidency. Democracy is all about giving people choices, and I believe Fingal County Council have done just that.

But on the same day the election process was given a legal clarification. Malcolm Byrne of Gorey, a Fianna Fáil member of Wexford County Council, proposed nominating Norris. However, the motion was quashed after the county secretary, Niall McDonnell, informed the chamber that the council could not pass a resolution nominating a candidate until the election order was made in September, before the November election. Co. Wexford would have been the first to vote on a nomination otherwise.

So while candidates would canvass, and in some cases address, local authorities, the formal nomination could not be given, whatever verbal assurances and pledges were made, until September. Councils could only pledge support for a nomination, and a formal nomination could only be made once the minister signed the order for the election.

The Fianna Fáil leader, Micheál Martin, said it was important that there be a 'new way to do politics' and confirmed that the parliamentary party would make a 'definitive party position on the nomination' the following month.

Fine Gael had instructed its councillors throughout the country—in many cases they held the balance of power on local authorities—not to vote for the nomination of any independent candidate. Councillor Paddy Belton of Longford County Council spoke openly to the media about the ban imposed on him by Fine Gael head office. Norris had asked to address the council, and the council agreed; but before his arrival the Fine Gael group had contacted the party's head office seeking advice.

'We got word from headquarters,' according to Belton, a farmer from Kenagh, about five miles outside the county town. 'The instruction we got was to oppose him if it was proposed for Longford local authority to support him.' Belton said he told Norris of the instruction they had received after Norris had addressed the meeting. Norris asked if they would consider abstaining. 'No,' said Belton, 'I said this was instructions from HQ.'

In Lower Mount Street, Micheál Martin took a different approach from that of his opposite number in Upper Mount Street, saying he would allow a free vote for Fianna Fáil councillors on nominations for the Áras.

It is the Fianna Fáil view that the people of this country are entitled to have as wide a choice for the office of President as possible and that this office should not be limited to the official nominations of the political parties. For this reason, I will not be taking the same approach as other parties as they seek to block the nomination of independent candidates and will permit party representatives to facilitate the candidacy of individuals who they believe should have the right to stand before the electorate.

Fianna Fáil also distanced itself from the former Taoiseach Bertie Ahern. Reading between the lines, it was clear there was no nomination available for him. 'I don't think that's something on the agenda at all,' said Micheál Martin firmly.

Fianna Fáil now had three options: to nominate its own party member as candidate; to offer support to an independent, such as Gallagher, who had already begun contacting Fianna Fáil members of the Oireachtas; or, radically, to set a precedent for the party by not running a candidate. Were the party to decide not to run a candidate it would be the first time since 1938 that it did not put forward a candidate, and in that instance Dr Douglas Hyde became the first President of Ireland in an uncontested election.

'Martin needs to make up his mind if Fianna Fáil is going to run a candidate,' Ahern said subsequently, telling the *Evening Herald* that 'if Fianna Fáil are going to nominate someone they'd want to do it soon, because it's May now and time is running out.' Reconciled to a lost cause, he said:

I definitely won't be putting my name on the list. I always said I'd have my mind made up by St Patrick's Day but I actually decided before that, as far back as January.

I don't have the funds, for a start, to mount a campaign. You need a lot of money for these things. I don't expect I would have the support either. When you look at Brian Lenihan's campaign in 1990, he went in with a 44 per cent approval rating and still didn't get it. Now with the party on 17 per cent approval after the election, even if you doubled it you still wouldn't come close to what Brian Lenihan had.

Ahern had been Lenihan's director of elections in his presidential bid. He predicted that if John Bruton

puts his name forward he could get it. Also Michael D. Higgins and David Norris have a very good chance and both are great speakers and very experienced, and would represent us well abroad.

As two former Taoisigh bowed out of the contest without ever formally entering it, Pat Cox, a former party leader and president of the European Parliament, dipped his toe into the political waters. A former member of Fianna Fáil, a founder-member of the Progressive Democrats and an MEP, he said he was open to a nomination and support from political parties. 'I'm open on all fronts after declaring an interest to see what's out there that might permit me to get a nomination and take to the field,' he said. Questioned, he said: 'I certainly would take some time to consider it . . . I am prepared to ask myself a question this week that wasn't even on my mind a week ago.'

The columnist Eamon Keane cast his eye over the candidates. Cox wouldn't set the Park alight, he wrote. Fine Gael MEP Seán Kelly had pushed through admirable reforms in the GAA, but was the Presidency a bridge too far? he asked, suggesting that Fine Gael might yet spring a surprise. Both Mairead McGuinness and John Bruton were more capable than charismatic. And had Fergus Finlay the same charisma as either Higgins or Norris?

> Thankfully Norris has the sort of devilment in him that you wish the other candidates had. Remember his reaction to Cardinal Desmond Connell's comments on the evils of homosexuality? Connell had previously written a thesis on how God acts through angels. Norris was succinct in his reply: Dr Connell may know everything there is to know about angels, but you can take it from me that he knows sweet f*** all about fairies.

A star of the 'Dragons' Den' programme, Seán Gallagher had already received the support of Senator Feargal Quinn and was canvassing hard to secure the nomination of nine other independents and hopefully to secure the balance of support required from ten Fianna Fáil Oireachtas members. He was also canvassing local authorities seeking their support—like Norris, adopting a belt-and-braces approach.

Gallagher said he was happy to take support across party lines, despite being a former member of the Fianna Fáil Ard-Chomhairle. At the launch by Console of its suicide bereavement and prevention service he said:

> If I or any other company was employing somebody they would not look at their political background. They would look at the role, what that role should be, and the skill sets required to be effective.

At the same event David Norris thanked Micheál Martin for allowing a free vote for Fianna Fáil councillors.

Micheál Martin has started the process of opening it up because he has said that people of substance should be allowed into the race. He has released the councillors. That's a beginning. I think he has further to go, but I thank him for it.

However, he questioned the reason for Fine Gael deliberately blocking him. 'My candidacy has raised questions which the Fine Gael party have to resolve for themselves,' he said.

———

Mary Hanafin, speaking at Fianna Fáil's Ard-Chomhairle meeting on the last Thursday of the month, said the party 'was in the business of contesting for the highest office in the land. You can't throw in the towel because there might not be another Presidential election for fourteen years.' It was construed as a clear signal that she was interested in seeking the party's nomination.

Mary Hanafin's family was steeped in Fianna Fáil. Her cousins were and had been councillors in Co. Tipperary, her brother John was a senator, and her father, Des, had been a long-time senator and fund-raiser for the party. He was also a staunch opponent of divorce and abortion and a founder of the Society for the Protection of Unborn Children. Mary Hanafin was one of three potential candidates to emerge from the Premier County and the first from Thurles. A former teacher who had been involved in politics since she was fifteen—the nuns in her boarding-school allowed her out in the middle of the week to attend local cumann meetings—she had also served as a Dublin city councillor. As a former Minister for Education, Minister for Social Welfare and also Minister for Tourism she was considered a strong contender for the party leadership after Brian Cowen stepped aside, but she lost her Dún Laoghaire seat in the Fianna Fáil general election bloodbath.

Until the leadership and the sub-committee made up its mind about whether or not to run a candidate, Hanafin would continue to figure in online debates and media speculation as a possible candidate both for the Áras and for the by-election seat in Dublin West after the death of Brian Lenihan.

The former minister Éamon Ó Cuív delivered what was unknowingly a similar, and ironic, message to the Ard-Chomhairle meeting, saying that Sinn Féin would never run a candidate in East Belfast if its only concern was electoral defeat.

The same meeting heard that the party was more than €2 million in debt, and the party leader, Martin, advised people to 'live in the real world', which suggested that he was leaning towards not running a candidate. Hanafin would argue the case subsequently, saying, 'Even if you don't win it, that's not the point: it's about being part of the democratic process—that's what we are.'

——

Next door to the Dáil, in the National Library, Mary Davis had called a press conference for Thursday 27 May. Her web site went live, and a Facebook presence followed shortly. Announcing her decision to seek a nomination from county councils throughout the country, she confirmed that she would write to them seeking their support. In the coming months she would travel the country, embarking on a time-consuming personal canvass of as many council members as she could manage, calling to their homes or meeting in local hotels or in council offices.

Among the members of her team was her husband, Julian, a founding director of one of the biggest public relations companies in the country, Fleishman-Hillard. The campaign chairperson, Peter Fitzgerald, was a former deputy commissioner of the Garda Síochána; others included Ryan Meader—a former adviser to the Green Party minister John Gormley— and the Newbridge councillor Fiona O'Loughlin. The PR consultant Toni Wall would be the tour advance party. In the back room offering advice was the former Fianna Fáil general secretary Martin Mackin, while Suzanne Coogan, former PR adviser to the Minister for Defence, Willie O'Dea, handled the media.

Davis, speaking in front of a light-blue backdrop, said,

I'm standing as an independent: I don't have any political affiliations, I've never had all my life. So I'll be looking for support across all political parties when I go to talk to county councillors over the coming weeks and months.

She said she intended running an 'Obama-style' grass-roots campaign based on local communities. 'I've always been supported by communities at local levels. That is why I'm seeking county council nominations, so I intend to raise money in that way as well.'

Davis was awarded the Person of the Year award in 2003 for bringing the hugely successful Special Olympics to Ireland—the first time they were held outside the United States—and mobilising and motivating communities in cities, towns and villages throughout the country. As the managing director of Special Olympics Europe and Eurasia she had a formidable informal network that went into every community of host towns and villages in the country, while internationally she had demonstrated considerable diplomatic and representational skills. Her arrival on the electoral stage was a source of concern for all the candidates as they worked out her demographic appeal and prospects.

Davis announced that she would adopt a theme of 'building communities', saying that all her life she has 'been committed to the values of equality, fairness, respect, empowerment and involvement. I believe these values are very relevant to the times we live in and to the office as President.'

Davis, like other candidates, was concerned at the head-start and the free run that Norris had won by declaring his interest publicly and early. A series of soft interviews had followed his declaration, and now those eyeing up the race knew that they would be playing catch-up.

A few days after her declaration of intent, Davis appeared on the Pat Kenny programme in a mini-debate during which, according to the following day's *Irish Independent*, she became the latest presidential hopeful to put their foot in it, damaging their campaign.

In 2004 Davis had been appointed by President McAleese to the Council of State, which provides advice to the President. When questioned about referring a Finance Bill to the Supreme Court when President if she thought it was unfair, Davis said she would. 'If it's not fair, if it's not equal for people, no, I will not sign it into law. I will refer it,' she said.

She was taken to task immediately by a member of the studio audience, who pointed out that the President is not allowed to refer any bills to the Supreme Court simply because it is regarded as unfair: a bill could be referred only if it was unconstitutional. Under article 26 of the Constitution, the President doesn't have the power to refer a money bill—for example, the budget as implemented by the passing of the annual Finance Bill—to the Supreme Court, and it would simply pass into law if the President did not sign it.

While the gaffe raised questions about Davis's understanding of her obligations and her role as a member of the Council of State, her election team was able to breathe a sigh of relief, as there was minimal negative comment. One adviser suggested that the issue was not one that most people would engage with and that it was one of the benefits of being so far out from the election date that the public's curiosity was engaged in learning about the candidates but had not progressed to a detailed examination of their experience or background.

In the Labour Party camp, both Finlay and Higgins had been canvassing members of the parliamentary party in the corridors and over coffee in Leinster House. Each candidate had until 3 June to secure the nomination of at least one Labour Party constituency council to enter the race. Sixteen days later the TDs, MEPs, senators and Executive Board members would hold a selection convention. For Finlay,

> when I started out to make contact with each of the sixty or so people who have a vote in this contest, I said to myself if this is going nowhere I will know pretty quickly . . . I have had conversations with about two-thirds of them, and I don't think anyone could call the result. I am more than sufficiently encouraged. I think the outcome is unpredictable.

A straw poll suggested that Finlay was drawing support from a number of new parliamentary party members and those with advocacy links, while Higgins's support came from the party hierarchy and the left wing of the party. Higgins had already secured the support of Brendan Howlin, Minister for Public Expenditure and Reform, who would propose him at the selection convention, and Kathleen Lynch, Minister of State at the Department of Health, who would second his nomination.

But with only a few days to qualify for the convention, the RTE journalist and former senator Kathleen O'Meara announced that she would contest the election. Originally from Shinrone, Co. Offaly, she had been a town councillor in Nenagh, Co. Tipperary, was a senator from 1997 to 2007, elected on the Agriculture panel, and was a former adviser to the Minister of State at the Department of Finance, Eithne FitzGerald (Labour Party), a daughter-in-law of the former Taoiseach Garret FitzGerald. A triplet, O'Meara is a sister of the journalist Aileen O'Meara. She was the head of advocacy and communications with the Irish Cancer Society in Dublin but returned home to Nenagh at the weekends. She had also unsuccessfully contested three general elections for a seat in North Tipperary.

> This presidential election is taking place during one of the most difficult and challenging times in this nation's history, but also at a time when many citizens are asking who we are as a nation, what are our values, what do we cherish and who do we need to be to build our nation again . . . I want to build a project, a national engagement, a conversation which would take place in every community in Ireland, asking those questions and hearing from the people themselves about who they want us, Ireland, to be.

This vision would be given expression in a new proclamation, she said, to be declared in 2016, the centenary of the Proclamation of the Irish Republic. She said the Proclamation was ambitious and inspiring. However,

> we did not cherish all the children of the nation equally, for instance, and still don't. And we have had to concede sovereignty in the face of a financial failure, in order to survive and continue to exist . . . Amidst the wreckage we are now in, it is an opportunity to start again, to preserve the best of what we have created and build a new vision to take this nation forward. The theme of the next presidency, under my leadership, would be building the nation. This is why I am seeking this nomination.

——————

In his negotiations with the party hierarchy, John Bruton emphasised his economic and diplomatic expertise and experience. He also opened a discussion about extending the powers of the President. However, this did not sit comfortably with Enda Kenny and senior party members, sparking fears of a President eclipsing the Government.

The negotiations spilled into the public domain when Mairead McGuinness issued a statement in which she said that any increase in powers for the President could lead to 'an unhealthy and corrosive tension between the President and the Government and could also render the office prey to lobbyists and pressure groups.' This last reference could also be taken as a criticism of the new rival, Pat Cox, who had worked as an EU lobbyist in Brussels.

Within a fortnight Bruton had made it clear to the party leadership that he was not going to allow his name to go forward. Instead he would concentrate on his work with the Irish Financial Services Centre. As he cryptically explained to the *Sunday Times* when confronted about his decision not to allow his name go forward, 'if I had any internal communications with members of the party I wouldn't be discussing them with the media. I have been asked those questions in public and I have given those answers in public. What I have said is what I have said. There is nothing to add.'

There had been extensive discussions within Fine Gael about the electoral support for John Bruton as the agreed party candidate, rather than a potentially damaging raising of old divisions at a selection convention. Bruton was considered a strong candidate for the party, as its national standing would translate into a landslide vote for him. However, the MEPs McGuinness and Kelly were both keen for a contest, and consensus was unlikely.

Bruton had been holding talks with the party hierarchy with two specific aims: to get an agreed coalition candidate and to seek an expansion of the role of President. His discussions with party leaders emphasised article 10 of the Constitution, which allowed for additional powers and functions to be conferred on the President by law. However, this fundamental change in the role of the Presidency put the political antennae of party leaders on high alert, as they could see a President Bruton commanding the national and international stage rather than a Taoiseach, Kenny.

The talks were going nowhere. Bruton decided to pull out of the race and issued a brief statement at the end of the month.

I discussed the matter thoroughly with the party's representatives. I promised to reflect carefully on the request and respond . . . I did so about ten days ago [mid-May 2011] when I said, with regret, that I did not wish my name to be among those considered.

Another opinion poll that weekend included withdrawn, declared and speculative candidates. Bruton, who had just withdrawn, was polling poorly and was in second place, at 11 per cent, but the runaway winner was Norris, at 41 per cent. The other candidates were bunched in two groups: Higgins at 9 per cent, Finlay at 8 per cent and Cox at 7 per cent; Crowley polling a poor 5 per cent, Gallagher at 3 per cent and McGuinness at 2 per cent.

A few days later Seán Kelly ruled himself out after months of speculation that he would contest the Fine Gael convention. He made his formal announcement on RTE's 'Morning Ireland', explaining that he had both personal and political reasons.

It was my own decision. Serious momentum was starting to build up behind me, but I felt that I could make a bigger contribution to Europe and Munster by withdrawing from the race. The last thing they [the electorate] want is a candidate who isn't committed to the job. My gut instinct is not to go with it.

Kelly also said that his father had died the previous month, that his mother was living alone and that he still had some family in school, all considerations that had influenced his decision.

Chapter 5 ∾

| THE PARADE RING

The withdrawal of Bruton and Kelly focused the minds of senior party members in Fine Gael, particularly the troika of the Minister for the Environment, Phil Hogan, the Taoiseach, Enda Kenny, and the deputy director of elections, Frank Flannery.

Fine Gael had never had a candidate elected to the Presidency, but if it could transfer its strength and support as shown in the opinion polls, for both party and leader, it could easily win the office. The question was who its candidate should be—and, perhaps more to the point, who should decide what was best for the party: a swell from the grass roots or an 'informed' decree from Mount Street?

Fine Gael had commissioned research, not about who the public wanted as a candidate but about what qualities they wanted from a candidate. John Bruton ticked all the boxes; the number 2 selection was Pat Cox. Now, with Bruton out of the contest, there was only one choice if it was to secure the Park for the first time. Reflecting the old adage about a week being a long time in politics, an afternoon—at a wedding—was to influence Fine Gael's tilt at the Presidency.

On the day of their thirty-first wedding anniversary, Friday 3 June, Gay and Norma Mitchell were at the wedding in Donegal of Fine Gael's Dublin regional organiser, Colm Jordan, to a local woman, Alison Hamilton. Jordan took up a new position with Alan Shatter when the latter was appointed Minister for Justice.

At the reception in Lough Eske Castle Hotel, the Mitchells were seated at the dinner with the former minister Nora Owen and her husband, the Dublin

TDs Terence Flanagan and Eoghan Murphy and the chairperson of the party's Executive Council, Brian Murphy, a former adviser to Mitchell who now worked in the office of Leo Varadkar, Minister for Transport. Also seated nearby were the ministers Frances Fitzgerald and Alan Shatter, the minister of state Brian Hayes and the Dublin councillor Neale Richmond, who was previously an assistant to Mitchell.

The Presidency was a topic of conversation among the politicians: the nomination of Cox had been in the news that morning, John Bruton had withdrawn from the race, and Mairead McGuinness was still seeking the nomination.

As dinner progressed, one of the guests suggested that either Nora Owen— a sister of Mary Banotti, who had unsuccessfully carried the Fine Gael standard in the Presidential election fourteen years earlier—or Gay Mitchell should put their name forward.

Gabriel 'Gay' Mitchell (59) was first elected to the Dáil in 1981 for the sprawling Dublin South-Central constituency, which includes Terenure, Crumlin, Walkinstown and Ballyfermot. He gave up his seat in 2007, saying he wanted to concentrate his energies on the European Parliament, to which he was first elected in 2004. He had previously served as Lord Mayor of Dublin, during which time he launched an initiative to bring the Olympic Games to Dublin, and was Minister of State for European Affairs from 1994 to 1997. He lost out in the party's leadership contest in 2002 to Enda Kenny.

On the four-hour journey back to Dublin his wife, Norma, took the steering-wheel, while Mitchell canvassed friends, party colleagues and its leader, Kenny, for their opinion about him making a bid for the Presidency. In a statement seven days later he announced his decision.

I have been giving serious consideration to the possibility of running for President. Yesterday I attended the funeral of Declan Costello whose political principles and approach to public service convinced me to join Fine Gael at the age of 16. Since then my political conviction is informed by a Christian Democratic ethos, based on four pillars: rights and responsibilities, enterprise and social justice.

Declan Costello, who had died at the age of eighty-four, was the son of the former Taoiseach John A. Costello, served in the Dáil for twenty years, was first elected in 1951 for Fine Gael, served as Attorney-General and later became president of the High Court. He pushed Fine Gael to the left in the 1960s and persuaded the party to publish his document 'Towards a Just Society', which was taken up as party policy by Garret FitzGerald. The former Taoiseach John Bruton would also cite him as his inspiration for entering politics.

Mitchell went into detail about twenty-six years of service as a Fine Gael TD and about his various political roles, but he made no reference to his decision, six months earlier, not to run for the Áras. He said he believed in unity in diversity but not in

> a diversity that includes only the politically correct . . . I want to play my part in ensuring that Ireland's views are heard where it matters and that they are heeded. This may require more perspiration than inspiration, and I believe I have the experience and the stamina to advance Ireland's cause.

Setting out a narrative that would be repeated throughout his campaign, he continued:

> My life's journey has brought me from the home of my widowed mother in Inchicore to the Dáil, the Mansion House and Brussels. From the President's study, which I visited many times as a minister, the floodlights of CIE works, where I worked as a boy, are visible as a clear landmark. If I am elected President this landmark shall be a daily reminder of where I came from and that my sworn duty is to serve the welfare of the people as well as to uphold the Constitution and the law.

Though he had contested the leadership of Fine Gael in 2002 with Kenny, now Taoiseach, in the leadership heave before the 2011 general election Mitchell threw his support behind Kenny and was also credited with corralling the support of all four Fine Gael MEPs.

Mitchell had an otherwise perfect and formidable record of winning political contests. During a career of thirty-one years he had won fourteen elections: eight general elections, to retain his seat, four local elections and two European elections. This meant that on average he was on the hustings every two years. He had also campaigned as director of elections in referendum campaigns and in by-elections.

The first member of the Fine Gael parliamentary party to offer public support for Mitchell's candidacy was Catherine Byrne, a Dublin South-Central TD who inherited her seat from him.

Meanwhile, Pat Cox moved swiftly. He had been in continuous contact with senior members of the party, and when told of Mitchell's decision to run he confirmed that he was willing to do what was necessary to secure the nomination, namely to join Fine Gael. It was an audacious political parachute for a former member of Fianna Fáil and unsuccessful local election candidate for the party in 1979, a staunch ally of the former minister Des O'Malley and a founding member of the Progressive Democrats.

Cox had initially mused out loud about whether he would allow his name go forward for a nomination. The seeming arrogance of his comments, which gave the impression that all the party had to do was to convince him to run under its standard, annoyed long-standing Fine Gael members, and also suggested that he had a 'done deal' with Mount Street.

Cox had an impressive national and international CV, but he was politically promiscuous, having served three times as an MEP, twice for the Progressive Democrats and finally as an independent. In 2002 he was elected president of the European Parliament and in 2009 he campaigned for the Fianna Fáil MEP Eoin Ryan in Dublin, who lost his seat.

In the run-up to the general election, with opinion polls predicting a Fine Gael victory, Cox volunteered his services to Fine Gael. There he helped put together a plan of action for the first hundred days of office—a significant plan that would grant the party credibility as it took office for the first time in more than a decade—aimed at enthusing the social partners, the electorate and, increasingly significant, Europe. The first hundred days in office of any political party had become a diary-marking for political and specialist correspondents.

In the cosy cockpit of planning for a future electoral endorsement in the Fine Gael offices in Leinster House, and in the nearby head office in Mount Street, it would be frequently suggested to Cox that he might make the leap into constituency politics and become a candidate. But this was not on his agenda. However, his service would obviously require subsequent recognition. In a statement issued on 7 June, Cox said:

> I am informed that having stood as a candidate for Dáil Éireann and the European Parliament 'other than as a Fine Gael candidate' requires that the question of party membership 'shall not be considered without the approval in writing of the Executive Council' . . . I have written to the General Secretary of Fine Gael, Mr Tom Curran, requesting such written approval. Pending the result of these deliberations I have no further comment to make at this time.

Then he went on a previously arranged holiday for a week to walk part of the ancient St James pilgrimage trail to Santiago de Compostela in Spain.

Questioned on a visit to Cork, Enda Kenny said he was not backing any of his party's three declared candidates.

> Clearly the opportunity for Fine Gael here is stronger than it used to be— put it that way. And obviously the units of the party will decide by vote who our chosen candidate will be. What I want is a candidate who will win.

Kenny's public statement of non-endorsement came after Mitchell had demanded the leader's neutrality in the contest.

——

On Sunday 19 June the sixty-two members of the Labour Party electoral college piled into the wood-panelled Oak Room of the Mansion House, its walls decorated with the coats of arms of each of the city's former Lord Mayors. The party's thirty-seven TDs, twelve senators and three MEPs, together with the party's Executive Board, prepared to vote.

That morning's papers had tipped Michael D. Higgins to win but suggested also that Fergus Finlay was a realistic threat. Kathleen O'Meara was given little hope. It was reported that, when asked about her chances, having failed three times to win a Dáil seat, she responded: 'So did Mary Robinson. There are many people who run for election several times. Sometimes we have to play the right game.'

The party leader, Eamon Gilmore, opened the good-humoured convention with a pledge that 'the candidate that we select will of course be a candidate for whom we all campaign.'

Finlay was first up and recited his CV before speaking about his vision for the office.

> It's easy to be cynical about the Presidency, but it is an office which is the exclusive property of the people, which costs the same to run each year as it costs to build just under three hundred yards of motorway and which can yield enormous benefits to the people.

The country needed a working President, he said, 'a President whose sleeves are rolled up every day of the week.' With some hint of premonition of the coming months, he said: 'This contest will be tense and exciting. Careers will be made and damaged by the outcome.'

In his entertaining book about his previous time in Government, *Snakes and Ladders*, Finlay set out his failings as a vote-catcher and his election superstitions, which he had obviously overcome in putting his name forward for the presidential nomination.

> I was doing what I always do during an election—living on coffee and cigarettes in head office. I have a superstition about elections—I've always been convinced that if I ask anyone for a vote we'll lose the seat. In fifteen years in active politics, I never once knocked on a door to ask anyone to vote for the party. I couldn't do it now to save my life.

Higgins asserted confidently that it is 'possible to both possess a vision and at the same time achieve practical results,' adding that his campaign would be about 'building an inclusive citizenship in a creative society appropriate to a republic.' He said that he hoped the campaign would allow the public to move 'beyond recriminations' about who caused the economic crisis to how the country could redefine itself according to its strengths.

Convention day was 'daunting', O'Meara told the meeting. It was also Father's Day, she reminded them, saying she was glad her father hadn't had to witness the arrival of the International Monetary Fund eight months earlier. Dissolving into tears, she said:

> My father, who was born in 1917, was raised through the Civil War and the War of Independence. He worked hard, like many others, to build this country, and he loved it and believed in it. And I thought, thank God he's not here to see this.

She recalled later that 'it was very emotional for me, it was personal and it was difficult,' saying that her son had to leave Ireland to find work in Australia.

The count was decisive. O'Meara won 7 votes, Finlay 18, but Higgins was the clear winner with 37.

Gilmore spoke to the media after the convention. Higgins, from the same county, had been a mentor and strong supporter in earlier days in the party and had twice proposed him in leadership contests. Gilmore recognised the lack of control that he, or Labour Party head office, would have over the campaign and candidate.

> This is not a campaign that the Labour Party intends to micromanage, to control what Michael D has to say. We're going to respect from today Michael D's independence as a candidate, the same way as we will respect Michael D's independence as President when he's elected.

It was a recognition of tensions that would emerge, but that never flared into public view, between Higgins's hand-picked team and Labour Party head office. On one occasion Higgins would flounce out of the office after a row.

Higgins's ambition for the Park was more than twenty years old, but the planning for the 2011 election began twenty months before the vote. In the summer of 2010 Kevin O'Driscoll, an old friend of Higgins and his former programme manager during Higgins's tenure as Minister for Arts, Culture and the Gaeltacht, called to visit him in hospital as he recovered from an operation on his knees. Higgins had previously expressed an interest in running for

President, but now he told O'Driscoll that he was going to run the following year and that he was going to retire from the Dáil.

Over the coming months they would discuss putting together a team and a policy platform. They were joined by the retired civil servant Chris O'Grady, who had worked in the film section of the Department of Arts when Higgins was minister and would be an important speech-writer. In May 2011 O'Driscoll, who would be his election agent, was on holiday in Antibes in the south of France, and he invited Higgins and O'Grady to join him in the Mediterranean sun, where they put the finishing touches to a shadow campaign.

Alice Mary Higgins, the candidate's daughter, was central to the management of the campaign as joint deputy director of elections with her colleague Councillor Brian McDowell, a member of the party staff.

The former Labour Party press officer Tony Heffernan would be coaxed out of retirement for the campaign. Greg Sparks (accountant), Morgan O'Sullivan, David Leach (national organiser), Ita McAuliffe (general secretary), Michael Treacy (parliamentary adviser) and Shauneen Armstrong completed the team. Mags Murphy looked after the tour logistics.

Constantly at his elbow during the campaign was Higgins's wife, Sabina Coyne, who supervised the Galway campaign with their son Daniel, which would deliver 60 per cent of the vote in the county. Another son, John, made a campaign video featuring his father through the decades. The core team met for the first time a fortnight after the selection convention and from then on once a week in the Mansion House.

A sliding scale of financial contributions was also drawn up by head office, requiring contributions to the campaign of €2,000 each from ministers and MEPs, €1,500 for ministers of state, €1,000 from Dáil deputies, €700 from each senator and €500 from party councillors. The Labour Party was to contribute approximately €320,000 to the campaign.

The Fine Gael aspirant Pat Cox was subsequently admitted to membership of the St Luke's Branch of the party in the Cork North-Central constituency, and two weeks later he confirmed at a press conference in Dublin that he had his nomination papers signed by twenty members of the Oireachtas, thirty of the party's county councillors and five of the National Executive for the convention planned for the following month.

The Fine Gael electoral college gives 70 per cent of the votes to TDs, senators and MEPs, 20 per cent to the councillors and 10 per cent to the Executive Council.

Cox's parachuting into the party, and his support from the party hierarchy, had raised tensions in the party. He was seen by some as an opportunist 'blow-in', despite his valuable international reputation.

Mairead McGuinness, who had made it clear that she joined the party when it was 'neither popular nor profitable', was still relatively new in the party, while Mitchell, despite his feisty image, had served the party long and loyally. Bruton had been the original favoured candidate, but now there would be a dog-fight for the nomination, with no overt guidance from the party leadership.

In the *Irish Times*, Stephen Collins in his Saturday column described the presidential election campaign as the strangest in the history of the country.

> Fine Gael probably has the most to lose if it gets it wrong. It became the biggest party in local government for the first time in 2009 and the biggest in the Dáil for the first time in February and so the Presidency should be its for the taking.

He added that some of Mitchell's strongest supporters came from the ranks of those who had tried to depose Kenny only a year earlier. He continued:

> While he has Kenny supporters, the potential for opening old wounds is there. 'There is every chance now that we will revert to type, have an all-out internal war and then run a disastrous campaign,' said one experienced party activist.

In the following day's *Sunday Independent*, John Drennan wrote how the election would reveal the true state of our politics.

> Rather like the great struggle between Mary Robinson and Brian Lenihan Snr, which morphed into a battle between the patriarchal Old and a better New Ireland, or the triumph of McAleese, which signified the return of FF to the centre of the national stage, this current campaign will also send out a number of key political messages.
>
> In spite of all the feigned indifference, Mr Kenny is more than keen to strengthen FG's imprint on the institutions of the State, for should FG secure the Presidency the great purpose of stealing FF's clothes to such an extent that FG becomes the new natural party of government will be complete.

Across the page, Eamon Delaney warned that allowing Cox to be considered for the race might prove a fatal move for Fine Gael. Bluntly he asked:

> Has Fine Gael lost its mind? . . . Mitchell is a populist, sure-footed, with long experience of politics—Irish politics—and, crucially, he has a vision for the job, which McGuinness doesn't appear to have. He is politically

right of centre and, most importantly, a big vote-getter—the biggest nationally. All due respects to Pat Cox, but what does he stand for?

Delaney went some way towards answering his own question.

> He appears arrogant: cold and careerist. I was in the company of some ex-PDs recently who rated his intellect and ability but their comments gave the impression of someone with an immense sense of entitlement.
>
> Indeed his ego was already evident in those media interviews where he first offered himself as a candidate, including all the Hamlet soul-searching stuff about 'having a dialogue with himself' about whether to enter the great contest . . .
>
> Mairead McGuinness represents another equally feisty FG element and could have strong rural appeal, but she is too studied and too cautious, and seems to be waiting to kick into action as a key replica of Robinson/McAleese . . .
>
> As for Cox, he may have the ability, but he is too cool and detached. One feels that his ambition is his own, as opposed to one shared by the country and, crucially in this case, the Fine Gael party who have to get him elected.

The *Sunday Times* published a substantial editorial that cautioned that, with Fine Gael scoring a poll rating of more than 40 per cent, the presidential election was theirs to lose.

> But failing to persuade John Bruton, a former Taoiseach, to stand has been a blow. The party's response, making overtures to Pat Cox, could backfire. Mr Cox, a former president of the European Parliament, will be regarded by many of the Fine Gael faithful as a blow-in, a fair description of a person who was formerly a member of the Progressive Democrats. Mairead McGuinness, who gave up the prospect of a near-certain seat in the general election, had expected to be the party's choice. She will not be pleased by Mr Cox's intervention, and nor will Gay Mitchell, a formidable operator, who has put his name forward.
>
> Not only has Mr Cox upset the balance of power in Fine Gael but his devotion to Brussels could be a lightning rod for the growing number disaffected by the EU who believe that Ireland's interests are no longer aligned with those of Germany and France. It could be Lisbon all over again.

McGuinness had been busy canvassing the electoral college and made a virtue of her Fine Gael credentials when questioned about how her campaign was progressing. She had been meeting party members since she announced her campaign, but it was too soon to identify the leader in the three-horse race. Savvy politicians will never hex their own campaign by saying they are leading, or annoy an electorate into either complacency or anger at a show of confidence or arrogance. Taking a swipe at Cox, McGuinness said that

> the vibe from the grass roots is extremely solid for my campaign. I've always believed that you build solid from the grass roots up, you don't do it from the top down . . . I was perhaps out of the stall way earlier. But the fact is I have been out there; people are saying to me that they knew me from way back. I was interested in contesting the Presidency on the basis of what I have to offer.

Liam Twomey, a Wexford TD, referred to the resentment against Cox when he confirmed to the *Sunday Business Post* that the former MEP and minister of state Avril Doyle would announce in a couple of days that she would seek the party's nomination. According to Twomey—like John the Baptist, heralding his candidate—after listening to 'some hard-hitting' comments about Cox's entry into the race, Doyle believed that she offered 'the same ability, appeal and experience' but that she

> has also dedicated her life to Fine Gael at national and European level and would bring this to the campaign . . . Avril has huge regard for Pat Cox, but feels that within the electoral college he has lost momentum, and she shares many of the characteristics of Pat Cox.

The Fine Gael stage was becoming crowded. Doyle's candidacy would reignite the fierce rivalry between McGuinness and Doyle that had characterised a previous election in Leinster for a seat in the European Parliament. In the event they both won seats in the Leinster constituency, as their campaigns and public skirmishing kept them in the headlines throughout the campaign. However, three of the candidates were now from the east, a consideration that might give Cox, from Cork, an edge.

Formally announcing that she would be running, Doyle emphasised her Fine Gael credentials and her service to the party and said she was unique in being born and raised in Dublin but having been living and working in Wexford for thirty years.

> I believe I'm the one who can most credibly represent urban and rural Ireland and all the best traditions of Fine Gael . . . I believe the experience and drive I represent offers my party the best chance of electing a Fine Gael President for the first time.

On Thursday 30 June the *Irish Independent* published a survey of the four Fine Gael candidates as they prepared to address the parliamentary party at a special meeting convened in their new party rooms in Leinster House. They were given eight minutes each to make a pitch for the vote of their parliamentary colleagues.

The large room on the top floor of the block is reached from a lift beside the Dáil canteen or from the floor above outside the chief whip's office. It was a trophy room in the Oireachtas complex, as it had been the Fianna Fáil meeting-room before its numbers were reduced by three-quarters and it reluctantly had to hand over the keys. Party representatives had produced tape measures as they argued about representation and heads per square metre in an attempt to decide who should retain or move into the most prestigious rooms.

It was all to play for in the battle for the Fine Gael ticket, said the *Independent* on its front page. However, the paper found that Mairead McGuinness was leading her rivals, as ten members of the parliamentary party declared for her, although many TDs and senators did not respond to the request to declare for their preferred candidate. 'There are twelve to fifteen turnips in the party waiting for a sign from the leadership,' said one anonymous TD. 'I don't see Pat Cox getting going unless the leadership comes out and backs him.' The term 'turnip' was being used by parliamentary party members to describe backbenchers who went along with the dictates of the hierarchy, while those who resisted were termed 'parsnips'. Neither was complimentary, but they pointed up some internal division or, at a minimum, dissatisfaction.

A senior party TD was quoted as saying: 'Mairead thinks Kenny is backing her; Gay thinks he's backing him; Cox is the anointed one; and Avril wouldn't be in it if she didn't think she had his blessing.'

The political editor, Fionnan Sheahan, summed up the phone survey, saying that each candidate faced their own obstacles in the battle to win support. He said that McGuinness was not universally popular within the party, that Mitchell was not strong in rural areas, that Doyle had left it too late to enter the campaign and that Cox was an outsider.

———

Only hours after Michael D. Higgins became the first political-party nominee for the Áras, the publisher Niall O'Dowd flew into Dublin from the United States to formally announce his interest in seeking a nomination for the Presidency from both Fianna Fáil and Sinn Féin. O'Dowd (58) was born in Thurles, Co. Tipperary, was raised in Drogheda and studied at UCD. His older brother Fergus is Minister of State at the Department of Communications, Energy and Natural Resources and at the Department of the Environment, Community and Local Government, with responsibility for the 'New Era Project'; he also held a number of senior positions on the Fine Gael front bench and was formerly a senator and Mayor of Drogheda.

Over the coming days Niall O'Dowd would run a storming campaign, meeting the media and potential political sponsors—the opposite to his experience in the United States, where he had been centrally involved in the Democratic Party's campaign for the Clintons. He founded a newspaper, the *Irishman*, in California before moving to New York, where he would establish an Irish-themed magazine and the newspaper *Irish Voice* and the hub site Irishcentral.com.

Politically active, he established the Irish-Americans for Clinton campaign in 1991 and led an Irish-American delegation to Northern Ireland after Clinton was elected. He was also an intermediary between Sinn Féin and the White House during the peace process and helped secure an American visa for the party president, Gerry Adams, in 1994.

O'Dowd has consistently worked on behalf of Irish emigrants to the United States and created the US-Ireland Forum, a forerunner of the Diaspora Forum hosted by the Irish Government, in 2009. He remains close to the Clintons and served on Hillary Clinton's Finance Committee for her 2008 presidential campaign.

In April 2011, at the inaugural Irish American Hall of Fame luncheon in New York, the former president Bill Clinton said his involvement in the Northern Ireland issue was on the initiative of O'Dowd.

O'Dowd declared his interest in the post while he was in the United States after he was approached by a number of people during the visit to Ireland by President Obama, who felt O'Dowd could be an independent candidate who would work with the Irish diaspora. He would refuse to identify the people who urged him to go forward, only saying that he had not approached the Clintons at any time for their support as he considered his potential bid.

O'Dowd's decision to seek support for a run sparked an article from Walter Ellis, a former diplomatic correspondent and correspondent in Brussels and Belfast for the *Irish Times*, who lives in both France and the United States, questioning his credentials. It also referred to O'Dowd taking the American oath of allegiance. Ellis wrote combatively that O'Dowd

> must be the first aspirant to Áras an Uachtaráin who sees Ireland and the Irish as a brand, not a nation . . . According to an article published on Irish Central [an Irish-interest portal established by O'Dowd] this week, he would, as president, call on the power of the Irish diaspora and bring it to

bear on the country's crippled economy. He would rally the world's wealthiest Irish people and encourage them to invest in Ireland, North and South, believing that, 'all things being equal', heritage clinches the deal.

Like most Irish-Americans, O'Dowd has an atavistic disdain for Britain and its royal family. Of Queen Elizabeth's State visit he wrote in March: 'Myself, I wouldn't cross the road to see her, but I think on balance it is a good thing . . . hopefully.'

Prince William, he wrote in November, was 'a member of the lucky sperm club'.

Kate Middleton, now the Duchess of Cambridge, was 'a good stud mare', who would be judged by whether or not she produced 'young colts' to secure the bloodline.

The recent royal wedding was 'a fitting circus for a fading empire'. Perhaps as well then that he was not in the Áras when Her Majesty came to call.

A veteran supporter of the peace process, O'Dowd is rightly credited with helping obtain US visas for former leaders of the IRA and for pricking the interest of President Clinton in a cause whose time had come. For he remains at heart an old-time republican.

According to O'Dowd, 'the reality is you gotta fish where the fish are, and the only votes for me are with Fianna Fáil and Sinn Féin.' He initially met the general secretary of Fianna Fáil, Seán Dorgan, and also Mary Lou McDonald and Gerry Adams of Sinn Féin. He ruled out the possibility of getting a nomination from county councils: that was not possible for him due to time constraints, as he had to tend his business interests. He said he would announce the success of his talks. 'I'm not going to spend a whole lot of time dilly-dallying over this decision. I will make my decision in a week or two as to whether or not I will go forward with this effort.'

O'Dowd blogged on his Irishcentral.com site saying he never thought taking the oath of allegiance when he became an American citizen would be thrown at him as something negative. There would be criticisms in the coming days about where his allegiance would or should lie after taking the oath, while the debate forgot that a previous President, Éamon de Valera, had been an American citizen by birth. O'Dowd wrote that

the presenter on Newstalk radio zeroes right in on it after a British writer for the *Irish Times* raised the issue. It seems a spurious argument, given that I have worked on Irish issues and have always been entirely comfortable with my allegiance to both countries. I will yield to no one my right to be Irish . . . Overall, it has been a fascinating experience.

He then recounted how he dealt with the Ellis article as put to him by Pat Kenny.

> In the event the interview is fair but tough. The *Irish Times* screed by London *Times* obituary writer Walter Ellis accused me of being anti-British Royal family and too extreme gets an airing but I am comfortable answering the questions.
>
> If the worst my opponents can throw at me is that I question the magnificence of the British Royal family to an audience in the Irish Republic I am on pretty safe grounds . . .
>
> The major declared candidates for this job are running on lifelong resumes as politicians, several from the now discredited European Parliament. The last thing Irish people want to hear right now are politicians given the mess the country is in. There is also a dearth of ideas among those candidates, with mostly touchy feely yak yak about national conversations and kumbaya sentiments.
>
> I take the tack that I can help with jobs, tourism and education.

In setting out his stall he said he would be a 'travelling salesman' for Ireland and that the role could drive more American investment in Ireland.

> I don't accept for a minute that the job is meaningless. I think it's a powerfully uplifting office at a time when Ireland's image abroad needs every bit of help it can get.

Ten days after he arrived in Ireland, O'Dowd had blitzed radio programmes and met representatives of Sinn Féin and Fianna Fáil. After some reflection he told the media he was not going to run for the Park, saying he had stopped believing he could win. Without saying it, clearly the support was not forthcoming.

> I have been given a fair hearing and am content that the issue of how the next president, with the help of the Diaspora, can help secure jobs and stop the involuntary emigration of Ireland's young people has been raised. I want to thank those who had promised support and to give an undertaking that I will continue to work on behalf of Irish and emigrant issues in my current capacity.

O'Dowd also said he could not compete financially with the political parties.

> The race costs about €480,000 to run a proper national campaign. The main political parties can easily raise that.

The logistical challenges of running for an office as an independent against established political parties is incredible. It is a complicated system which overwhelmingly favours the big guns in the main political parties such as Fine Gael and Labour. Bottom line: unless they are completely terrible candidates either the Labour or Fine Gael contender will win the race. Quite simply, I believe the race is not winnable for an independent, any independent, no matter what the current polls say.

Gerry Adams of Sinn Féin would later confirm that he had advised O'Dowd to pull out of the contest.

I strongly advised O'Dowd not to stand, because he is a friend of mine. He didn't really know what he was letting himself in for, and, as an independent, it is difficult. It is a very undemocratic system.

Ten days later O'Dowd would write for www.thejournal.ie saying that the power elites in Ireland don't want to acknowledge the great contribution made by Irish emigrants to their native land, because to do so would be to admit that the state has failed them.

I think we Irish abroad threaten the status quo in a way that is quite surprising even to me. The *Irish Times* did their readers the single courtesy of printing, unbidden, the pledge each person takes on taking American citizenship. Even though the Irish state recognises dual citizenship, the august *Irish Times* clearly does not.

He added that since 1840 more than half the people born in Ireland had emigrated. Their descendants make up the 70-million-strong diaspora around the world.

O'Dowd went on to quote a letter about Irish economic emigrants that Paul Hill, one of the Guildford Four, had written to him when he announced that he was not going to contest the race.

I worked with these men on the buildings of London, many lived in bedsits which were no more than hovels, yet every week the first port of call for these men was the post office, Ireland was never forgotten. Those pointing the finger today never give those men a thought as they passed away penniless on the streets of London.

O'Dowd concluded:

There is no emigrant senator, no minister for immigrant affairs, quite the contrary, a determination to block any voting rights or any real participation in the dialogue. I quickly realised the race was not winnable, running against the vastly superior firepower of the major parties who set all the rules. Like a lot of things in Ireland, I discovered the cards are held where only the insiders can deal them.

He would later endorse the Sinn Féin candidate as one of the great arbiters of the Irish peace process.

On Thursday 7 July, Phil Hogan, the Fine Gael strategist and Minister for the Environment, 'bumped into' Pat Cox in Dublin and posed for photographs with him for the lucky photographers who 'happened' to be nearby. It was seen as a set-up, despite protestations to the contrary and a clear endorsement from Mount Street for Cox's campaign. Party sources denied that he was being shown favouritism. 'It was a chance encounter, which should not be interpreted as support for Mr Cox's campaign.'

Meanwhile, Avril Doyle announced that she was pulling out of the contest, saying she was 'unlikely to secure the nomination, notwithstanding the fact that I retain the support of a sizeable number of the parliamentary party.' She said she was acting in the best interests of the party, and that she would not be endorsing any candidate before the convention.

The *Irish Independent* reported that senior Fine Gael figures were contacting undecided members of the parliamentary party in the run-up to the convention. They said that head office had carried out an opinion poll and that it showed Cox and McGuinness securing 22 per cent of the vote each, with Mitchell trailing at 14 per cent. One TD said that head office was 'terrified' of the prospect of Mitchell winning the nomination, and that they preferred Cox but would settle for McGuinness instead of Mitchell.

Fine Gael never released the market research. However, the reported figures are believed to have shown Norris leading the field, with all three Fine Gael candidates trailing.

Twenty-one years earlier Fine Gael head office had commissioned the Market Research Bureau of Ireland to conduct an opinion poll to assess the likely candidates, including Brian Lenihan (senior) and Mary Robinson, and the potential Fine Gael candidates, Peter Barry, Avril Doyle and, its eventual candidate, Austin Currie. Any rating below 3.5 would translate into certain defeat at the polls. Lenihan topped the poll with 3.91, Robinson scored 3.7, Barry and John Wilson 2.94, Doyle 2.86 and Currie, trailing last, 2.74. Despite scoring the lowest, Currie was selected as its official—and, as it turned out, unsuccessful—candidate.

Convinced that he was being undermined with an opinion poll and a phone campaign, Mitchell fired off an angry letter to head office complaining about party bias and favouritism.

On Saturday 9 July, Fine Gael's electoral college, with 650 delegates, gathered in the Regency Hotel in Whitehall, Dublin. Frances Fitzgerald, Minister for Children and a Dublin North-West TD, proposed Mitchell, saying that Fine Gael had never won the Presidency but that it could do so now. John Bruton, who had earlier withdrawn from the party's nomination process, had signed Mitchell's nomination papers. Mitchell told delegates that he would campaign on the four pillars of his political philosophy—'rights, responsibilities, enterprise and social justice'—and added that 'we need to return to a less harsh and more merciful society.'

Party delegates were still buoyed up by the result of the general election and by continuing support in the opinion polls for the party. Enda Kenny spoke to the crowded room as votes were being counted. 'Fine Gael doesn't have any right to this Presidency . . . it's something we have to win.' Then he momentarily forgot his own caution: 'As we speak, the future of Áras an Uachtaráin—potentially—is being counted in the next room.'

Brian Murphy, chairperson of the Executive Council of Fine Gael, announced the elimination of Cox after he received less than 25 per cent of the first vote. By 5 p.m. he was able to announce Mitchell as the Fine Gael presidential candidate, as he had taken 55 per cent of the vote, to McGuinness's 45 per cent.

Kenny's face fell as the result was announced and, according to reporters, he could barely disguise his disappointment. At a press conference after the vote Mitchell revealed that he was going to take a week's holiday before throwing himself into the campaign. Publicly rebuking him, Kenny said: 'Take your holiday and enjoy it, because, believe you me, when you come back you better be ready for one hell of a campaign.'

Mitchell said he would attend the Patrick MacGill Summer School in the Glenties, Co. Donegal, before taking off to the Mediterranean for a week on a holiday that was already booked.

Mitchell's strong canvassing skills and his service to the party had won him the nomination, and he wasn't going to let the party forget how Cox had been favoured over his candidacy.

We are the hierarchy, the parliamentary party. The executive council made a very firm point. They re-established themselves and made a very firm point as to who makes the decisions.

A journalist challenged Kenny, saying he looked disappointed with the result. 'Am I supposed to be going around grinning like a Cheshire cat at everything?' Kenny replied tartly.

The next edition of the *Phoenix* had Mitchell and Kenny on the cover, with a speech bubble from Mitchell saying, 'There'll be a gay in the Park for sure.' Kenny's bubble replied: 'But it won't be you.'

A number of profiles of Mitchell were published in the wake of his selection. It was said in the *Daily Mail* that he was

> the shock choice of Fine Gael as its presidential candidate; a man who, according to many in the party, achieved the nomination because he wasn't Pat Cox rather than because he was Gay Mitchell.
>
> Mitchell is a combative—some might even say prickly—politician with some pretty eyebrow-raising views about Ireland, including his support for a radical anti-abortionist who murdered a doctor in the US.

This was a reference to an event in 2003 when Mitchell, who consistently campaigned against the death penalty, called on the Governor of Florida, Jeb Bush, to spare the life of Paul Jennings Hill, who in 1994 murdered a doctor and his bodyguard because the doctor performed abortions. Hill was executed by lethal injection. Mitchell had also campaigned to prevent the execution of Louis Joe Truesdale, Junior, the rapist and murderer of a teenager.

Mitchell made the headlines again in 2010 when he invited the radical anti-abortion activist Dr Alveda King (a niece of Dr Martin Luther King) to Dublin, where she met senior members of Fine Gael, including Kenny. The *Mail* also reminded readers of his notorious cousin George Mitchell, 'the Penguin', a drug-runner and criminal who had been disowned by the family.

For Harry McGee of the *Irish Times*, Mitchell had the CV and history of a self-made man who had risen through the ranks of the party. McGee quoted an admirer as saying, 'He may be prickly, but there is huge admiration for loyalty, his pedigree and what he has achieved over the past thirty years.'

However, some party handlers saw him as a nightmare candidate, with his strong views and with no cross-demographic appeal. A close supporter of Mitchell offered the opinion that

> the perception of Fine Gael for fifty years was that we were too rural and too local. Now they are giving out because he is too much of a Dub and too working class. There are a number of TDs in Dublin who did not back him because there is a vestigial snobbery in the party. They give out about his attitude, but it's they who have to change.

| THE PEOPLE'S FAVOURITE

The broadcaster Gay Byrne was with his wife, Kathleen Watkins, at their holiday home in the Rosses, Co. Donegal, when his mobile phone rang on Saturday 6 August. It was the Fianna Fáil leader, Micheál Martin. Martin was also on holiday, in Skibbereen, Co Cork, at the other end of the country.

Byrne had celebrated his seventy-seventh birthday the previous day. His daughters had been among the first to ring and congratulate him: Suzy, who was on holiday in France, and Crona and her husband, from their home in Killaloe, Co. Clare.

It was Crona's phone call that had intrigued Byrne most. She told her father that during the previous week she had been 'bombarded' with calls from a local TD, Timmy Dooley. He had eventually arranged to meet her near his home village of Tulla, close to Ennis.

Dooley was one of six members of a sub-committee set up by Micheál Martin to explore the party's options before the coming presidential election. Always affable, humorous and self-deprecating, and a shrewd political operator, he was well known as the eyes and ears of the leader in the parliamentary party.

As it turned out, Martin had entrusted Dooley with sounding out Gay Byrne to see whether he would be prepared to run for the Áras on the Fianna Fáil ticket. At their meeting, Dooley floated this with Crona and asked her to approach her father.

At any other time in recent Irish history, endorsement by Fianna Fáil would have virtually guaranteed the Presidency to a candidate. But these times were different. Fianna Fáil had carried the blame for Ireland's economic meltdown, and the brand was now toxic with the electorate. In the general election a few months earlier there had been a collapse in the Fianna Fáil vote and the loss of three-quarters of its seats.

Before the general election an unprecedented number of former Fianna Fáil stalwarts, under no illusions about how they were likely to fare, had retired. Consequently, Fianna Fáil did not field a sufficient number of candidates to form a Government, even if by some miracle every one of them had been elected. In the event, the overbearingly dominant political party since the foundation of the state lost a staggering fifty-eight seats and was able to return only twenty TDs to the Dáil.

When the presidential election began to appear on the horizon, Fianna Fáil was more than €2.1 million in debt and still limping along in the opinion polls. There was a heated debate within the party about whether anyone should be selected to run at all—a previously unthinkable prospect for Fianna Fáil. If, irrespective of the party's dire financial state, the decision was 'yes', who on earth should it be? Indeed, given how the party was viewed by the country, who would be brave enough?

A number of senior Fianna Fáil politicians had let it be known that they would be available if called on by the party. Senator Mary White, owner of Lir Chocolates and wife of Padraic White, former managing director of the Industrial Development Authority and a policy adviser to the party, had previously expressed an interest in running.

The MEP for the Ireland South constituency, Brian Crowley, a hugely popular vote-winner throughout Munster, had also made it clear that he was interested in running, long before the vote meltdown, in an interview on 'The Late Late Show'.

Éamon Ó Cuív, a former Minister for the Gaeltacht and Minister for Social Protection, had an eye to destiny and history and was interested in holding the same office as his grandfather and the party's founder, Éamon de Valera.

Another former minister, Mary Hanafin, was also considered a possible late entrant for a Fianna Fáil nomination. Until a sub-committee appointed by the leadership produced its report and recommendation on the presidential race, she would continue to figure in online debates and in media speculation.

Polling carried out privately by Fianna Fáil to test the public mood showed that even the party's biggest vote-catcher, Brian Crowley, could gain only a 9 per cent approval, such was the hostility to the party. This surprisingly poor rating showed that he could not get elected.

However, publicly the party was reserving its position. After all, it was argued, Mary McAleese had been selected only five weeks before polling day in the last presidential election fourteen years earlier, and so there was time to consider and watch events unfold.

To the many members of the party who expressed their frustration on social media about the internal decision-making process it seemed that the party was dithering. Their frustration was further heightened when their comments, supposedly made in an internal and closed forum, were quoted in the media.

As the Dáil broke for the summer recess in July, Martin appointed a six-member parliamentary committee to consider the party's options. It consisted of himself, Éamon Ó Cuív (Galway West), a potential candidate, Dara Calleary (Mayo), Niall Collins (Limerick), Timmy Dooley (Clare), Seán Ó Fearghail (Kildare South) and one senator, Darragh O'Brien (Malahide, Co. Dublin).

One month later Dooley was to phone Gay Byrne's daughter, who in turn spoke to Byrne. His response was lukewarm and he was to claim later that his daughter had 'jokingly referred to it once or twice.'

Dooley, as a conduit, served three purposes: an approach to Byrne could be considered informal and unofficial, even though Dooley was a member of the Presidency Committee; it allowed Byrne time to think about the offer; and it kept the party leader at a deniable arm's length. The danger was that, unless tightly controlled, the approach might become public knowledge before the candidate had fully made a commitment. The public revelation could irk party members as well as the Presidency Committee, but a rejection by the candidate because their cover was blown, or because they decided this was not an offer they could accept, could prove highly embarrassing and, within the party, divisive.

In retrospect, putting Byrne forward as a candidate must have seemed like an obvious choice, a 'stroke' even. He was a household name, much-loved among the public, a good communicator and a good candidate.

————

In Co. Clare you could pick up 4FM. The new radio station broadcast into four cities—Dublin, Cork, Limerick and Galway—and was aimed at listeners aged forty and older who liked classic hits.

It cost twenty cents to cast a vote in any opinion poll on 'The David Harvey Show' on 4FM. Harvey, a highly experienced broadcaster with an easy manner, knew how to engage with his audience for his afternoon chat show, and on Wednesday 3 August he effectually launched a new candidate for the Áras with his provocative question: 'Who would you trust as the ninth President of Ireland?'

A woman who identified herself simply as Caroline suggested that they should include Gay Byrne, the host of 'The Late Late Show', which had dominated the television ratings during its 37-year run on RTE. It was the world's longest-running chat show. Texters and callers offered other options, including already-declared candidates.

Byrne topped the poll, with 47 per cent, the declared candidate Mary Davis took 16 per cent, the television presenter Mary Kennedy 11 per cent, the journalist Miriam O'Callaghan 9 per cent and the former supermarket owner Feargal Quinn 8 per cent. The pundit, retailer and cocaine-and-prostitute-scandal figure Ben Dunne trailed at 5 per cent, with others picking up just 4 per cent.

On Friday, Byrne was celebrating his birthday, and the latest presenter of 'The Late Late Show', Ryan Tubridy, had Byrne as a guest on his morning radio programme on 2FM, on which he was quizzed about his reaction to the phone-in poll. Byrne said that his name

wasn't even mentioned, and I got 46 per cent, and the nearest one was Mary Davis, at 16 per cent. It was extraordinary, as my name wasn't put forward at all. It's quite amazing and complimentary and very nice.

Asked the obvious question—would he run for President?—he gave an open-ended answer.

I would have to take some considerable persuasion. It hasn't been on my horizon. I would rather go on doing what I am doing with 'For One Night Only' [an RTE television interview programme] and 'The Meaning of Life' [a religious-philosophical interview programme] and my Lyric FM programme on Sunday afternoon [a jazz DJ programme].

It is kind of encouraging and it is kind of stupefying. I don't know where it came from or how it came. Let the clamour continue . . . Could we leave this question and come back to it at a later date and see what happens?

His refusal to rule out making a bid for the Presidency unleashed a storm of media speculation over the coming days. That coverage was to incite speculation within Fianna Fáil that perhaps Byrne could be the talisman for the resurrection of the party.

When Micheál Martin rang him on Saturday evening it was a surprise to Byrne. Martin tantalised him with the offer of another birthday present: the possibility of the keys to Áras an Uachtaráin.

Martin put his offer in the simplest of terms. If Byrne wanted to run as an independent candidate Fianna Fáil would provide the twenty nominations from members of the parliamentary party required to secure a nomination—

thus ruling out the gruelling tour of county councils in the hope of securing four nominations.

No time limit for a response was suggested. While there would be media pressure for a response when the offer was eventually made public, there was no political imperative to respond, as nominations would not close until September, which was still some weeks away.

The following day the off-lead front-page story of the *Sunday Independent* quoted Byrne directly, having interviewed him before Martin's phone call.

> I would have to consider it seriously . . . But I would have to consult with she who must be obeyed as well, because any mention of presidency would mean a huge disruption in our lives.

It was only days after David Norris had been forced to withdraw from the race, and it was the nearest confirmation that Byrne was open to make a run for the Áras. His comments also suggested that, perhaps dutifully, he would consider making the sacrifice of running and of perhaps taking up office for his country and its people. It was a folksy, considerate, humorous quotation that nodded towards the required self-sacrifice. It was also a considered sound-bite from one of the country's most respected and experienced communicators. It was duly splashed on the front page, under a picture of Gaybo and a teaser for the opinion poll inside announcing that 'Gay Byrne gets the Norris vote.'

The newspaper also reported an unnamed Fianna Fáil spokesperson as saying, 'Gay Byrne would make an excellent candidate.' But it added that the party had yet to decide whether it would nominate its own candidate or back an independent one.

The withdrawal of Norris, announced the previous Tuesday, gave the *Sunday Independent* time to commission an opinion poll from Quantum Research on the Norris decision and another on voting intentions. It included declared runners and added the speculative runners, Dana and Gay Byrne.

The Áras race dominated coverage in the best-selling Sunday broadsheet, and the headline over the opinion poll presaged the tone of coverage for the coming days. 'Gay Byrne is people's choice although he's not officially in the race . . . yet.'

The nationwide opinion poll consisted of a random selection of five hundred homes telephoned by professional researchers. Quantum emphasised that it was was not a phone-in poll in which the possibility existed for political parties and special-interest groups to influence the outcome.

It was a definitive result: Byrne topped the poll, with 34 per cent of the vote. In four previous opinion polls only David Norris had polled higher (and in only one, lower). Norris took 39 per cent on 5 June, then 30 per cent on 19 June, 37 per cent on 3 July, and finally 42 per cent—exactly twice his nearest rival, the newly declared candidate Gay Mitchell. In the August poll that included Byrne, Mitchell had dropped back 6 points to 21 per cent and was trailed by Michael D. Higgins at 16 per cent, with Mary Davis, Seán Gallagher and Dana trailing at 11, 10 and 8 per cent, respectively.

However, inside the paper the potentially more significant quotations about Byrne 'not having the stomach' for campaigning or 'auditioning' weren't seized upon for headlines. For Byrne,

> as I say, I'm not the sort of person who will get on a bus and go around the country asking people for votes, and I'm not the sort of person who wants to go and be interviewed by county councils. So where that leaves us I don't know.

This seemed less thought through than his front-page comment, but it clearly suggested that he would prefer an Oireachtas nomination rather than the reversal of his previous role of interviewer to become interviewee.

The following day Bruce Arnold, the well-known *Irish Independent* columnist, seized on Byrne's words.

> Do we have a new Presidential candidate in Gay Byrne? Characteristically he is putting his toe in the water to see if it is too hot for him, and waiting for the noise of approval that will send him on his way.
>
> His position is an entirely passive one. Everything he has said so far indicates that, while David Norris was the front runner—as he was— Byrne would not be seeking the job. With all that changed, it suddenly seems a good idea, half-decided by the opinion polls, a deal that could be clinched by Fianna Fáil support. A gentle mindless canter to the Áras would follow.

It was perhaps a harsh judgement on someone who was genuinely considering his options, and it was, as Arnold notes, characteristic of Byrne's career of feeling the public mood and reflecting that in his unmissable Saturday night television programme and weekly morning radio programme. That nous resulted in him reflecting and expertly understanding society's zeitgeist and being informed and confident enough to challenge it.

Arnold's colleague Sam Smyth, an experienced and authoritative political commentator, wrote an article in the *Independent* setting out the scale of the task facing Byrne and the type of organisation and spending he would need in order to mount a professional campaign. But he too couldn't help but wonder about Byrne's commitment. He questioned whether Byrne could put together a team to provide 24-hour media relations, a campaign manager, regional campaign managers, a team of volunteers, researchers, speech-writers, social media campaigners and, crucially, a fund-raiser. He described it as a 'Herculean task'.

> With a deadline of less than three months, Byrne would require almost supernatural powers to put it all together before polling day . . . Veteran politicians believe Byrne would have little difficulty getting the four local authorities or the 20 politicians required to nominate him as a candidate. Neither would he have a lot of difficulty raising whatever money is required to fund a campaign. But putting together a competent organisation and a credible campaign team would present enormous difficulties, even if he wasn't facing such a tight deadline.

And then the crunch:

> And if he was very serious about running, he would have abandoned his walking holiday and hot-footed it back to Dublin yesterday.

————

On the day of the 4FM opinion poll both Dana, the Eurovision singer and former presidential candidate, and the GAA commentator Mícheál Ó Muircheartaigh confirmed that they were considering allowing their names be put forward for the Áras.

Dana was on a two-week holiday in Los Angeles, but her brother John Brown, who managed her previous campaigns, said she would make a decision on her return. Pressure had mounted on her to run after Norris withdrew his candidacy. According to Brown, she wasn't

> ruling anything in or out. I spoke to her, and it is something that has moved up in her decision-making process. A few politicians have also approached her about running.

Dana (53) ran as independent in 1997, having received the support of five county councils. She polled more than 175,000 first-preference votes, a respectable 14 per cent, to finish third. She was subsequently elected MEP for Connacht-Ulster. When she lost the seat in 2004 she declared with some good humour: 'Like Schwarzenegger, I'll be back.'

The *Catholic Voice* immediately declared for Dana. Its publisher, Anthony Murphy, said:

It is time for a clean pair of hands. We need change and we need a politician we can trust to keep their promises. Dana is emerging as the only choice for President of Ireland.

————

Gay Byrne's affection for Co. Donegal, where he had a holiday home and regularly visited, was well known. His summer holidays were carved in stone, and representatives of the media seeking him knew his summer-holiday habits.

The Gay Byrne for President story was a 'silly season' gift to the media. It was a showbiz phenomenon, a story hanging on a possible decision about a titan of the television who revelled and played in the spotlight after a lifetime of prompting and exploring major debates about social change, the economy and every other topic that excited human interest.

It was no surprise, then, that every inflection, comment, consideration and opinion poll would add fuel to what was a bonfire of speculation. This wasn't a story about politics: it was pure showbiz, not only about Byrne but about people who had shared the spotlight with him or who were his glittering celebrity colleagues—and it sold newspapers.

The *Irish Daily Star* that day, however, was much more encouraging. Its main headline read 'Gaybo has x factor', and it quoted the pop mogul Louis Walsh on the front page. Referring to the record-breaking talent programme, Walsh said with his usual effusiveness:

I think he would be impossible to beat in an election. Gaybo has the x factor; I'd love him to get the gig. I hope he's going to run, because he would definitely be the best candidate out there.

An article inside the paper was provocatively and humorously headlined 'Louis: Gay would kick Áras with Late Late election bid.' In an adjoining column the *Star* continued to show its mischievousness as it described five 'scandals' that could 'Byrne him.' Knowing that Walsh managed the group Boyzone, the paper cited the debut of the pop sensations on 'The Late Late Show', hosted by Byrne, and asked, tongue firmly in cheek:

Six boys were forced into revealing clobber and subjected to strobe lighting to induce an epileptic dance display that scared everyone. Their debut stands as one of the most shocking episodes in Byrne's career. But is it enough to finish his bid for the Áras?

George Hook, the RTE rugby pundit, Newstalk drive-time presenter and Fine Gael supporter, was his usual popularly opinionated self in another article in the same paper.

> The whole thing of the position is becoming a personality contest and that is not what it is about. I think people are thinking that anyone can be President. That is actually crap because the presidency is the third house of the Oireachtas.

Asked if he thought Byrne could be a good President, he replied bluntly:

> No, I don't. Whether we like it or not, this is a quasi-political office.

The following day DonegalDaily.com, a news and magazine web site recently launched by the senior journalists Greg Harkin and Stephen Maguire, reported that Fianna Fáil had 'finally' come out and backed Gay Byrne for the Presidency. 'Mr Byrne, who is on holiday in Dungloe at the moment, admitted that he was "thinking about it" when asked if he planned to run for the Áras.'

They quoted Donegal North-East's new Fianna Fáil deputy, Charlie McConalogue, a local farmer and former organiser and researcher in Fianna Fáil head office. Before the 2011 general election the party held four of the six seats in the two constituencies in the county; McConalogue now was the only Fianna Fáil candidate elected in the county. He suggested that Byrne would be a 'great candidate'.

However, it was that same Monday's edition of the *Limerick Leader* that revealed that the Clare TD Timmy Dooley had been pressing Gay Byrne's daughter to ask her to convince him to run for the Áras. It was a news story that would put both Byrne and Martin under pressure now that the offer had become public—Byrne to come under pressure to decide, and Martin, now exposed, to hope that his approach would be successful. A leading member of the party was quoted anonymously in the *Limerick Leader* as saying that

> Timmy has been bombarding her with calls. Gay is one of the five people identified by Fianna Fáil. He first said that at 77 he felt too old but that could all change as the momentum is now with him.

It then quoted the former Government minister and Limerick TD Willie O'Dea, who endorsed Byrne as a candidate.

He has to get a nomination for President, and if that is the case I think that we could do it for him in the morning. I don't think we would have any problem with it.

His party colleague in the adjoining constituency of Limerick County, Niall Collins TD, said, 'He is the most favoured candidate.'

As every pundit or celebrity in the country, whether A-league or z-league, rushed to have their opinion aired or to let it be known that they were available if the country called, it seemed that the only person in the country who remained silent on the issue was the Fianna Fáil leader, who remained in isolation as he continued his family holiday in west Cork.

Clearly conscious of the publicity storm they had created and of its profile-raising potential for a new station, 4FM organised another opinion poll on Monday the 8th. The results were perhaps predictable and influenced by the blanket positive coverage of Gaybo as a presidential candidate. A staggering 58 per cent of texters to the station put him at the top of the poll. The Ryan Tubridy show on 2FM also ran a text opinion poll on the same day, which showed that 54 per cent of listeners wanted him to run for the Presidency.

The following day Byrne, who had now returned to Dublin from his holiday to consult family, friends and advisers, told the *Irish Independent*: 'That means 46 per cent don't want me to run. I'm talking to people, hearing what they have to say, then I will decide what I'm doing.'

The *Irish Daily Mail* trumpeted the 4FM poll on Tuesday: 'Go on, give us Gaybo', it headlined its front page. However, on the letters page of the same paper Dr Bernadette Flanagan of Buncrana, Co. Donegal, wrote to set out a series of qualifications for the office of President, including the ability to act as guardian of the Constitution, international political experience, compassion and humility. She said she had found the ideal candidate in Rosemary Scallon (Dana), who she had met as chairperson of a meeting of European delegates in Brussels. Then she gave sub-editors and commentators a future hostage to fortune and humour when she finished her letter by saying, 'Don't dismiss her as the Lark in the Park.'

The morning papers carried numerous endorsements of Byrne, which had been canvassed by reporters. The best-selling author Maeve Binchy said, 'He has a huge rapport with the people of Ireland.' His RTE colleague Jimmy Magee, the sports broadcaster, admitted that Byrne's age could be a drawback but offered his support, saying that 'Gay would be a an excellent communicator, a great public speaker—great at working an audience in the old show-business sense.' The Donegal country-and-western star Daniel O'Donnell said, 'I can't think of anyone who would represent us better.'

The former Longford-Westmeath TD, Fianna Fáil minister and sister of former candidate Brian Lenihan (senior), Mary O'Rourke, who failed to retain her seat in the 2011 election, endorsed him, saying, 'I'm in favour. He would handle himself and the country very well.' A few days earlier she was quoted in the *Examiner* as ruling herself out as a possible candidate. A regular media contributor, popular among radio producers and commissioning editors for describing a political situation candidly, O'Rourke was against her party running its own candidate. In typical forthright fashion, and perhaps a bit exasperated, she said, 'I just don't see why we have to contest everything. We should give it a break, for goodness' sake.'

———

As shoppers in Eason's at Mahon Point Shopping Centre in Cork, billed as Munster's largest shopping centre, read the glowing endorsements of Gay Byrne in Wednesday's newspapers, the Euro-pop superstars Jedward (the identical twins John and Edward Grimes) were signing copies of their newly launched album *Victory* a few yards away. Surrounded by hundreds of noisy fans, they were asked by reporters about the presidential campaign. They rubbished any ageism arguments and said they would give Gaybo their vote.

Then they put forward a new political proposition: if they themselves were to run, they said, Gaybo would have no chance. 'If we were allowed to contest the election we would totally win,' Edward said. But at twenty, below the constitutionally required thirty-five years of age, they were excluded. 'We need a referendum to get the age limit down to twenty,' said Edward, excusing themselves from a showdown. Consequent discussions of the 'what if' variety were to centre on the old versus the new.

The argument went that, if Gaybo ran, the question was who would vote for him: people aged over forty-five who probably remembered his television and radio programmes and welcomed his later sporadic return to the screen and Lyric FM; some younger people might vote for him for his work with the Road Safety Authority in reducing road deaths. Older people traditionally vote in far greater numbers at the polling booths.

If Jedward were allowed to run, and if it was a text vote? No contest. A technology, pop-music and social-media savvy generation would swamp the vote—and it would be a shared Presidency—or not, if you could tell them apart!

While the media continued to speculate about Byrne's intentions there was growing criticism within Fianna Fáil of Micheál Martin's solo run in offering to support him. The six-member committee established before the Dáil's summer recess still had not met to consider whether or not to run or alternatively to support an independent candidate. On social media networking sites, Fianna Fáil members were equally divided into those critical and those supportive of the Byrne overture.

However, the debate began to broaden out into the reason for senior members not being part of the selection process. Why, for example, were the former ministers Éamon Ó Cuív and Mary Hanafin and the MEP Brian Crowley not given the first option of party support, and why had Martin taken such a high-risk course of action?

With this solo run, it was also being questioned why Martin would invest so much of his own credibility in making the overture. Surely an intermediary, such as Dooley, should not have been given the task of securing Byrne and then unveiling him once agreement had been reached.

By approaching Byrne with almost unseemly haste, Martin ran a number of risks. He risked the ire of Fianna Fáil members who would prefer to see loyal party members put forward as candidates for selection by the parliamentary party. He also failed to secure a commitment from Byrne and consequently risked a public rebuff and the resulting difficulty in selecting a candidate who would inevitably be dubbed a second choice for the party. Were Byrne not to run, Martin could find himself unwilling to support any other candidate, or he could select a Fianna Fáil candidate—a decision likely to further divide opinion among the grass roots.

Unless Martin was to allow the parliamentary party to endorse other candidates, Byrne would be seen as endorsed by Fianna Fáil. And, while not their candidate—as he would argue—their reputation hung on the shoulders of an unaccountable independent. In addition to these risks, even if Byrne was nominated there was no guarantee that he would win the election, so providing further collateral damage to Fianna Fáil. The news web site BreakingNews.ie reported that

> it is believed there is some argument within the Fianna Fáil party as to whether it should put forward its own candidate for the presidential election . . . Some members of the party are said to be angry Micheál Martin did not consult them beforehand when offering support to Byrne.

A former Minister of State at the Department of Finance, Martin Mansergh—another victim of the general election cull, who had lost his South Tipperary seat—confirmed that a 'lively discussion' was under way in the party and that no decision had been made about whether it would put forward its own candidate. But he supported Byrne. 'He is a national institution; I think he would be a very worthy candidate.'

One party member posted on an online discussion page for members of Fianna Fáil, echoing the frustration of other contributors:

> A couple of posters have very reasonably asked why is stopping FG an end in itself, is it just tribalism? FG have been on a roll from 2004 to 2011 (starting from when they wisely chose not to contest the 2004 presidential election), they doubled their council seats, became the biggest local authority party in the country, beat Fianna Fáil in a national election for the first time, more than doubled their Dáil seats and won most first-preference votes than ever in their history.
>
> The one thing they have never won is the Presidency, and that is why it matters so dearly to them this time around. Psychology is as much a factor in electoral politics as is policy and if FF are to reverse our decline we must halt the myth of FG as the coming dominant force in Irish politics.

The former minister Éamon Ó Cuív, who had announced an interest in the post, told the media of his disappointment about the approach to Byrne. Even though he was a member of the Presidential Election Committee (which had not yet met), he explained:

> I was not aware of it. Nobody contacted me about it, but I'm not making any further comment on that.
>
> The first decision Fianna Fáil needs to be making is whether we are running a candidate or not. We haven't even got as far as answering that question. I would consider that issue if and when Fianna Fáil decided whether it will put up a candidate.

A number of Ó Cuív's party colleagues were also quoted and offered support to Byrne.

Willie O'Dea, the former Minister for Defence, said that Byrne would be an 'outstanding candidate and an excellent President' and that the public were seeking someone outside the political system.

In the neighbouring constituency to Ó Cuív, Galway East, Michael Kitt TD appeared to be ambivalent, saying the candidate didn't necessarily have to be a party member and pointing to the former Fianna Fáil candidate Mary McAleese. He said the party leader was

> entitled to sound anybody out . . . There are a lot of people within the party with incredible ability, standards and stature. But there are also individuals from outside our ranks who are impressive and of very high standing.

The *Irish Daily Mail*, which had been giving blanket coverage to the election, appeared to be losing patience with the process. In its editorial it said that with only a few weeks to go, the final line-up of candidates was unclear. It added that Byrne's 'rumbustious' comments on Europe appeared to suggest that he had made up his mind, while Ó Cuív had only been 'murmuring half-heartedly' about his own interest in the Áras.

> The reluctance of two major potential candidates to lay their cards on the table is of concern on two fronts. Not only does it leave the electorate in a rather ridiculous position, it also sends out a less than impressive portent of what we can expect if either is elected to the Áras. As in so many aspects of public life these days, the time for indecision is over.

By contrast, the editorial of the *Irish Daily Star* dubbed Byrne 'a serious contender'. It said that

> it wasn't until Gay threw his lot in with the Government's road safety campaign that lives started to be saved and families spared the heartbreak of senseless deaths. He oozes old-fashioned decency, common sense, charm, courtesy—but is also politically instinctive, savvy and streetwise.

The media storm continued to rage around Byrne, despite his continued assertion that he was consulting friends and family and that he would take his time before making an announcement.

The traditional silly season in August was well under way as the courts, the Dáil and Seanad and local authority meetings went into recess for the summer. While some candidates took the opportunity to recharge their batteries before the campaigns formally kicked off—candidates such as Gay Mitchell and Mary Davis, with short breaks—they effactually excluded themselves from media scrutiny but left the field open for a late potential entrant to dominate the headlines.

Gaybo, however, was guaranteed front-page coverage. He was a recognised national figure, an entertainer and showbiz personality who now added the sulphur of politics to the story about personalities in a race for the country's biggest prize. At a time when the only other story capturing the headlines was the rioting and looting in cities in England, he was the only Irish story for Irish media.

That same evening, Wednesday 10 August, the media pack who had ambushed Pat Kenny spotted Byrne and his wife arriving for the opening night of the rock and roll musical *Grease*. As they rushed to surround him, fiddling with microphones, Smartphones and cameras to record him, he was typically relaxed, at the centre of attention on the metaphorical studio floor again. Dressed in a dark suit, light-grey shirt and red-and-green patterned tie, he was ever the showman, hand behind his ear to have a question repeated, tilting his head for emphasis as Kathleen stood smiling at his shoulder.

What he was to say to the media would launch a debate that was to keep his name to the fore for days to come, for both positive and negative reasons— neither of which would upset a man whose career had prospered on self-promoting controversy. But the first question was, predictably, the question on everyone's lips: would he run for the Presidency?

> We're still consulting and we're talking to various people, and there's no time limit. Nobody has ever given me a time limit as to when I should make a decision. Nobody has said we need your 'yes' or 'no' by twelve noon on Friday. So I'm taking as long as it takes, and I would imagine I have certainly another few days' thinking and talking to people about it.

If he did decide to run, he told the anxious gaggle of reporters, it would be as an independent.

> Fianna Fáil have very little to do with it. I would be an independent runner if it comes to that, and they've assured me of that situation and all of that, so forget about that.

To the next question he answered that he had been overwhelmed by the messages of support he had received.

> No political party officially has approached me, but there have been rumours and approaches and whispers and all of that sort of thing. There would appear to be more offers [of money and support] than I can cope with from all sorts of people . . .

However, that support and his showings in opinion polls were not going to influence his decision on whether to run or not.

> I am absolutely overwhelmed by the messages of good will and regards and affection from all over the country. I am not fooled by that, for one single minute, because I have been in the business far too long. But nonetheless it's very, very gratifying and satisfying and delightful.

It was at this stage that an experienced press officer would have stepped in and ended the media opportunity. Why? Because the main issue had been addressed and effectively dealt with. Any further comment could diminish the central message, and the opportunity would have been lost. Furthermore, an undisciplined interviewee who was willing to be distracted off-message and to field unrelated questions—even with the intention of being the media's best friend by facilitating them—could damage themselves unintentionally as answers to questions became gaffes, uninformed answers or even offensive remarks.

The following day's *Irish Daily Mail* described the next moment:

> When he was asked whether his dislike for the single currency and Lisbon Treaty would become a topical subject for him in office, he appeared evasive at first.
>
> Then without a moment's hesitation, he said: 'It might be, it might not. I haven't changed my mind.
>
> 'What we're seeing now in Europe as far as I'm concerned is a culmination of all my concerns about it down through the years. I never thought we'd reach the disastrous stage we are at at the moment in Europe in my lifetime.
>
> 'I thought it would eventually come in my grandchildren's time, but it's come much, much quicker than even I could have realised, and it's happening even as we speak.'

It was a repetition of an opinion he had previously made public. Prompted to reveal his concerns, he said:

> Those concerns are—I think it's a crazy notion from the very beginning. We crossed the Rubicon when we joined the single currency. I think there is no backing out now, but it's a mad, mad world and we're being run by mad people in Brussels.

Those comments dominated the headlines. The *Mail* scrapped its earlier draft for its front page and instead splashed a picture of Byrne being interviewed and three paragraphs of text, a main headline reading 'Gaybo: We're being run by mad people in Brussels' and a smaller headline over it: 'TV host makes controversial attack on EU—and all but launches his bid for the Áras.'

Perhaps more controversial was the fact that Byrne had long been a critic of the EU project and in 2008 opposed the Lisbon Treaty, whose stated aim was 'to complete the process started by the Treaty of Amsterdam and by the Treaty of Nice with a view to enhancing the efficiency and democratic legitimacy of the Union and to improving the coherence of its action.' It put him on a collision course with Fianna Fáil in Government and its director of elections, the then Minister for Foreign Affairs, Micheál Martin.

In his column in the *Sunday Independent* three years earlier Byrne had said he would be voting No in the forthcoming referendum. And with withering criticism he dismissed the whole process as

> so sneaky, dishonest, underhanded and sinister that I now have neither faith nor trust in the whole approach. I don't believe a word from the mouths of any of the 'Yes' brigade and I have deep scepticism about any of their promises or undertakings.
>
> What we are being asked to vote on is a series of amendments to amendments to revisions to an existing Constitution.
>
> I feel desperately sorry for my grandchildren that certifiable lunatics in Brussels will dictate every single aspect of their lives . . .
>
> One other thing, I'll guarantee within six months of Ireland voting 'Yes' our special corporate tax rate will be gone, not because of 'harmonisation' but because of 'competition barriers'. And our veto? We'll be none too politely told to stick it you know where and whistle Dixie to it.

It wasn't the only time he clashed with the Fianna Fáil viewpoint. The retired editor of the *Irish Independent*, Vinny Doyle, had been the Government's first choice as chairperson of the newly established Road Safety Authority. When Doyle declined the post Byrne was offered it, and accepted. In 2007 he again professed views that were contrary to Fianna Fáil's when he called for a debate on the legalisation of certain drugs. 'This is a mighty chasm for me to leap,' he said at the time, 'but I've come to the conclusion that the possibility of legalising drugs should be looked at.' But the Taoiseach of the day, Bertie Ahern, slapped down his comments, saying he was 'totally and fundamentally opposed to the legislation of any drugs in any respects.'

Byrne also clashed with the next Taoiseach, Brian Cowen, commenting on how he should have communicated the economic crisis.

> I question whether you can be Taoiseach and still sit up and have a pint in the local pub. That is what I would have told him, had I been asked. What everyone is crying out for is leadership.
>
> What I would have recommended Cowen to do, at the latest in midsummer 2009, is that he should have been on the television every night at nine o'clock instead of the news. Not being interviewed but there to camera, explaining how bad things are. And then he should have explained what we will do about it and that it is going to be ghastly and that he will be the most hated man in the world.

Yet when the publicity bandwagon started to roll for Byrne, Cowen's successor, Micheál Martin, contacted him directly.

As the dominant voice in broadcasting and media in Ireland, Byrne's outspoken and informed views held powerful sway among public opinion. While he wasn't party-political, as he asserted, he held a number of strong opinions that were political in content and social effect. On his radio programme he fulminated over the years against a series of targets. He admitted that as a broadcaster a lot of the 'crabbiness and thunderstruck apoplexy is feigned. It comes out of something genuine, but the manner in which it is delivered is a performance.'

Topics he has campaigned for—or at least for which he raised a debate —include the birching of offenders, the reduction of high taxation, the non-introduction of a property tax (over which he clashed with both Gay Mitchell and Michael D. Higgins) and the introduction of divorce. He was suspicious of the European Union and the high cost of living, at one stage urging shoppers to cross the border to pick up bargains in Newry.

The following day, Thursday 11 August, the *Evening Herald* also carried the 'stinging attack' and described it as 'Gay's first controversy over "mad EU" comment.' However, the article concentrated on Fianna Fáil, ruling out suggestions that it would fund Byrne's potential campaign.

Byrne's wife, Kathleen Watkins, came from a strong Fianna Fáil background, a point made to reporters by supporters of other candidates in the field. Had her Fianna Fáil influence rubbed off on him?

> Fianna Fáil have very little to do with it. I will be an independent candidate if it comes to that. They've assured me about that. I've always remained completely unpolitical. That's why people love me.

The developer and promoter Harry Crosbie, owner of the Grand Canal Theatre and O2 Theatre, a friend of Byrne's, joined him as he spoke to reporters. He told them that both he and the RTE radio presenter Joe Duffy, who had been a reporter on Byrne's morning radio programme for many years, had joined Byrne for a drink before the premiere and urged him to run for the Presidency. 'Go, Gaybo, go, that's what I'll say. I think people love him, and they cry out for him in the night,' he said.

To which Byrne quipped, 'He's already offered me €50 without conditions!'

Crosbie would later offer to host a concert at his O2 Theatre, which, it was estimated, with a maximum capacity of 14,000 and tickets at €50, would raise €700,000—almost the maximum spending allowed for a presidential campaign. It was suggested that top-name acts—perhaps U2, who had presented Byrne with a Harley-Davidson motorbike on his final 'Late Late Show' in 1999—would play free of charge.

Funding a campaign with a spending ceiling of €750,000 was always going to be an issue, but Byrne had said he had received lots of offers of financial support. He was also RTE's top presenter and top earner, with a famed Saturday night chat show and a weekday morning chat show, both of which were major earners for RTE.

In his autobiography, *The Time of My Life*, in a chapter entitled 'The Betrayal', Byrne spoke of his friendship with Russell Murphy, his accountant.

> He was one of my closest friends, a father figure, yet he embezzled my life's savings. After he died I found that not only was all my money gone but I was in serious debt.

Byrne chronicles fondly his memories of this larger-than-life character who was blessed with a deep and sonorous voice, great generosity and a pithy wit and charm. He was an attentive and generous godfather to Crona, and when Suzy's godfather died Murphy 'adopted' her as a godchild too. It emerged after Murphy's death that he had been taking clients' funds for the last eight years of his life and that £1½ million was missing. 'And unfortunately for me,' wrote Byrne, 'I was one of them.' He felt bitterly betrayed.

Byrne didn't say how much he had been swindled out of, or how much in debt Murphy had left him. The Revenue Commissioners reminded him that Murphy had been his accountant and not theirs, and they could not be responsible for tax cheques that Byrne had made out in good faith to Murphy but that were never passed on. He was in tax arrears for ten years.

Murphy had also taken out a loan of £65,000 on Byrne's house in Dublin, though not on his Donegal cottage, but he had made some repayments in the last two years of his life.

> This good man from this good bank would not tell me how much was outstanding. All he would say was that the loan was now 'manageable'. (Mind you, he didn't say whether it was manageable for them or for me!)

What Byrne was to reveal next passed without comment at the time his book was published but would have led to intense scrutiny by the media were he to run for the highest office in the land. Times had changed, and all banking issues, particularly special treatment by bankers, would have prompted a round of queries as the media dug into Byrne's business dealings. He continued:

He asked me to write him a letter setting out my side of the story. I wrote the letter and delivered it. The man from the bank rang me at 'The Late Late' office and told me the debt had been written off. I could come down and collect the deeds on the house any time I liked, on condition that I never revealed either his name or that of his bank. I saved the information for Kathleen until I got home that evening. The situation called for a few tears of relief.

In public Byrne spoke only occasionally about the theft of his life's savings, but when he did he never discussed the amount, only speaking with understandable bitterness about the betrayal. Over the next twelve years, he redoubled his efforts to build a pension chest. Like most high earners, he had his own company to channel his RTE fees in the most tax-efficient way.

In 2008 the Irish banks spectacularly collapsed, and Byrne found himself among the thousands of private investors who had put their belief and their savings into the supposed blue-chip companies. 'What has happened in this country is putting me under pressure,' he revealed a few weeks before his name was publicly speculated on as a presidential candidate.

> I never had a pension in RTE, so we invested in what we believed were blue-chip stocks—AIB, Bank of Ireland, Anglo—and all of them have been wiped out.

He was one of the more famous faces, looking extremely downcast, pictured at an extraordinary general meeting of the shareholders of Anglo Irish Bank in 2009 as they were officially informed of the new bargain-basement values of their shares, which had previously soared year after year, vastly outperforming the markets of the 'Celtic Tiger' years.

He also invested in the Quinlan Private group, run by a former tax inspector and then developer, Derek Quinlan, which cut a swathe through Irish and European property markets but whose investment values crashed. Byrne's only public comments about these investments, which are now in the portfolio of the National Assets Management Agency, are that they are under 'severe pressure' and are 'a millstone around our necks.'

Quinlan, a large-framed, affable man, is a friend of Byrne and is known to have other wealthy showbiz investors, including the founders of Riverdance, John McColgan and Moya Doherty. Quinlan would put together a syndicate of people to buy a property—one of them the famed Savoy Hotel in London—and then open his contact book to seek support from investors and banks. Byrne and others have not provided details about which investments they made. According to Byrne, speaking with remarkable honesty as a culture of blame and finger-pointing sprang up throughout the country (and invariably with the finger pointed at someone else):

> Again and again journalists seem to think that Derek Quinlan was running some sort of Bernie Madoff scheme. But he wasn't involved in anything of that kind at all.
>
> We went in with our eyes open. He took a fee and his company ran the property, collecting the rents and doing all that. The problem we now have is that when the original loans were made the buildings were valued at a certain figure. The loans are being repaid, the tenants are paying their rent, but the banks have changed the 'loan to value' ratio, saying the buildings are only worth half the original amount that was borrowed.
>
> All you can say is 'Well done, Sherlock', but because the building is no longer worth what it was they are saying, 'We need more money', and that is how they are screwing everybody. The loan-to-value thing should be tested in the High Court. It has been the ruination of so many people, and that is the nub of the problem. Yes, it is putting us under pressure.
>
> I had a long run of very good years. I invested in absolutely watertight stuff: AIB, Anglo Irish and Guinness, all the stuff you were told couldn't go wrong. And that is all gone! It is wiped out. And it is the same all over the country for people of my age and older. My sole worry is that Kathleen will have enough to see her through.
>
> But nobody has been made accountable. And we thought we were paying these high-flying guys enormous sums of money because they were experts. And now we know that they knew nothing more than we did.
>
> The situation is serious. I am frightened for people of my generation. They have introduced this constant, low-level anxiety into our lives, which we could well do without. It all hangs on a thread anyhow.

A presidential campaign would need money and someone with deep pockets, or a lot of generous friends, as the maximum anyone could now spend on their campaign was €750,000 and the most an individual could donate was €2,500 under the new limits introduced by the Minister for the Environment and Local Government, Phil Hogan. However, the potential Labour Party candidate for the Park, Fergus Finlay, estimated that a minimum requirement would be at least €500,000, to include posters, travel and staffing.

While Byrne's own company, Gabbro, had available funds of €312,000, according to accounts submitted for 2010, a self-funded campaign would require as much again. The media put the question to Fianna Fáil, which was offering him a nomination. Would Fianna Fáil financially back him? 'No' was the short answer: it was restricted in its spending. The party spokesperson said that it couldn't just 'write Gay Byrne a cheque for €200,000 and say "go for President." The most we could give him as an entity is €2,500, but it's all speculative at this point.'

Unaware of the media kerfuffle about Byrne's attendance at the rock and roll musical, Vincent Browne had submitted his regular column that evening for the *Irish Times*. Opinionated, and dismissive of guests at times to the point of rudeness, he was always more entertaining than any guest on his panel while discussing the issues of the day on his late-night programme on TV3. The opinions of Browne, a former young Fine Gaeler fascinated by politics and with a long memory for detail, were always a source of interest, delight, controversy or insight, depending on the issue of the day.

The following morning's *Irish Times* opinion page carried Browne's feature article, provocatively headed 'Gay would star in the Áras, not on the hustings.' The article, which started off with an endorsement of Byrne and then meandered into a discussion about the 'odd office', revealed that, although Byrne's name had first surfaced publicly on the 4FM radio phone-in poll, Browne had in fact raised the issue of his running for office previously with Byrne.

> Gay Byrne would be a fine president. Perhaps more than anybody else contemplated now for the Presidency, he would represent the values and instincts of the Irish people: decent, conservative, cautious, respectful.
>
> He would grow in office, learning the tone of the presidency and the protocols. Were he to be declared a candidate, I think he would rate far ahead of all the others in any poll because of the high regard people have for him and the affection he enjoys from the public. That is, initially, he would fare spectacularly in the polls.
>
> As a friend of many years and as someone who gave him encouragement a few months ago to think about running, I am now fearful of what the campaign might do to him and to his sense of contentment.
>
> For I think he would not be a good campaigner. He probably would make gaffes, like any candidate would, but he would not be good at correcting the gaffes. I don't think he would be good on the hustings, defining what kind of presidency he would offer. There are no skeletons in Gay's cupboard; in fact he may not have a cupboard, but that is not the point.
>
> In short, Gay probably would be a bad candidate, but very probably a very good President, if fortunate enough to be elected.

Browne, who had the good humour to allow himself to be mocked in comedy sketches on his own programme, was a double-edged sword. He was strongly opinionated, and his endorsement and analysis would always be open to debate. His analysis of Byrne finding himself in an unfamiliar and opposite role—as interviewee rather than scrutineer—would be one that would not sit comfortably with him, he ventured, and it would be one that would be difficult for him to adjust to, particularly for a candidate who could be prickly when faced with criticism.

The *Irish Times* letters page had been filled during August with a variety of comments and opinions about the presidential election. 'With a growing number of people past the average age for life expectancy convulsing the country with a will-he-or-won't-he tilt at the presidency, should we consider a constitutional amendment inserting an upper age limit for the office to complement the lower age limit already in place?', asked Patrick Cotter of St Stephen's Street, Cork.

Chapter 7 ⌒

| # THE TIPSTERS

Four thousand years ago a Babylonian priest plunged a ceremonial knife into a sheep and tore out its liver. It was a regular occurrence and part of the holy role of the high priests. The liver was considered to be the source of blood in the animal's body and the basis of life. The organ was divided into different parts, each dedicated to a separate deity. By analysing each section of it the priests would, through its presentation and condition, interpret the will of the gods.

The Babylonian priest was a forerunner of the soothsayers, taking different forms and using different techniques to connect with the gods, using sacred rites and sacrifices to foretell the future. Extispicy, the study of organs for the purpose of divination, was hinted at in the Bible, and a refined form, haruspicy, continued through the Roman and Etruscan eras, when it was used to predict future events.

Lightning-strikes and the flights of flocks of birds (augury) were also used to divine the will of the gods. More than three thousand years ago the Oracle of Delphi was the most important shrine in Greece. People came from all over Greece and the Mediterranean to consult the priestess of Apollo, Pythia, to have questions about their future answered. She answered cryptically—much like astrologers in today's newspaper columns—and, fortunately, if the supplicant didn't like her answer she was prepared, for a second fee, to give a second opinion.

Throughout history humans have been fascinated, frightened and optimistic about what the future holds. For ancient kings and commanders, an informed prediction could launch an army or rein it back until the moment 'augured' well. Today's politicians, whose grasp of power or fight for power depends on predicting the will of their constituents and the country at large, are obsessed with opinion polls. They have the same reverence for the results that the ancients surely carried in their hearts.

A winning poll will be barely referred to, even in hushed tones, for fear of bringing bad luck or of reversing the result in the next poll by displaying the confidence it secretly provides. A bad poll will be dismissed as a 'snapshot in time', and mitigating factors will be evoked, through gritted teeth, and issues pointed to that will, or can, be changed.

Because of the sophistication of polling techniques today, opinion polls are treated with the reverence once accorded to a haruspex with fresh chicken blood on his hands. Today, in Dublin, the new breed of haruspex sits in ordinary office buildings, behind computer screens. Instead of a pen of sheep or coop of hens ready for slaughter, their raw materials are census data, demographic breakdowns, access to call centres, statistical databases and a range of other information and supports.

The managing director of REDC, Richard Colwell, is young and enthusiastic in his manner; he sits forward confidently to engage with his clients, his warmth of manner belying the anonymity of his office. His office furniture is smart and functional; a computer and a stack of files sit on his desk. There are no distracting windows or pictures on his white walls: one, made of glass, looks out over an open-plan office. The only possible clue to his profession as an augur is the glass roof overhead—which looks straight to the heavens.

He set up REDC (Research, Evaluation, Direction, Clarity) in 2003, and since then it has had a series of the most recent successes in the political sphere: four of the five most accurate pre-election opinion polls in 2007. (The final poll had an average sample error of 1.4 per cent.) In 2009 it successfully predicted the result of the second referendum on the Lisbon Treaty, and in the local elections it had an average error of only 2.1 per cent—as accurate as the exit poll.

The *Sunday Business Post* has published monthly REDC political-satisfaction tracking polls, which are eagerly anticipated by politicians and political anoraks. One-off polls can occasionally be wrong, for a variety of reasons—rogue polls—whereas a change in attitudes in a tracking poll can be measured against specific events or subsequently identified as a significant change in trend.

Richard emphasises that the strength of opinion-polling is that it is as accurate as possible and reflects the country by means of quotas it establishes, based on census data for sex, age, region and social class.

No polling is 100 per cent accurate by its nature, but for a national poll we interview our established quota, which gives us a plus or minus 3 per cent margin of error. Why not interview more? Because were we to interview two thousand people the time it would take and the cost would be prohibitive and only decrease that to a margin of 1 to 2 per cent.

Statistical theory proves that in a random poll of a thousand people, nineteen times out of every twenty the result will be accurate. The science is in ensuring that the sample is randomly generated, with carefully constructed questions and prompts. From those interviewed, about one in four sets of answers is selected for inclusion in the poll, based on a quota set by the company in accordance with constantly updated census and demographic data and previous experience.

A typical national political poll would be carried out by REDC at the beginning of the week and issued on Thursday the same week. Polls are conducted on both mobile and land-line phones. Only 2 per cent of the population have neither a land line nor a mobile phone, while 25 per cent have mobile only. The sample is divided equally between land-line owners and mobile owners, and polling is conducted from 2 to 9 p.m. so as to include those working regular hours and shift hours. Numbers are generated from 'seed' numbers from directories. A number is randomly selected and then a 1, 2 or 4 substituted for the last digit to provide a number for the call centre.

On Thursday 11 August the bookmakers Paddy Power released to RTE's one o'clock radio news the result of an opinion poll they had commissioned from REDC. It was fascinating, prompting debate and conjecture, as it included people in, out and ruled out of the race for the Park.

The result showed that almost 40 per cent said they would have voted for David Norris, who had withdrawn from the race a week earlier. Gay Byrne came in second—even though he still hadn't announced his decision on whether to run—with 28 per cent, with a strong showing of support from young people and from women. Michael D. Higgins followed, with 21 per cent, while Gay Mitchell for Fine Gael polled 13 per cent, with a strong showing in Dublin, where he had previously topped the poll to win a Dublin seat in the European Parliament. On a similar showing of 13 per cent was Brian Crowley, who also was not a runner, despite having expressed interest in the Presidency. As expected, he polled particularly well in Munster, where he had topped the poll in June 2004, receiving an impressive 125,539 votes and being elected on the first count. Seán Gallagher and Mary Davis both trailed, at 12 and 7 per cent, respectively. Dana, whose name had been featured as a possible contender, scored 6 per cent.

Byrne reacted cagily to the opinion poll.

All I will say is that it's very heartening and satisfying that so many people think so well of me, and I'm very grateful for that. But I don't think it proves that the people of Ireland are behind me—it proves that some are. I'm fully aware that there's a great number of people out there that bloody detest me.

He admitted surprise at scoring so highly in the popularity stakes with young people.

Women, maybe, but young people? That's very surprising. I wouldn't have thought that's where my support was. I know from huge experience that poll and votes and opinions change vastly as we go along the line. I'm talking to people and getting all kinds of advice and all kinds of help and have all sorts of interested parties talking to me. But there's no time limit on when I must make a decision, so I'm taking my time.

He went on to say that he would make a decision within the next week.

Definitely in the next week. I think so. It has to be done. I don't want to drag it on.

Michael D. Higgins responded diplomatically while managing to emphasise his own credentials and to raise doubts about Byrne's political abilities.

I know from all of my time—I was Minister for Broadcasting—he is one our most distinguished professional broadcasters, with enormous audiences over a very long lifetime. He will find politics and the background of issues very different to dealing with the issues of the day.

The following morning, Friday the 12th, Sam Smyth in the *Irish Independent* again offered Byrne some advice, this time drawing his attention to the scrutiny he would inevitably come under and to the political dichotomy he could face as head of state and as an avowed opponent of the EU, which, with the IMF, was bailing out the country.

Referring to the 'mad people in Brussels' remark, he said Byrne was 'an old pro who delivered a very glib remark designed to make maximum impact in yesterday's headlines, and it achieved the desired result.' But he cautioned that

Europhiles will switch to adversarial interviewer mode and question his credentials to make such withering judgements about a subject in which he has so spectacularly failed: finance.

Recalling his double failure with pension plans, Byrne can be certain someone will rework Oscar Wilde's quip about losing one parent being unfortunate but two being careless.

Asked about a possible alternative to the EU, most would expect a potential presidential candidate's answer to use more grey matter than purple prose. And he would be expected to come up with a detailed inventory of his views on most subjects, although the EU will attract most interest after his anti-EU comments and yesterday's poll. The one fact that can't be avoided is this: if the EU hadn't been there to dig us out last year, this state would have been bankrupt.

The EU and IMF pitched in a net €68 billion last year to allow civil servants, nurses, teachers, Gardaí and others to draw wages from the exchequer.

As a potential president, the media—and the other candidates—would want nothing less than full disclosure of his financial dealings. After all, mainstream elected politicians are expected to declare everything they own or have beneficial interest in. Full disclosure of all their income from salaries, pensions or investments is mandatory, not only for them but for their spouses.

Gay Byrne has been very candid about his personal finances, although most people would feel that having to make public their tax returns is grossly prurient and intrusive. But crossing over to the world of elected politics requires the candidate to suspend their sensitivities about privacy and personal space.

Unlike members of the Oireachtas and their spouses, who had strict rules applied to them about reporting their financial affairs and interests to the Standards in Public Office Commission—which then made them public—the business or property interests of presidential candidates do not have to be declared. The only requirement is that details of election expenses and donations received be reported.

A consideration for every candidate would be the rewards of office: lavish accommodation in a mansion with private grounds set in the largest enclosed parkland in any European capital, armed Garda security, round-the-clock chauffeur, use of the Government jet, overseas travel with five-star accommodation, invitations to hot-ticket events, and expenses, in addition to the salary of €325,508.

At this time the *Daily Star* trumpeted an exclusive story saying that President Mary McAleese would leave office with a pension pot of €7 million, equalling an annual pension of just over €162,000, or €3,100 a week for life. However, it also noted that she had taken a number of self-imposed pay cuts since 2008, reducing her salary to €250,000. Comments by Peter Mullen of the Irish National Teachers' Organisation, drily noting that the President's annual pension would pay for the hiring of five primary teachers at an entry-level salary of slightly less than €30,000 a year, were also recorded. The editorial in the *Star* was typically blunt:

> For a society that's crippled with debt, unemployment, cutbacks and multi-billion-euro bail-out repayments, the massive pension is ridiculous. Many taxpayers haven't the price of a pint, literally, yet the President will soon pocket enough each week before tax to buy 700 pints in Dublin's poshest pubs.
>
> The Government is laying off special-needs assistants and increasing class sizes, yet it can stand over a massive €3,100 a week to keep the President in luxury for the rest of her life. For most people, their pensions are hammered—but not for our President and politicians. It seems there's one recession for ordinary folk—and no recession at all for the Golden Circle.

In the same day's *Irish Independent*, Sam Smyth continued his articles about Gay Byrne, noting that 'others who have reversed their position from curious interviewer to reluctant interviewee have had serious regrets—and not just his colleague, George Lee.'

Lee, a former economics editor with RTE, was unveiled two years earlier as Fine Gael's by-election parachute candidate for Dublin South after the death in July 2008 of the Fianna Fáil minister Séamus Brennan, who had held six ministerial and three minister of state positions since 1987. Lee was an opinionated commentator who had previously worked in the Central Bank as an economist and had won popular approval as he cautioned against Government fiscal policies before the crash. On the campaign trail he was met with excited crowds, glad-handed and kissed by enthusiastic voters. They were looking for change and hope, and they channelled that demand into Lee. As expected, he easily topped the poll, sweeping into office on the first count. It was a harbinger for Fine Gael and an accurate reflection of the public mood and support for the party for the 2011 general election result.

Lee, however, who had enjoyed the limelight in RTE and on the campaign trail, was relegated to the backbenches. He felt that his input and undoubted professional expertise were not being utilised by the party in the formulation of Fine Gael's economic policy for the looming general election. Disillusioned, in a bolt out of the blue he resigned not just from Fine Gael but from Dáil Éireann. Fortunately for him he was able to return to RTE as a business reporter, as he had made his decision within the twelve-month window provided for his leave arrangement. Any later and he would have had to resign from RTE. The importance of 'minding the talent' had been lost by Fine Gael in Lee's case.

Ironically, the man Lee had replaced in Dublin South, Séamus Brennan, was Government chief whip in the previous Fianna Fáil-PD Government, which had to rely on a three-line whip and on the crucial make-or-break votes of four independent candidates. Brennan made sure they were given access to ministers and were minded and mentored to ensure that they supported the Government in what was to become a full five-year term.

Across the Liffey, in the plush new *Irish Times* building, the columnist Fintan O'Toole also offered his analysis of where Byrne's campaign would have to go—and what it would have to avoid. He argued that there were two Byrnes: Gaybo the television host, which was a carefully crafted persona, and the intensely private Gay Byrne.

He referred the other evening to 'all the love and affection from all over the country' that's been wafting his way.

But who is it that the Irish people really love? Is it Gaybo or Gabriel Byrne? Given they don't really know the man himself—a man who has retained his privacy throughout a lifetime of fame—the love is surely for the persona rather than the person.

Gaybo is not a man but an image. That image is of someone who floats above Irish life without ever being entirely a part of it. The paradox is that Byrne had such a huge effect on attitudes in Ireland from the 1960s onwards because he perfected the art of appearing not to be trying to affect anything.

He made himself into an Irish Everyman, able to open up discussion on any issue because he seemed to have no personal stake in it. On his radio show especially he became the nation's father confessor, listening calmly and without judgment to all of its sins and anxieties, its private agonies and dark secrets.

This is precisely what attracts many people to the idea of President Gaybo. In this time of deep anxiety there is an allure to the idea of a father confessor in the park who is calm, unruffled, dapper, smooth, stoical—the reverse image of our bedraggled, overwrought, scared-stiff selves.

O'Toole, who was firmly on the left of political opinion, said that Byrne could never be considered as a neutral and would have to address his status as an independent, as in his autobiography he revealed that he voted Fianna Fáil. O'Toole also believed that it would be impossible for Gaybo to clock up thousands of hours behind an on-air microphone without his views emerging occasionally. 'And what has emerged is a bog-standard, unreflective and instinctive right-winger,' he said in a scathing judgement.

So while the nation may be turning its lonely eyes to Dr Gaybo, the suave man who is above it all, it will first have to push past Mr Byrne, the mere mortal who votes Fianna Fáil, hates taxes, thinks Brussels is full of mad people and can get irritated by uppity women . . .

If he could get through the long months of a campaign as Gaybo, with Mr Byrne locked safely in the attic, it would be the greatest performance of his brilliant career.

The opinion page article on Friday 12 August was illustrated by Martyn Turner, with a cartoon of Byrne in front of a full-length mirror clutching the results of the opinion poll. The cartoon was titled 'The style icon President', and its speech bubble said, 'Once more, I find myself in the presence of greatness.' This was a reference to his voice-over radio advertisement for Newbridge Silverware's Museum of Style Icons, which included the film stars Audrey Hepburn and Marilyn Monroe, among others.

———

Further south of the city, in Donnybrook, all the daily papers were strewn on a square coffee table and on the two leather sofas in the reception areas on the ground floor of the RTE radio centre. There had been nominal coverage of any candidate other than Byrne in the print media, such was the megawatt bulb that bathed his 'will he, won't he' game of speculation.

The *Irish Examiner* published a report that the independent candidate Seán Gallagher had moved to sever his links with Fianna Fáil, saying he didn't want to be 'demonised' because of his past links and that it was 'nonsense' that he had any links at present. According to Gallagher, 'I was a member of the party and I think it's really dangerous and disappointing that the media and others might now try to demonise people who were voluntary members of a political organisation.' Gallagher confirmed that he was involved in Ógra Fianna Fáil in the 1980s but said he had no links with the party between 1993 and 2007. He had directed the re-election campaign of Séamus Kirk in Co. Louth, chairperson of the Fianna Fáil parliamentary party, and attended two Fianna Fáil Ard-Chomhairle meetings in 2009.

He was non-committal about the party's former Taoisigh. On Bertie Ahern he said: 'I'm sure he has done some good, and he has done some things that are not so good.' On Ahern's successor, Brian Cowen, he said: 'I guess what Brian Cowen was doing and his Cabinet were doing was based on what was in front of them; they were making the best decisions they felt at the time. Maybe in hindsight, there were decisions that could have been made differently.' The headline over the comments was balder: 'Gallagher anxious to sever his links with FF.'

Gallagher hit out at Pat Kenny's series of interviews of candidates, criticising the phone calls he had received about his links with Fianna Fáil.

That was an ambush . . . And somebody was well tutored to come in on that line . . . They said I had made it a secret . . . Where is this story that I'm a sort of proxy Fianna Fáil candidate?

———

It took Gay Mitchell just fifteen minutes to get to RTE from his home in Rathmines. He passed the television building on the right-hand side of the entrance road and wound round the administration building to the radio centre. He was familiar with both buildings: the TV centre which housed the newsroom and where 'Morning Ireland' and the 'News at One' were broadcast from in cramped studios, and the radio centre.

The radio producer arrived in reception to escort him through the sliding doors and down the staircase into the underground suite of studios that flanked the central courtyard. He was ushered through the heavy, sound-proof door into the producer's room, which looked through a large window into the studio, where the presenter Myles Dungan was filling in for the holidaying Kenny.

The Pat Kenny show had opened a weekly Friday morning debate about the Presidency by inviting each of the candidates into the studio to talk about their campaign. As this was a heavyweight news programme, no candidate could afford to pass up the opportunity to set out their stall for the listening political correspondents and opinion-formers on one of the top ten radio programmes in the country, attracting audiences of more than 300,000.

Mitchell had already prompted considerable media interest. He had bucked the Fine Gael leader's preference for Pat Cox to secure the party's nomination. A formidable vote-catcher, he was also on the right wing of his party, firmly anti-abortion, with strong views on marriage and homosexuality. He was also, unfortunately, a cousin of a well-known Dublin criminal. These had all prompted a media trawl of the archives and a rehash of the past. Despite Fine Gael's dominance in opinion polls, the last REDC poll put him in third place, with only 13 per cent of the vote.

In the studio, Mitchell was to face down those issues in the first substantial radio interview of his campaign. Defending his ratings, he said that people are not engaged with this election. When the real election comes people will engage and, as happened in every other presidential election, these polls will wax and wane . . . I wouldn't go to the bank and take a mortgage out on these figures.

He also urged caution in taking comfort in high opinion poll figures in the early stages of the campaign, before the electorate engaged with and analysed the candidates on offer. Fourteen years earlier the Labour Party presidential candidate Adi Roche, the charity organiser of the Chernobyl Children's Project and a popular media figure, polled 38 per cent in the earlier stages of the campaign, but on election day she took only 7 per cent of the vote. It was a mantra he would repeat again and again.

A confirmed Europhile, Mitchell, not surprisingly, dismissed Byrne's 'mad people in Brussels' comment.

I think we have a serious problem when we start blaming other people, particularly when we start blaming the people who have given us the tools to dramatically change this country.

The interview continued:

Dungan: In relation not specifically to Alveda King [who has extreme views on homosexuality and religion], you've quite emphatically said that you do not agree with anybody who says God hates homosexuals; but people are asking, Would you be prepared to go a step further? And what is your attitude towards gay marriage?

Mitchell: Well, first of all, I don't want to do anything that weakens marriage. Secondly, I supported partnership for gay people—no problem with that. And, thirdly, let the hare sit—let's see if there's any problems with this, how this works out . . . Let's not caricature gay people as being different than the rest of us. They're not different than the rest of us. Gay people have different views about this.

Dungan: But they have different rights; this is what they say.

Mitchell: No, no, some of them . . .

Dungan [interrupting]: Lesser rights.

Mitchell: No, no, let's . . . We—we shouldn't be saying—we would never say, for example, heterosexual people say this, or heterosexual people say that. There are people in the gay community that are quite happy that they've got—that this has been achieved. Now let's—let the hare sit on this, let's see how this works out, what problems there are with it, and let's be reasonable and open-minded about it . . . But I do not want to do anything that will weaken marriage. Incidentally, because I support different forms of relationships, people who are single parents, people who are . . . people who are living in, in, in relations that they're not married. But I think marriage is the ideal, and I think there's something very supportive of my view that people think marriage is so worth while that they want to have it. I'm open-minded on the idea, in time—not now. I want to see how this—

Dungan [interrupting]: How does increasing the rights of people who are involved in civil partnership in relation to adoption, in relation to children—how does that weaken marriage?

Mitchell: I don't know. And I'm not saying it weakens marriage. I don't want to do anything that weakens marriage. I want to take our time about this. I supported gay partnership—

Dungan [correcting him]: Civil partnership.

Mitchell: Civil partnership, rather, on the basis that this was going to solve a problem. People asked for it, and I supported it, and I have no misgivings about supporting it. Let's just see how this works out, and we'll talk about where we go from here; but let's do it calmly, let's do it respectfully, let's do it by discussion.

The interview moved on, taking a question, phoned in to the studio, asking Mitchell to confirm whether or not he was the first cousin of George Mitchell, 'the Penguin'.

I'm the first cousin of an ambassador. I'm the first cousin of people who've been involved in the security forces of the state, people who were married to the security forces of the state, people who were school principals, teachers, farmers. I've no responsibility for any of them, and none of them have responsibility for me. And I think it's actually not a proper question to be put to a candidate on a radio programme, to be perfectly honest.

But Dungan wouldn't leave it there. 'But I mean, is it—are you or are you not?'

I don't think you should put that question to me. This is a matter of record. I've nothing, nothing to do with my cousins. I have cousins who play international rugby for Ireland. None of them have anything to do with me.

For Mitchell, though clearly annoyed about the questions he had to face, it was better to deal with these issues early in the campaign and before a public still arguably in a holiday frame of mind, with schools closed and August threatening to become warm and summery, engaged with the campaign, as at the end of the campaign voters' minds focused.

――――

As Mitchell left RTE, Seán Gallagher was on a walkabout in Ennis as part of his public consultation 'listening tour'. A 300-strong group of cyclists were taking a break while on their four-day charity Tour de Munster, a fund-raiser for Down Syndrome Ireland. Gallagher had spotted the international cyclist Seán Kelly and reacted like an old pro on the campaign trail, making a beeline for him and posing with him for the photographers who were accompanying him. Staying on-message, Gallagher wouldn't be drawn on Gay Byrne's possible entry into the field.

> There has been lots of speculation about people entering the race, and for me, I am focused on my own campaign, meeting people around the country.

When asked how he would finance his campaign, he took a novel approach and offered an invitation to his competitors.

> It's very much like a start-up business: it will be low-cost, it will be run on a very low budget. It is absolutely obscene that vast amounts of money are thrown towards campaigns to become President. There are enough avenues through the media to get your message across without spending lots of money.
> I have really serious reservations about spending silly money on posters. To be wasting that money is offensive to people in terms of people being unable to pay their mortgages and being in negative equity. I would like to see that issue of posters debated amongst the candidates.

The cost of the campaign was an issue that he would address again in the campaign. The other issue that had trailed him through the print media and on the airwaves was brought up again. But Gallagher was taking a firm line.

> It hasn't come up on the ground at all. I'm standing as an independent. There are tens of thousands of people in Fianna Fáil. There are great people in Fianna Fáil, as there are in every other political party, and we need to stop demonising people for being voluntary members of a political party.

Later that day the unrest in Fianna Fáil about the party leader's solo run in offering support for Gay Byrne was to surface as reporters spoke to some members of the parliamentary party. And the following day that bubbling unrest in Fianna Fáil, which had first surfaced in social media, had grown into a front-page story in the *Irish Times*.

Senator Ned O'Sullivan of Co. Kerry was the most outspoken. 'I am unhappy that there seems to be an impression abroad that an outsider will have a better chance than one of our own. Are we a party or are we not?' He said the party needed to put up a candidate who would be proud to wear the party logo. It was interpreted as an implicit criticism of Micheál Martin's offer of support to Byrne as an independent. O'Sullivan said that if Byrne went before the Fianna Fáil parliamentary party, along with other aspiring candidates, and was selected, he would have his support. But, he said, Fianna Fáil needed to stop 'shadow-boxing'.

Another Kerry senator, Mark Daly, said he was in favour of the party choosing its own candidate and professed his preference for Brian Crowley, to whom Daly had formerly been a political assistant.

A solicitor from Bantry, Co. Cork, Denis O'Donovan, had served as a TD for one term when he was chairperson of the prestigious Oireachtas Joint Committee on the Constitution. However, he lost his seat in 2007 and was now on his fourth term as a senator. Crowley, he said, should have been given first refusal.

Senator Mary White criticised the 'spinning' of the Byrne candidacy by the party hierarchy as unfair and undemocratic. 'Gay Byrne is an outstanding person. But I believe that no decision should take place outside the parliamentary party.'

None of the four senators had been on a list of ten preferred Fianna Fáil candidates circulated to Fianna Fáil councillors for consideration by Micheál Martin in the recent Senate elections.

John Browne, a Wexford TD and former minister of state, now chairperson of the Fianna Fáil parliamentary party, and Michael Moynihan, a Cork North-West TD, expressed similar opinions. However, the former minister Willie O'Dea was taking a typically robust attitude to the problem, promoting a strong line in defence of his party and of Martin. He confirmed that some time earlier he had received a letter from Brian Crowley seeking his support and that of his parliamentary party members for his candidacy.

When I got his letter, out of respect for Brian, because I've great personal admiration for him, I rang him, and I told him my view was that we shouldn't run a candidate. I'm still of the view we shouldn't.

An internal candidate would be a very bad idea. It's only six months since the most catastrophic general election result in the history of the party, and we haven't even begun to recover from that. Running an internal candidate and getting a very, very bad result would be a shattering blow for the party's morale.

The Fianna Fáil party was beginning to publicly splinter. Fault lines were now publicly showing over Martin's solo run with Byrne even before they knew what the broadcaster would decide. There was also deep dissatisfaction about the way in which Brian Crowley had been overlooked.

For Martin it was the first real test of his leadership and his ability to impose discipline. And it was about to get worse.

Chapter 8 ∾

THE PRESIDENTIAL ENDORSEMENT

The following day, Saturday 13 August, Gay Byrne was again to dominate the news. The initiative was his. He dialled the confidential number Micheál Martin had given him during their initial discussion a week earlier. Martin was still on holiday with his family in west Cork. Martin replied simply: 'That's your decision, that's fine, and thank you very much.'

It was a very brief conversation, and Byrne couldn't tell whether Martin was annoyed or upset. Later asked to characterise the conversation, Byrne said he couldn't. 'I told him, and I don't know whether the man was disappointed or not. I called him first out of manners and courtesy, because he was the one who obviously made the offer of backing me at the time.' Then Byrne made an announcement to the media: 'I just decided not to run, period.'

It was a simple declaration that would end intense speculation and spark another furious round of commentary, not least on Byrne's motivation but also on what the decision would mean for Fianna Fáil, and for Martin's leadership in particular.

Byrne always gave good quotations and sound-bites to the media, and, as approachable as ever, he embarked on a round of interviews, anxious to state his case.

The *Sunday World*, the country's largest-selling Sunday newspaper, with a sale of almost 250,000, claimed that he broke the news to it first.

Okay, look, I used to write for you guys, and for old time's sake I'll tell you now I won't be running.

Ah, I made up my mind a couple of days ago but I just wanted to keep all the family involved, and that included my daughter who is in France at the moment. So, I spoke to her on the phone and that was that, they were all kept in the loop and as soon as I had that chat, it was all over.

He had felt 'under considerable pressure' to run, but now that he had made his decision he could draw a sigh of relief: the 'clamour' was over.

And out of respect for the office and the role, I had to give it my serious consideration, especially after the poll results always put my name on top, but I sat down with people who are all well versed in these matters and spoke at length about what it involved and decided it wasn't, in the end, for me.

While he had 'no worries' about probes of his financial and business affairs, he was concerned about possible scrutiny of his family.

Yes, I would be concerned, and that's all the subject of discussion and what I've been considering over the past number of weeks.

He paraphrased what he had already told the *Sunday World* to other media:

When I discovered there was a lot of interest in me running for president I realised I knew nothing about the role and sought the advice of a number of people. Unfortunately, because of the time of year it is, a lot of these people were on holidays, so it took me a while to get their advice—that is why it has taken me up to ten days to make up my mind. My family also played a big role in this decision. At this time, I don't think the job is for me.

And I do not believe that I am what the Irish people are looking for in a president at this time.

Age was not an issue for him, even at seventy-seven, but it might be for others, he said. Nor had it anything to do with his health. (A month earlier he had been rushed to hospital, fearing death, as he couldn't breathe.)

My decision has had nothing whatsoever to do with that. That was simply a bad infection I had at the time, which many people get, but I am well recovered.

He reiterated his thanks for all the messages of support he had received as he deliberated. Commenting on the volume of phone calls and messages, he said,

'I will never get around to thanking all the people who have contacted me offering support.'

The top columnist of the *Sunday World*, Des Ekin, reminded readers that some years previously the paper had asked a major polling company to find out the ten most loved and most hated public figures in Ireland. 'Astonishingly, Gay Byrne emerged as a clear winner in both categories.' According to Ekin,

> Gaybo has no nasty skeletons in his cupboard, but such exposure would have been anathema for a private and reserved individual. After his withdrawal, the real Gay Byrne will remain an enigma.
>
> As the fuss subsides, Gay will probably derive a mischievous enjoyment from the fact that he can still surprise us, keep us guessing, and drive us crazy after all these years.

A competing tabloid, the *Irish Sunday Mirror*, was robust in its front-page coverage. 'Gaybo chickens out' was its main headline, two others being 'Millions let down as RTE legend bottles presidency battle' and 'Runaway poll leader insists: I'm not what the Irish people want.' The first three sentences of the story summed it all up.

> The presidency race was blown wide open last night after big favourite Gay Byrne bowed out. The broadcaster has stunned his supporters all over the country by declaring that he doesn't want a job he was odds on to win. His bombshell decision has shocked the nation and left his main backer, Fianna Fáil leader Micheál Martin, with egg on his face.

At the other end of the Sunday newspaper market, the *Sunday Times* published an analysis of the Byrne debacle. It reported that TDs and senators had received calls from councillors and grass-roots members expressing disappointment that an independent had been given the nod ahead of a party member. One bitter quotation reflected the deep level of dismay felt by some party members: 'One said to me, "I'd vote for Gay Mitchell before I'd vote for Gay Byrne."'

However, an official party spokesperson was quoted after the Byrne decision was made known saying they would be meeting in September to discuss their strategy. 'They'll decide whether they want to run an internal candidate, support an independent candidate or not run a candidate at all. No decision on any of that has yet been made.'

The official response suggested a process of consultation, part of the process of rebuilding the party with a national tour by Martin that would end in September with a visit to each constituency to meet party members. By omission, however, it admitted that the sub-committee established to consider the decision about running candidates had not met and that the offer, now a political mess, had not embraced, or been informed by, consultation.

Under an entertaining headline that echoed the catchphrase of 'The Late Late Show', 'To whom it concerns—I'm out,' the *Sunday Times* reported the thinking of strategists in Martin's office, who insisted that Fianna Fáil's best strategy was to support a candidate outside the fold who wasn't tainted by the Cowen era, and ideally to back a winning candidate who would also be supported by the independent TDs and senators who had previously offered their support to Norris.

The independent TD Finian McGrath had worked to achieve a cohesion between the diverse independents elected to the Dáil only a few months earlier. Under his leadership they had drawn up a list of ten names that they would consider supporting for the Presidency. According to McGrath,

> we had a list of ten people we thought would potentially be good candidates, and Byrne's name was on that list. From informal chats I've had with other independents, there were definitely some open to supporting him.

Had Byrne taken up Martin's offer he might have also secured the support of the independents. That would have had two benefits: giving Martin political cover and, for Byrne, broadening his base of political loyalty, allowing him to maintain his credentials as an independent candidate.

Now, with Byrne out, McGrath was looking for a candidate to support and was hardly effusive about the other nominees on his list. He told the *Sunday Times* that, 'at this stage, the other people on the list aren't exactly banging down my door. Unless some other super-duper candidate comes on the pitch, I'll have to move on to the next-best thing.'

——

The Andrews family had dominated public life for three generations and were viewed as Fianna Fáil blue-bloods. C. S. 'Todd' Andrews had been an active member of the IRA during the War of Independence, in which he had been an internee and a hunger-striker, and took part on the Republican side in the Civil War. His son Niall was a TD, minister of state and MEP for Dublin, and his son David was a long-term TD for Dún Laoghaire and served in different departments, including Foreign Affairs. Niall's son Chris became a Dublin TD in the previous Dáil, and David's son Barry was Minister of State for Children from 2008. Both lost their seats in the 2011 general election.

In an uncharacteristic outburst, the mild-mannered Chris responded to the *Sunday Independent*, labelling the Byrne approach that 'poisonous short-termism, the very thing that had brought the party to a historical low.' He went on to the record to say that the decision to back Byrne was yet another example of the attitude of seeking 'shortcuts to success that dishonour the party's origins and demean the profession of politics.'

The comments were a reflection of some of the debate that was going on within the party and among its grass roots. Other senior party members were to be quoted in the coming days but remained anonymous. These sources described the Byrne approach as damaging to the party, and Martin said it was 'profoundly embarrassing.'

However, Timmy Dooley, who had made the initial approach to Crona Byrne, countered these comments in the *Sunday Independent*, saying that the party would have been forced 'to do even more side-stepping if it had refused to back "Gay, the people's choice" when he emerged into the frame.'

The Laois TD Seán Fleming told of a recent meeting of party activists in his own constituency attended by Martin as part of his national consultation tour. Two-thirds of those present were against running a candidate, saying that they weren't going to win and that it would be better to concentrate efforts and funding on building the party for the next local elections. Fleming, an accountant who could do his sums, said, 'We're not going to win it. We're not going to be second, we're fighting for third or fourth.'

'The last thing we want,' said Dooley, emphasising the point, 'the last thing we want is to end up fighting it out with Dana.'

———

Frank McNamara was a precociously talented musician from Thurles, Co. Tipperary, who at the tender age of nineteen shot to national fame when he was appointed studio pianist for 'The Late Late Show'. He went on to become a composer and musical director for the programme in 1979, and most recently he presented 'Weekend Classics' on Lyric FM, the station on which Gay Byrne hosted a Sunday jazz programme. With a number of strings to his bow, McNamara was an apt choice to write a full-page tribute to his friend and boss for decades.

Gay probably made the right decision for his own sake. Every quip he uttered over the years, every comment made, every letter written, would have been trawled and scrutinised for the slightest hint of something that could be spun into a story. With the party political machines in full swing, and ever-willing media anxious for market share, who in his right mind would voluntarily bring upon himself the inevitable savagery that would follow a declaration of intent to run for President? While I totally understand why Gay decided not to run, I am saddened at what we have lost.

McNamara had been a familiar figure on TV in living-rooms around the country. The Progressive Democrats, led by Mary Harney, were identifying celebrity candidates to run in the 2007 general election and recruited him to run in Dublin South-Central, the former political home of Gay Mitchell.

Politics was new to him, and sixteen candidates from all and no parties sought the votes of the people in that very diverse constituency, which includes Terenure, Crumlin, Kimmage, Inchicore, Kilmainham, Walkinstown and Ballyfermot. It was a bruising experience. With a quota of 7,992 votes, Fianna Fáil took two seats, and the Labour Party, Fine Gael and Sinn Féin one each. McNamara came fourth-last, with 474 votes.

With the insight of a former candidate, he concluded his tribute, borrowing a key word from Gaybo:

> On the one hand the public appears to be clamouring for a President who is not affiliated to one of the main parties. On the other hand the main parties are eager to cling to what was once their exclusive gift to put one of their friends in the Park. The void between the rulers and the will of the people grows ever greater.

Ever on the ball, the bookies Paddy Power, who offered sports odds but also regularly offered odds on politics or anything that captured public attention, now placed Michael D. Higgins as favourite, at 8:11. Gay Mitchell was in second place at 7:2, Seán Gallagher was popular at 10:1, Brian Crowley at 14:1, Mary Davis at 16:1 and Éamon Ó Cuív at 20:1. Three other names—Dana, Martin McAleese (husband of Mary McAleese) and Martin McGuinness, who had been nominated by Sinn Féin—were each quoted at 25:1.

Brendan O'Connor in his *Sunday Independent* column took a pop at the *Irish Times* for doing a 'hatchet job' on Byrne. He said that the paper

> took issue with the fact that Gay had claimed to be apolitical but in fact, shock horror, it turned out he had many views on things, and, more worryingly, many of these views were not left-wing, which made them 'controversial', and worse again, 'right-wing'. And we all know that to accuse a potential president of right-wing views is a fatal blow in this country. Because although this is a right-wing, capitalist, western country

where the vast majority of people vote for parties that are centrist or right wing, in Fintan O'Toole's Ireland 'right-wing' means evil . . .

Gay would not have been going into this election with the clamour he wanted. He would have been entering a potential dogfight. And having seen just a taste of what the dogfight might entail in the media last week, he clearly decided he would be mad to sully his position as father of the nation by subjecting himself to it.

Echoing the comments of Vincent Browne a few days earlier, who had suggested that Byrne would be a good President but a bad candidate—one not up to the rigours of campaigning—O'Connor added: 'And the unfortunate thing about how this election has gone thus far, is probably that the best candidate will win it, and not necessarily the best President.'

The newly elected senator John Crown, a consultant oncologist elected on the National University panel, used his column in the same paper to suggest that the presidential contest could be seen as one of the least consequential electoral exercises. However, it would be instructive for future political students, he said. He slammed Fianna Fáil for offering support to Byrne in contravention of its support for the European Union, which Byrne firmly opposed. And Fine Gael was not spared either for opposing Norris's bid, saying it suggested 'a certain contempt for democracy.' He railed that our politicians

hire armies of public relations consultants to maintain their reputational status. They would do well to pay attention to their responsibilities for maintaining the reputation of the democratic system of government itself.

Now more than ever we need political leaders who are more concerned about statesmanship and less about electoral stunt-mongering.

This presidential election would be a good start.

Fianna Fáil responded formally to Byrne's announcement with a brief statement.

As was fully demonstrated in this week's opinion poll, there was very wide public support for Gay Byrne's potential candidacy. Gay Byrne has many fine qualities and would have made an excellent candidate. However, we respect his personal decision not to stand in the presidential election.

As to who the party will support, the process remains that a decision will be taken on this matter by the parliamentary party next month.

While the Sunday-paper-buying public munched their breakfast toast and drank their breakfast tea as they read the myriad stories and opinions about

Byrne, he was on the radio. He was talking to the chat-show presenter Claire Byrne (no relation), who was filling in for the doyenne of RTE radio, Marian Finucane. Byrne decided he was

> just pestered to death. I completely accept that the campaign process is the campaign process, and it's the silly season, and it's August, and newspapers and media are looking for some type of story. I really felt that I was in the middle of a firestorm.
>
> To give you an example, one young woman from a newspaper rang me yesterday and asked, 'Have you made up your mind?' I said, 'I'll give you my decision when I make up my mind and when the decision is made.' She said, 'What's the hold-up?' There was a fair amount of indignation in her voice, as if I was getting between her and her dinner. And I had to explain to her that I just had to have consultation with people, because I knew nothing about this situation, and I had to consult with people who did know something about this situation, and I decided there and then that I would put an end to all this. So there you go, it's over.
>
> The race for the Presidency is not a sprint, it's a marathon, and it was going to go on for a long, long time, and I didn't have the stomach for all of that. It was a totally and completely new concept to me, because in truth I never dreamed about being President. I never thought about it: it never occurred to me. It never came up, even on my long-range radar of what way my life would go.

He signed off by thanking all the 'good people' who had wished him well and wishing good luck to the four contenders already in the field. He added that he felt his former RTE colleague sports commentator Mícheál Ó Muircheartaigh was the most popular man in Ireland and that, if he ran, his money was on him. To the final question, 'Any regrets?' he replied definitively. 'None. Once the decision was made. Thank you, and goodbye.'

The following morning, Monday 15 August, the editorial in the *Irish Examiner* rapped Micheál Martin on the knuckles over his approach to Byrne.

> No matter what spin Martin's office might offer, he made a very public error of judgement that will cast a shadow over his leadership. It will provoke antipathy and resentment among colleagues who are probably entitled to believe that they should be allowed to challenge for the party's nomination in the Áras race.

It compared Bertie Ahern's sure-footed and careful approach in securing the party's nomination for Mary McAleese with the Byrne fiasco. It was also probably the only recent positive press reference Ahern had received since the country's financial collapse, for which he was pilloried. It continued:

> Where Mr Ahern was ruthless and utterly focused, Mr Martin was wildly optimistic and opportunist. He was also far less respectful of his party's traditions and colleagues with presidential ambitions than he should have been.

That same day the *Evening Herald* published a column by Fergus Finlay, the defeated Labour Party contender, in which he said that Byrne had had two choices if he ran: to organise his own campaign team or to let Fianna Fáil organise it for him. The former wasn't a runner, he suggested, as he'd need an experienced political manager. 'In America you can buy that kind of expertise,' he said, 'but not here.' No, the only alternative was to let Fianna Fáil run his campaign—the preparation, the slogans, the message—which meant that it would end up owning him. For Finlay,

> you might get over that if you won—but you'd have to win. Gay Byrne was being pushed into a race that he couldn't, at any level, afford to lose. Not for the first time, Gay Byrne made the right career choice. That's how he has survived for so long.

Fine Gael and Fianna Fáil had both employed American political consultants in their various general election campaigns, during which they paid particular attention to the big picture and to messaging. But Finlay was proved wrong, as the independent candidates would all recruit the services of professional PR and political operatives to bolster their campaign teams. Mary Davis and Seán Gallagher had recruited former Fianna Fáil and ministerial press officers; Gay Mitchell had recruited the press officer of the former Green Party minister John Gormley.

A cadre of former back-room operatives from all parties had grown over the past twenty years as people employed by the three main parties moved into the private sector and specifically into public-relations companies. In the recent general elections the core strategising and implementation for Fianna Fáil and Fine Gael was carried out by experienced current and former staff members and a cadre of volunteers around the country.

In the same edition of the *Evening Herald* that Finlay's column appeared, Willie O'Dea was quoted as maintaining his support for an independent candidate rather than for someone from within the ranks of the party. But he opened up a potential new line of thought, referring not only to supporting an independent who might yet emerge but possibly to someone who was already declared, which by implication was either Gallagher or Davis.

> There is nobody in Fianna Fáil who can be elected President given the way the party is still seen by voters. There is no possibility whatsoever in my mind of us electing a Fianna Fáil President. It would be a bad mistake nominating our own candidate.
>
> I still believe we should look to an independent candidate that is already in the race or else support a completely new candidate that may emerge.

A few days later he would tell the *Irish Times* that he would have no problem getting behind a good external candidate but 'won't be beating the bushes' to find one. Asked what he thought about the four candidates in the field already, he said, 'Mary Davis is well qualified to be President.'

O'Dea's colleague in Limerick County, Niall Collins, had proved his own election expertise by achieving the highest percentage vote for any Fianna Fáil candidate in the general election. He echoed O'Dea's view:

> I can't identify anybody within our own ranks who I feel could potentially win the contest. Obviously there are people who could carry out the role and the job as President of Ireland quite successfully, but I don't think that they're in a position where they could win the election.

Now that Gay Byrne had exited the political stage, existing candidates and potential candidates began to win back more media coverage.

———

The only hard news story in the race was Gay Mitchell's support for two condemned men on death row in the United States, and the media probed for the content of the letters after the revelation of Norris's letter of support for his lover had led to his resignation. Until there was clarity, Mitchell would also be a target.

A secondary debate had emerged about the use and the cost of posters. Gallagher had called on candidates not to use posters, as they would be part of the cost that candidates could possibly recoup if they received enough votes to be reimbursed by the taxpayers. 'There are many outlets in which we can communicate our message without plastering unsightly posters on every telegraph pole in our cities, towns and rural areas.' But he would later draw fire from Davis, who said that he had postered advertising space on rubbish bins in shopping centres while calling for a no-poster campaign from other candidates.

Davis would also later defend her decision to run a national poster campaign, saying it was necessary for candidate recognition. Unlike politicians, she had not featured previously in such campaigns and so had not benefited from being in the public eye as they had over the years. Her posters showed her in a red dress, which some commentators likened to advertisements for the cereal Special K, which put itself forward as important in a slimming diet. (Thankful for the reference, the cereal company sent a hamper of its products to the campaign headquarters, which Davis subsequently donated to a charity.)

Davis also denied that her photograph was airbrushed when critics suggested that it bore no resemblance to the 56-year-old woman. After the campaign she said that

the pictures weren't airbrushed. I've said this *ad nauseam*. No matter how many times I said it, the same questions were asked again and again. If you looked closely you'd see all the lines were there. But of course as the campaign progressed you were looking more and more tired; but the pictures weren't airbrushed.

Michael D. Higgins said that posters were a traditional part of the electoral process and played a significant role in creating awareness among the public. Only Gallagher and Dana failed to put up posters on poles.

Surprisingly, the content of the posters would be the next issue in an increasingly fractious campaign, and it boiled over into the public domain in early September. Davis had been using the slogan *Pride at home, respect abroad* for weeks, according to her campaign team. On Friday 9 September she launched her posters, as well as a web site and leaflets carrying the slogan, with a photo call. However, Mitchell's web site and leaflets, which were promoted at the Galway think-in (a parliamentary party seminar before the autumn Dáil session), had the same slogan. According to a Mitchell spokesperson, they were 'something that we have been using for quite a while.'

'Don't you just hate when you come up with a brilliant slogan—and it turns out to be exactly the same as your rivals'?' asked www.thejournal.ie, which used the words 'oops' and 'snap' to promote its article. Mitchell's team responded to the site that imitation was the best form of flattery.

The issue of who was first with the slogan was never resolved, but there were dark mutterings that Fine Gael had adopted the slogan as a 'flak' attack on Davis. The Davis campaign said they had used the slogan first, as she launched her campaign in May and it had featured in local media advertising, including, most recently, the *Sligo Champion*. 'It is exactly what we stand for. I certainly have no intention of changing the slogan,' said Davis. 'What Fine Gael do is up to them. I don't think they stole it, I think it's merely a coincidence.'

Describing it as a 'bizarre coincidence,' Mitchell's director of elections, Charlie Flanagan TD, said: 'It's our slogan. The literature is in the public domain for some time now. The slogan has appeared on election literature and paraphernalia for weeks. I'd be surprised to see it feature in another candidate's material.'

While Davis had already printed her posters, Fine Gael had so far provided only canvassing materials for its TDs and its organisation. Davis stuck to her guns, and Mitchell changed his slogan. He would produce two versions, for different markets, one of him wearing a smart suit and a second wearing a windcheater with a tractor in the background.

On www.thejournal.ie, via Twitter, there were comments that ranged from entertained to outraged and deeply sceptical. Fitzpatrick tweeted:

> Well done Mary Davis. With a slight moderation both candidates can be accommodated. For Gay: Pride at home? Respect abroad? For Mary: Pride at home. Respect the Broad.

Darragh Yay Doyle on Facebook unearthed a startling reference.

> Not sure if this adds to it, but from Barry Goldwater in a 1964 US Presidential campaign leaflet comes a similar phrase: 'A crusade which will restore pride and self reliance and respect abroad.'

Mícheál O'Neill on Facebook was pithy: 'Is that "Gay Pride at home"?'

On the campaign trail in the sprawling Blanchardstown Shopping Centre, west of Dublin, Mitchell, accompanied by the former Taoiseach John Bruton, was again asked when he would release copies of the letters he sent pleading for the lives of two men on death row in the United States. The cases of the double killer Paul Jennings Hill and the murderer and rapist Louis Joe Truesdale had followed him around since Norris had quit the race for the Presidency. Mitchell 'just doesn't have time to dig back through his extensive files; he's been putting out several dozen letters a week for the past thirty years,' said his campaign spokesperson, who reiterated that Mitchell did not condone their crimes and that he was solely motivated by his opposition to the death penalty. 'Gay Mitchell is implacably opposed to the death penalty, always and everywhere. He is in the company of Amnesty International, Mary Robinson and others.'

Mitchell's record on the death penalty was consistent. He had previously objected to the Nigerian ambassador in Ireland in 2002 over the sentencing to death by stoning of a woman, Amina Lawal, under Sharia law. Her death sentence was overturned the following year. In another campaign four years earlier he had handed in a letter of opposition to the American embassy to coincide with the execution of the 500th prisoner in the United States since 1976, Louis Joe Truesdale.

Justin Moran of Amnesty International had given Mitchell his support, saying the organisation was in favour of politicians campaigning with them on the issue. 'In general, we absolutely encourage people like Gay Mitchell to raise their support for the abolition of the death penalty in the USA or other countries.'

In the *Irish Independent*, Michael Brennan, the paper's deputy political editor, asked Higgins's spokesperson if the candidate had sent similar letters. 'No specific letters come to mind, but any action taken would have been in the context of human rights campaigns, or joint decisions by the Oireachtas Foreign Affairs Committee,' she replied, adding that, although Higgins had been a lifelong supporter of Amnesty International and other groups opposed to the death penalty, he had not made any representations in any criminal or civil court case. 'He may have, from time to time, made representations to prison authorities regarding the welfare of individual prisoners on matters such as the provision of literacy services or other training services.' Ironically, both Mitchell and Higgins, as Dáil deputies, had served on the same Oireachtas committee when Mitchell chaired it.

———

At seventy years of age, Michael D. Higgins revealed that his 'rock and roll' years were over when he talked to the political correspondent of the *Star*, Catherine Halloran. He said he had given up the booze two years earlier and replaced it with yoga as he coped with early mornings and late nights writing speeches. But rock and roll didn't translate into having skeletons in his cupboard.

There is absolutely nothing in my past that in any way would impede me in being President.

I lost my taste for alcohol, really. But I did have my rock and roll years. I have lived a very full life. I am more active now than people half my age.

It is not about age. It is about what you are able to do. Look at people like Giovanni Trapattoni and Pablo Picasso—they have done some of their best work in their older years.

Not exactly rock and roll, but the iconic folk singer and social campaigner Christy Moore had also been asked by friends to consider standing. But he ruled himself out, saying he was supporting Michael D. 'He is a cultured man who has negotiated a difficult road in politics,' Moore said. He said he had always made decisions and stuck by them, ever since an irate bank manager had told him, as a junior member of the staff, that it was 'inappropriate' for clerks to sing in pubs, prompting him to opt for a life of music. 'He told me that I had choices to make, and I made them.'

The *Star* also revisited a brief comment by the colourful former Kerry South TD Jackie Healy-Rae the previous April. Healy-Rae, ten years older than Higgins, told Kerry Radio at the time that he was 'definitely considering it anyway, and that's no joke.'

'What now?' he was asked. 'I've changed my mind about it: I've ruled myself out. Yerra, there would have been too much hassle involved in it for me.'

———

While Higgins was happily talking about his earlier years, Mitchell was being taken to task for his. Trócaire, the Catholic overseas aid agency, had organised a conference in 1998 to which Mitchell was invited as a Fine Gael TD. Speaking about abortion, Mitchell read out the testimony of a survivor of a German death camp who had witnessed 'gas chambers built by learned engineers, children poisoned by educated physicians, infants killed by trained nurses, and women and babies shot and burned by high-school and college graduates.' He then walked into a controversy by saying that 'the above quote in relation to the concentration camps could easily apply to the millions of abortions which needlessly take place year after year.'

Thirteen years later Mitchell was held to account over those comments. He would also refer to his continued donations to Trócaire later in the campaign as he took another candidate to task over how they spent their money.

A spokesperson for Mitchell said he remained an unequivocal opponent of abortion but did not support anything that put the life of the mother in danger and 'wouldn't use such emotive language now, particularly in deference to the Jewish community.'

On LM/FM radio, which covers Cos. Louth and Meath and a huge commuter belt in north Co. Dublin, he pledged to release—if he could find them—copies of the letters he had sent pleading for the lives of the two notorious criminals. 'In particular, I don't think I know how someone who's pro-life can take somebody else's life. I think that's absolutely outrageous,' he said in the course of the interview.

The blogosphere and Twitter erupted again. Abusive and crass anonymous comments characterised much of what passed for discourse or debate. However, on politics.ie one contributor, Ciarán Ó Raghallaigh, provided some perspective on the controversy:

> The last presidential election in 1997 was in pre-internet days. Now, with the internet available to everyone, there is a huge potential for bad stuff to be dug up about all the candidates. Journalists, bloggers and forum users like our good selves are having and will continue to have a field day. The question is: will there be anyone left come late October whose character won't have been well and truly assassinated?

Among the dozens left on that one forum, 'Cpm' commented:

> I never thought I'd hear myself say it but Michael Twee is looking like the best candidate at this stage. Let's just put him in Áras an Uachtaráin, lock the doors so he can't get out, and try to forget about the whole horrid affair for seven years.

Mitchell was contacted by the *Irish Independent*, seeking his reaction to comments from the retired Fianna Fáil TD Ben Briscoe. Briscoe, like his politician father, Bob, was well connected to the Jewish political caucus in the United States, where both had raised political funds. When Briscoe retired in 2002 to his home in Co. Kildare, at the age of sixty-eight, he had served as a Fianna Fáil TD for thirty-seven years. He had followed faithfully in the footsteps of his father, a Dáil deputy from 1927 to 1965 and twice Lord Mayor of Dublin, but he had minimal contact with the party since his retirement.

Mitchell, Briscoe's constituency colleague, had served Dublin South-Central since 1981, and both had served on Dublin City Council and had been Lord Mayor. Asked his opinion on the election race by the *Irish Independent*, Briscoe was forthright: 'What was done to Gay Byrne was disgusting. He didn't know what he was getting into. It was a very bad call by Micheál Martin.' But whatever the political anoraks cared about Briscoe's attack on the party leader, his subsequent comments were to prove incendiary to Fianna Fáil members. He was asked who he would support in the race for the Áras now that Gaybo had been 'badly treated' and had pulled out of the race. 'I'm backing Gay Mitchell,' he said, 'because I served the people of Dublin with him for more than twenty years.'

A spokesperson for Mitchell was quoted in the following day's press as welcoming Briscoe's support and claiming that many grass-roots Fianna Fáil supporters were backing his candidacy. The comment was a straightforward bid for number 2s—an appeal across party lines that were defined by the Civil War.

Fianna Fáil bit their tongues and issued no official comment. However, Briscoe's mould-breaking endorsement of an opposition party's candidate provoked a storm of abuse and negative comment from party members on Twitter and on a Fianna Fáil internet discussion group.

———

Alison O'Connor, a columnist with the *Irish Independent*, offered the opinion that Gay Byrne had done the right thing in pulling out of the race and in doing what he was best at: being a broadcaster. She also set out the case for Micheál Martin's intervention in trying to get Byrne on board.

I say fair play to him for having a bit of a punt. If it had come off, it could have been viewed as a classically cheeky Fianna Fail stroke.

The party, desperately in need of any kind of a boost, hasn't had a bad week. As well as the positive publicity, it has made the important discovery that not everything the party touches, or is associated with, turns immediately toxic in terms of public opinion. So what if Micheál was so hands-on that he didn't bother with the fig leaf of asking someone else to make contact with Gay?

The man has a mammoth, if not impossible, task in attempting to rebuild Fianna Fail. It cannot be a case of politics as usual. It's going to take the application of a number of different approaches and attitudes before he finds some way forward. The party would be absolutely daft to run an official candidate for the presidency.

The bottom line here is that the race for the Aras is wide open. However unpredictable the mood, one apparent certainty is that people seem not to be sure what they want as long as it's different. But the campaign proper has yet to get started and we will have hopefully gotten over all the daftness by then.

The madness of the silly season was to abate over the coming week, with the candidates continuing their low-key ground war in the constituencies and with minimal national news coverage. The two big beasts, Byrne and Norris, were off the stage. Mitchell was dealing effectively with comments he had made more than a decade earlier, and his promise to release the two letters seeking clemency for convicted criminals on death row in the United States seemed to guarantee that there was no smoking gun or further controversy in their content.

19 June 2011. The Tánaiste and leader of the Labour Party, Eamon Gilmore, at the Mansion House, Dublin, with nominees Fergus Finlay, Kathleen O'Meara and Michael D. Higgins at the election of Higgins as the party's candidate for the Presidency. (© *Collins*)

9 July 2011. The presidential candidates Gay Mitchell MEP, Mairead McGuinness MEP and Pat Cox during the Fine Gael convention in the Regency Hotel, Dublin, to select the party's presidential candidate. (© *Collins*)

2 August 2011. Senator David Norris outside his home in Dublin after he announced that he was pulling out of the race amid revelations that he had sought leniency for his ex-partner, who had been convicted of statutory rape. (© *Julien Behal/PA Wire*)

10 August 2011. The RTE broadcaster Gay Byrne answering questions regarding his possible candidacy for the presidential election as his wife, Kathleen Watkins, listens at *Grease: The Musical* at the Grand Canal Theatre, Dublin. (© *Photocall Ireland*)

31 August 2011. Senator Darragh O'Brien, Micheál Martin (leader of Fianna Fáil), Éamon Ó Cuív TD and Seán Ó Fearghail TD outside the Dáil explaining why Fianna Fáil decided not to put forward a candidate in the presidential election. (© *Photocall Ireland*)

3 September 2011. Volunteers for Mary Davis's presidential campaign hand out free ponchos on the Saturday morning of the Electric Picnic music and arts festival.
(© *Photocall Ireland*)

18 September 2011. Michael D. Higgins with Dublin fans at the all-Ireland football final between Dublin and Kerry at Croke Park. (© *Collins*)

19 September 2011. Dana holds a copy of the Constitution of Ireland after she announced her intention to seek a nomination for the Presidency at a press conference at the Fitzwilliam Hotel, Dublin. (© *Niall Carson/PA Wire*)

27 September 2011. David Norris shakes hands with his fellow-candidate Michael D. Higgins as he celebrates at City Hall, Dublin, after receiving the backing of Dublin City Council, giving him the fourth nomination needed to enter the race. (© *Niall Carson/ PA Wire*)

11 October 2011. The businessman and independent presidential candidate Seán Gallagher at the Today FM presidential debate in the Sugar Club, Dublin. (© *Photocall Ireland*)

13 October 2011. The actor Colm Meaney, of *Star Trek* fame, who spoke at a rally for the Sinn Féin presidential candidate, Martin McGuinness, at the Mansion House, Dublin. (© *Michael Debets/Demotix/Press Association Images*)

17 October 2011. Martin McGuinness and Paddy Power at the Paddy Power bookmakers shop in Baggot Street, Dublin, where McGuinness placed a bet on himself becoming the next President of Ireland, with the winnings to go to Irish Guide Dogs for the Blind. (© *Collins*)

19 October 2011. Dana in Dublin beside the badly damaged tyre of her campaign car, after it suffered a puncture on a motorway. (© *Julien Behal/PA Wire*)

22 October 2011. Michael D. Higgins with his wife, Sabina Coyne, Nessa Childers MEP (daughter of the fourth president of Ireland, Erskine Childers) and Labour Party leader Eamon Gilmore during Higgins's walkabout in Grafton Street, Dublin. (© *Julien Behal/PA Wire*)

24 October 2011. The 'Frontline' presidential debate. (L to R) Dana (independent), Gay Mitchell MEP (Fine Gael), Michael D. Higgins (Labour Party), Mary Davis (independent), Senator David Norris (independent), Martin McGuinness (Sinn Féin) and Seán Gallagher (independent). (© *Photocall Ireland*)

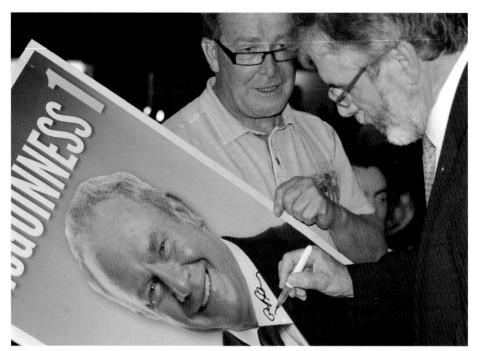

24 October 2011. Gerry Adams signing a Martin McGuinness election poster. (© *Art Widak/ Demotix/Press Association Images*)

24 October 2011. Mary Davis makes a point at the Mansion House, Dublin. (© *Art Widak/Demotix/ Press Association Images*)

24 October 2011. Gay Mitchell and Martin McGuinness lost in thought at the Mansion House, Dublin. (© *Art Widak/Demotix/Press Association Images*)

26 October 2011. Martin McGuinness in Ballyfermot, Dublin, during his final canvassing before polling day, with the local Sinn Féin TD Aengus Ó Snodaigh. (© *Julien Behal/PA Wire*)

27 October 2011. David Norris casts his vote in the presidential election at a polling station in Marlborough Street, Dublin. (© *Collins*)

27 October 2011. Gay Mitchell and his wife, Norma, at Kildare Place Primary School in Rathmines casting their votes in the presidential election. (© *Photocall Ireland*)

28 October 2011. Seán Gallagher with his wife, Trish, speaking to the media at Dublin Castle after he conceded defeat to Michael D. Higgins. (© *Niall Carson/PA Wire*)

28 October 2011. Michael D. Higgins and his wife at the announcement of the first-preference votes at the count centre in Dublin Castle. (© *Julien Behal/PA Wire*)

28 October 2011. Michael D. Higgins gets a kiss from his wife on stage at Dublin Castle before being announced as the new President of Ireland. (© *Photocall Ireland*)

29 October 2011. Michael D. Higgins is congratulated by the Taoiseach, Enda Kenny, after being declared ninth President of Ireland. (© *Peter Morrison/AP/Press Association*)

The two independents, Davis and Gallagher, also campaigned outside the capital and were more effective in the use of social media, constantly tweeting and updating their Facebook and web sites with photographs and text.

Another retired politician, Ivan Yates, had been the youngest politician in the Dáil for three terms as a Fine Gael TD for Wexford and as a former minister. His Celtic Bookmakers chain of more than forty shops throughout the country, employing 230 people, had gone into receivership earlier in the year. He presented the morning news programme on Newstalk, the rival to RTE's 'Morning Ireland'.

On Thursday 18 August he wrote his regular political opinion column for the *Examiner*. The campaign had been receiving 'hyperactive media attention', he said. The media were building up the candidates only to knock them down.

> It resembles one of the poorer Big Brother summer series. Evictions are coming fast and furious—David Norris and Gay Byrne were forced to leave the house, before they could be voted off.

Then, provocatively, he examined the campaign credentials of the candidates and cast doubt on Gay Mitchell's ability to reflect and gain support from the high standing of Fine Gael in the opinion polls and from its recent historic general election victory. This was to be blunt language from Yates, who had been Minister for Agriculture from 1994 to 1997, at the same time as his party colleague Mitchell held the role of Minister of State at the Department of the Taoiseach and Minister of State at the Department of Foreign Affairs with Special Responsibility for European Affairs.

> On paper the Fine Gael nominee should have a significant head start. Unfortunately for Mitchell, many consider him more suited to a frontline combative political post than a diplomatic one. He takes no prisoners. He is perceived as Dublin-centric. FG party leadership preferred either Cox or [Mairead] McGuinness. He may not obtain half of the FG current market share. He successfully exploited antipathy to party leadership in gaining the nomination. While the party will close ranks around him in coming weeks, this may not be enough to get him more than the line.

Yates was equally tough on the other candidates. Because of a bad back problem he often conducted interviews in the studio standing up rather than sitting across from his guests. A large man with a large voice and a unique interviewing manner, he could be at the least an unusual experience, and even an intimidating one, to any but the most experienced and self-confident guests.

He suggested that the change in the bookies' odds—from odds-against to odds-on 13:8 to 8:11, following the REDC Paddy Power poll of the previous week in favour of Higgins—was defining, and that the poll, which included second-preference and subsequent intentions, clearly made Higgins the favourite.

However, although reaching that conclusion, he also suggested that the retailer, independent senator, sometime television host and multimillionaire Feargal Quinn, who had recently sold the Superquinn chain of supermarkets, would make a credible candidate. He initially praised him and then somewhat damned him with the comment:

> He looks the part and has enthusiastic eloquence for every occasion. At 75 years of age, he's somewhat auld—but ageism is now a criminal offence. We could do a lot worse.

The following day another radio presenter, Matt Cooper, former editor of the *Sunday Tribune* and presenter of Today FM's 'Last Word', a drivetime afternoon programme, referred to the attendance of Mícheál Ó Muircheartaigh at the lunch hosted by President McAleese for Queen Elizabeth and Prince Philip on the first day of their visit to Ireland. Ó Muircheartaigh revealed to Cooper that he had interviewed the Queen's son, Prince Edward, in London a year earlier at, of all places, a greyhound track. Ó Muircheartaigh was also to act act as MC for the appearance in Dublin city centre of the American president, Barack Obama, on his whistle-stop tour of the country.

Ó Muircheartaigh was to flirt with the idea of running for the Presidency. On Monday 15 August the *Evening Herald* confirmed that he was now considering a late entry into the race. He said he would make a decision on whether to run 'shortly'.

> I haven't ruled out anything but even at the dogs last night [in Dundalk] I almost left with the number of people that were saying it to me. I will give it a bit of consideration but it's a major undertaking.
>
> I won't spend too much time. Usually when I give something a thought I make a decision [but] I have never been involved in a thing like this and it was never my intention.

The following day's papers carried his assertion that he had been approached by representatives of a number of political parties to stand in recent months, that he would only stand as an independent and that his decision would be made in the next ten days. He continually refused to say who had approached him from the main parties.

There are very good candidates declared already but I haven't approached anyone. I haven't been nominated and it's a difficult job to get a nomination. Maybe too difficult in the world that we're in today. If I stood, I would insist on standing as an independent. Politics never came into sport, and all shades of political opinion are represented, and for that reason I wouldn't stand representing any party, no matter what party it was. The only thing that got me interested in it is the people and the number of people who say they want me to be a part of it.

Take everyone now who's been nominated so far—they're very well known and I don't know if there's any point in spending money to get people who are already well known more well known.

He added that age shouldn't be an issue for any candidate.

On Sunday 19 September 2010 Ó Muircheartaigh had given his last broadcast when he covered the all-Ireland football final between Cork and Down from Croke Park. (Two days earlier he had celebrated his eightieth birthday by climbing Brandon Mountain, a few miles from his Kerry home.) Outside the stadium, canny hawkers were selling pocket radios to fans 'for Mícheál's last broadcast.' After the minor match Ó Muircheartaigh was led onto the pitch in front of a packed crowd of more than 81,000 people, and the president of the GAA, Christy Cooney, presented him with a framed oil painting of his beloved Brandon Mountain. Ó Muircheartaigh's fellow-commentator Marty Morrissey told the cheering crowd that 'Thursday was a momentous and yet a sad morning for Cumann Lúthchleas Gael, because the man we all love in RTE—our hero, our idol, our friend—had decided to hang up his microphone in a few weeks' time.'

According to Ó Muircheartaigh,

age was never a factor with me, and I'm involved with Third Age, an organisation started by Mary Nally to get people to remain active, people who had more or less retired in the literal meaning of the word, to get them to come back out, to be going places and doing things regardless of their age.

I think people should remain active for as long as they like. They should remain in employment as long as they feel they have something to offer, and I think more and more people are accepting that now.

Despite his active retirement, however, Ó Muircheartaigh became the second broadcaster to rule himself out of the race after an intense week of speculation about whether he could secure wide support. Now, just a few days after his eighty-first birthday, he said he would not be contesting for the Park.

I am honoured and humbled that so many people from all sections of society should have contacted me offering support and assistance. I want to thank them sincerely for their kind offers.

——

Meanwhile fierce debate raged on Fianna Fáil's confidential internet discussion group about Micheál Martin's handling of the presidential race. The flavour of many of the comments was that Éamon de Valera would be turning in his grave. The president of the University of Limerick Students' Union, Derek Daly, went a step further, labelling the party leader a 'disgrace' over his handling of the presidential election—comments that caused controversy when they ended up in the national press.

On the same day that the Queen of England was visiting Áras an Uachtaráin the social media campaign to have the former RTE presenter (now Lyric FM presenter) Marty Whelan nominated as a candidate had taken off, and it was reported in the print media. Whelan said he was 'enjoying the fun of it, and I think the people behind the campaign are having fun with it. I don't even have a Facebook page, to be honest, but it seems like I have a bit of support.' A few days later he made it clear that he was not seeking a nomination.

The columnist Shane Hegarty of the *Irish Times*, with his tongue firmly in cheek, begged to differ with Whelan's decision.

I actually think he'd be a pretty decent president. Years of practice at the Rose of Tralee and 'Fame and Fortune' mean he is perhaps the country's greatest expert at making Jovial Conversation with Mildly Bewildered Strangers. As far as I can tell, this is one of the key roles performed by presidents, another being Delaying the Irish Rugby Team from Starting Matches.

Ten days earlier a newly established Facebook page and Twitter site had attracted hundreds of people to 'like' it within a couple of hours. The page was the beginning of a campaign: Martin Sheen for President. This was the first of a series of celebrity campaigns, none of which existed in reality but all providing extra colour and entertainment. Sheen was the American actor who had famously starred in *Apocalypse Now* and, more relevantly, the blockbusting NBC series 'The West Wing', in which he played Josiah Bartlet, fictional President of the United States. The Facebook page was set up by Emmet Murphy, a native of Douglas, Cork, and was serious in tone—certainly not tongue-in-cheek—and contained numerous clips from the popular 'West Wing' series. It also attracted widespread press coverage in the United States. Sheen could qualify to run for President of Ireland because his mother, Mary Anne Phelan, was an Irish citizen. She was born in Borrisokane, Co. Tipperary, in 1903 and later married Francisco Estévez, Sheen's father.

The seventy-year-old actor is a well-known human rights activist and has been described as the best actor never to get an Oscar. A few years earlier he attended the National University of Ireland, Galway, as a mature student in English literature, philosophy and oceanography. During his stay in Barna, on the west coast, he got to know one of his local TDs, Michael D. Higgins.

———

On Monday 22 August the former TG4 weather presenter Dáithí Ó Sé was live on RTE1 presenting the annual Rose of Tralee programme. Over two nights, talented and beautiful women with Irish connections from all over the world would vie for the coveted title. The light-entertainment programme was full of dancing, music, poetry, recitations and craic. Politics was certainly not on the agenda. And canvassing for any candidate in any political race while live on air would be firmly frowned on.

That was until the Southern California Rose, Molly O'Keefe, came on stage. A television producer, she was fondly teased from the audience by family and friends as 'Mollywood'. She told the packed audience that she was a huge fan of Martin Sheen.

'Did you know there's a Facebook campaign to make him our next President?' asked the compere.

'I'm a fan. That doesn't surprise me at all. President Bartlet was a powerful man,' said the Rose of Hollywood, lending her support to the online campaign.

By the following Saturday more than five thousand people had signed up to the Martin Sheen for President site. However, at a public appearance in the United States with his son Emilio Estevez, Sheen insisted that he was flattered but had no intention of campaigning for the office. He subsequently issued a statement to the Facebook campaign confirming his decision and endorsing another candidate.

I am deeply moved and extremely flattered for the extraordinary interest in my proposed candidacy. And while I might be tempted to fantasize about being President of Ireland, I am totally unqualified for such a responsibility.

Frankly the bar has been set by two extraordinary Irish patriots in Mary Robinson and Mary McAleese. And I could not hope to better the quality of their service.

There is, however, one candidate that I most heartily support: my dear friend Michael Higgins. A vote for Michael is a real vote for Ireland. Sincerely, in gratitude, Ramón Estévez, a.k.a. Martin Sheen. Sláinte.

Facebook had also hosted another Sheen for President page, but it was for his troubled son Charlie—and for the American Presidency.

——

On the same day Mary Minihan of the *Irish Times* explored a previously little-discussed aspect of the Constitution of Ireland with the former presidential adviser Bríd Rosney, who continued to act for Mary Robinson, former President and now United Nations High Commissioner for Human Rights, who was also one of Nelson Mandela's select group of 'Elders'. Robinson had established her own foundation, the Mary Robinson Foundation—Climate Justice, and in that role, and as a patron of Oxfam, she had recently returned from Somalia, a country she had previously visited as President and that was again in the throes of a terrible famine.

Under article 12.4.4 of the Constitution, former or retiring Presidents 'may become candidates on their own nomination.' The other two avenues were for candidates to be nominated by twenty members of the Oireachtas or four local councils. Would Robinson consider entering the field again? She had been asked to consider her position and had been urged to put her name forward again, as confirmed by Rosney.

It would not be accurate to say she was inundated. It would be accurate to say her office is getting calls about it, and it's a live issue on Twitter, but she has made it clear she will not be nominating herself.

For the first time in weeks the Sunday papers carried nominal coverage of the race for the Áras. There was analysis and some comment but nothing to inflame or upset the candidates or their hawk-eyed teams of media advisers.

On Monday 29 August, Seán Gallagher set out his stall in an article written at the invitation of the *Irish Sun*. His message was honed, referring to his own unemployment—something that many in the lower social demographic groups who read the *Irish Sun* could associate with—and to his plan to support work initiatives and build on the country's successes. It was a positive message of hope and 'can do', and there was an absence of the woolliness of thought and aspiration that had been expressed by candidates previously. 'I've been unemployed through no fault of my own three times since the early eighties,' he wrote, saying that unemployment, which prompted feelings of despair and hopelessness, 'is eating away at the very fabric of society and of communities.' For Gallagher, unemployment

> was certainly the key issue that I have come across during my listening tour of the country. Of course I have been told that the President has no say in economic policy or financial matters. That is true. I understand the constitutional role of the first office. But I also understand that at times of crisis we need to play to our strengths. And make sure that we use all players on Team Ireland.
>
> That is why if nominated and subsequently elected President I will roll up my sleeves and get down to the task of making Ireland work . . . In order to help turn this ship of state around we need all hands on deck. Mine are willing and I believe able.

———

The *Sunday Independent* columnist Eilis O'Hanlon, in the absence of any news or new developments about the race for the Áras, provided a thought-provoking piece about the campaign so far and about the type of candidate the electorate would embrace come 27 October.

> All we need now is for Mr Tayto and Bosco to announce their candidacy and the rot would be complete. And it might just be an appropriate development too, since the presidency has, if we're honest, become a rather silly job.
>
> It wasn't always so. Until recently, the Aras was a retirement home for those who had done the State some service. As such, it had a certain dignity to it. They did their duty. They dined well.
>
> Then along came the Marys. Not so much a breath of fresh air as a gale: they gave the office glitz and glam.
>
> They made the presidency sexy.

While 'sexy' had never been a defining term for the Presidency, a reinvigoration and reinvention of the role by both women engendered a media fascination and column-inches of coverage.

Also, as part of the paparazzi endorsement, pictures at public engagements of the two President Marys had helped redefine the role as the dull and turgid pictures of the presenting of credentials of newly appointed ambassadors were complemented by pictures of a fashionable President at social and community events. Both Presidents had expanded the scope of their office outside the rigid role set by the Constitution, making it reflective of the people they represented and of an increasingly confident and aspirational country.

The Presidency, O'Hanlon contended, was all about saying nothing, however eloquently expressed.

Thousands of words all amounting in the end to: 'Ireland is lovely. Please visit/invest/don't kill us (delete as appropriate).' Constitutionally there's the occasional exciting opportunity to refer a bill to the Supreme court, oh joy, or dissolve the Dail—which has proved contentious in the past—but mostly it's having tea with foreigners and waving at friendly crowds.

Somewhere along the line, we decided, therefore, that we were content with anyone who was vaguely photogenic and looked good in a frock . . .

We want to be mothered by our presidents these days, so even though we're looking for a man to take over we want one who can read us a bedtime story and tuck us in rather than one who looks as if he'll send us to bed without any supper.

It could be that a candidate may emerge who can redefine the presidency in a robust way for the more muscular 21st century in the way that the Marys did so effectively for the soft, politically correct fag-end of the past century but I'd be lying if I said I was hopeful.

———

In the same edition the news pages revisited Gay Mitchell's stance on abortion and quizzed his spokesperson, John Downing, who was quoted as saying that Mitchell was 'disappointed and concerned' that more than four thousand Irish women went overseas each year for an abortion. 'Gay would prefer they sought help here, keep the child, and that they look for help here rather than feeling obliged to sneak off for abortions overseas,' he said. The colourful phrase was used in the headline.

He added that Mitchell's views were pro-life but were 'tempered by compassion' and that he was strongly concerned about the rights of the unborn but also about protecting the well-being of the mother.

| NON-DECLARED AT 25 TO 1

'**M**ichael D leads but 1-3 want David Norris for President', said the page 1 headline reporting on an opinion poll in the *Sunday Independent*. A sub-heading said that few people attached any negative images to him, despite controversy. The poll would send out political shock waves, igniting a new debate about Norris's decision to resign, and would also define the weaknesses and strengths of the candidates.

The Millward Brown Lansdowne poll on 4 September showed that Higgins commanded the lead, with 32 per cent of first-preference support, nine points ahead of Mitchell, followed by Norris, who had 18 per cent, despite having withdrawn from the race. It found that 34 per cent of the people asked would favour Norris re-entering the race. Jody Corcoran wrote:

> The Minister for the Environment, Community and Local Government, Phil Hogan, last week moved the order for the presidential election, which will be held on October 27. The closing date for nomination of candidates, however, is September 28, which gives Mr Norris almost four weeks to reconsider his position . . . The clear interpretation is that many people wish to see Mr Norris in the race for the presidency, even if they do not support him themselves.

Those polled were presented with a series of words with which to describe the candidates, both positively and negatively. They included *inspiring, proud to have, modern, trust, vibrant, honest, boring, conservative, uninspiring, old* and *unknown (unrecognised).*

Norris polled well, topping the poll as the most vibrant candidate, at 14 per cent, only one point behind Higgins, level-pegging at the top of the poll with Ó Muircheartaigh, tying in third place with Davis in reference to *honest*, behind Higgins and Ó Muircheartaigh, and was joint *best known* with Higgins. He barely featured when voters were asked if he was *boring* or *conservative* or even *old*.

An associate director of Millward Brown, Paul Moran, analysed the results. He explained:

> Incredibly, over two weeks after his withdrawal from the race, David Norris was still attracting the support of 18 per cent of the electorate (we included his name on our ballot to see if there was any residual support following his August 2 announcement). Evidently there is. Given his self-imposed exile for the month of August, as other candidates ratchet up their campaigns, his strategists must wonder what might have been.
>
> Is it that the electorate are seeking a return, or that they are not entirely comfortable with what is currently on offer? . . . Perhaps it is a case that they have seen the presidential menu, and have merely decided that what's on offer doesn't suit their palate.
>
> . . . Both Mary Davis and Sean Gallagher (at 13 per cent and 11 per cent respectively) are struggling to build any kind of momentum. If these results were to be replicated come October 27, they would swiftly be eliminated.

The results of the opinion poll were phoned to Norris in Cyprus by his former campaign co-ordinator, Liam McCabe. Norris tweeted about the poll and sparked speculation that he might re-enter. 'David Norris is greatly heartened by and appreciates the continued support being shown to him by the Irish public.'

One former supporter, however, the independent TD Finian McGrath, counselled him against returning to the race. 'I accept there is a genuine desire among a number of people for David Norris to run, but I wouldn't back him again,' he said. 'I think it would be the wrong decision, because I think, probably, something else would come out.'

The *Sunday Times* on the same day published another pulse-taking exercise, by Behaviour and Attitudes, which showed Higgins with a very strong lead of 35 per cent, twelve points clear of his nearest rival, Mitchell, with 23 per cent. Crowley, who had just withdrawn his name from any speculative lists, polled a respectable 17 per cent, ahead of Gallagher, with 13 per cent, and Davis, with 12 per cent. The poll was conducted using a random-dialling technique, surveying 1,001 voters in all forty-three constituencies.

Meanwhile in Sinn Féin there was a growing debate about running a candidate, as Fianna Fáil seemed to be about to leave the field open for a republican candidate. The following Saturday the party would meet in Belfast for its ard-fheis, where it was expected that the Presidency would be an issue for consideration.

A number of senior party figures, including the Dublin North-West TD Dessie Ellis and the party's chief whip, Aengus Ó Snodaigh, were putting their support behind a call from the Kerry TD Martin Ferris to field a candidate. The party president, Gerry Adams, and the Cavan-Monaghan TD, Caoimhghín Ó Caoláin, were understood to be uncommitted. 'We are a growing party in this state,' Ó Snodaigh told the *Sunday Times*, 'and if there are more people looking to support us we should put somebody in the field. It has to be somebody of calibre. Somebody who held an elected position now or previously needs to be considered for a job as important as President.'

When questioned he said he didn't believe that either Martin McGuinness (Deputy First Minister of Northern Ireland) or Gerry Adams could afford to leave their leadership positions. Ellis was in favour of choosing a candidate from Northern Ireland, while Paul Donnelly, a member of Fingal County Council and the Sinn Féin by-election candidate in Dublin West, suggested that Martin McGuinness, Mary Lou McDonald, the Dublin Central TD, or Michelle Gildernew, MP for Fermanagh South Tyrone and former Northern Ireland Minister of Agriculture, would make exceptional candidates.

In the same day's *Sunday Business Post*, Pearse Doherty of Sinn Féin was reported as saying that whether or not Fianna Fáil ran a candidate, Sinn Féin should join the race.

> It's important for us to remember that there is no candidate in the field that shares the values or thinking of Sinn Féin, with its all-Ireland agenda, which is highly critical of the austerity measures. Because of the field of candidates we have at the moment, and those candidates are in support of the direction this Government has taken, it is crucial that there is an alternative voice and that people have the opportunity to vote for that voice.

He refused to speculate on who they would consider as their candidate. 'The only thing we can say with certainty is that Gerry Adams will not be standing.'

———

To borrow a phrase from a previous candidate, 'on mature reflection' Gay Byrne had recently written about his decision not to contest the Presidency, and they were salutary words for all the candidates.

You could almost hear his legendary radio voice in the *Sunday Independent*. Revealing a deep hurt and disgust at how he had been treated by the media, he said:

There sure are some malevolent, malice-filled, dangerous souls who delight in the chance to destroy, undermine and denigrate, what I'd call the *News of the World* mentality—do anything for a story, and you end up with the hacking scandal . . .

In my case, these people had 40 years of Late Late Show and 30 years of The Gay Byrne Show to fall back on for ammunition, and they went scurrying to it with gusto.

Every five minutes there was some clown on the phone asking me could I stand over what I said on either show about such-and-such in 1976, 1983, or 1968.

I've been accustomed to pretty regular maulings by the press through the years, and I've always considered it part of the job, but for anyone new to the game it must be deeply upsetting. The level of misinformation, half-baked conjecture and loony theorising that goes on is breathtaking.

But Kim Bielenberg in the *Irish Independent* threw a bucket of cold water over Gaybo's preciousness.

Just as journalists were doing their duty when they reported on David Norris's views on paedophilia or Gay Mitchell's stance on the death penalty, they acted in the public interest in examining life on Planet Gaybo . . .

To compare the journalists who delved into his past with the guttersnipes who hacked the phone of murder victim Milly Dowler, as Gaybo did with his *News of the World* reference, was facile . . .

As one pundit pointed out, when Mary Robinson was running in 1990 she had to answer probing questions about her declared support for the nationalisation of banks, in part based on quotes from eight years previously.

The probing, but hardly malevolent, interviewer was none other than Gay Byrne himself . . .

We may complain about their hard necks, but at least most seasoned campaigners do not go around moaning about the media when they find that they don't have the stomach for a long fight.

———

Mary Davis secured her first local authority endorsement when Galway County Council gave her its support. The specially convened meeting carried the motion, with fourteen voting in favour and Fine Gael councillors abstaining. She was one of six independent candidates to address the council, the others being Seán Gallagher, Dr Pat Jones, Richard McSweeney, Dermot Mulqueen and Gary Smiley.

It was the first endorsement of a candidate by any local authority and was an important milestone in the race for the Park. 'I'm thrilled to have won the very first nomination here in Galway,' Davis said before posing for photographs in Eyre Square in front of the flared sails of the Galway Hooker installation. 'It's onwards and upwards from here.' Sligo County Council gave her a second nomination.

Later that Monday afternoon, 5 September, Meath County Council gave its support to Gallagher. In the evening Leitrim County Council also gave him its nomination after he was proposed by an independent councillor, Enda Stenson. On his web site Gallagher posted a thank-you note to both councils and gave details of his 'listening tour' so far: in seven weeks he had visited twenty counties and seventy towns and villages, had travelled almost 9,000 kilometres and visited more than twenty voluntary groups and charities and had spoken to more than thirty entrepreneurial groups, business networks and chambers of commerce.

Meanwhile, Mitchell was still battling with the past. Evelyn Eudy, the mother of a teenager who was shot and raped in the United States, condemned Mitchell's plea for the lifting of the death sentence for her daughter's killer, Louis Joe Truesdale, Jr. Eudy told the *Irish Independent* of her distress about Mitchell's letter. The killer was executed by lethal injection eighteen years later.

Mitchell was reported by the *Irish Independent* to be 'incensed' when interviewed by the paper, saying he did not know how many letters he had written pleading for the lives of people sentenced to death, and he asked for other candidates to set out their position in relation to the death penalty. People should be proud to have a candidate with the 'courage and moral fibre' to take a stand against the death penalty, he said.

On Facebook a new site was established, 'Stop Gay Mitchell from becoming President', which espoused a liberal agenda; by the end of August it had 1,478 likes.

However, an unlikely public endorsement praised Mitchell as 'an excellent parliamentarian, an excellent representative.' The support came from David Andrews, Fianna Fáil TD for Dún Laoghaire, a former Minister for Foreign Affairs and father of Barry Andrews, a former Minister of State for Children. He spoke highly of Mitchell on a visit to Galway but said that, 'in the absence of a Fianna Fáil candidate,' he was offering his support to his lifelong friend

Michael D. Higgins. 'I'm out of politics now and I'm a very strong supporter of the Fianna Fáil leader, Micheál Martin,' he said, but he would not be drawn on whether the party should run a candidate, as he was now, he said, 'out of the loop.'

Andrews, on the left wing of Fianna Fáil, recalled missions that he and Higgins had undertaken, including their unofficial visit to Iraq and Jordan with Paul Bradford of Fine Gael to lobby for the release of the twenty-six Irish employees of PARC who were being held captive by Saddam Hussein after the invasion of Kuwait in 1990. He recalled their other visits two years later to Somalia and the trips Higgins had made with Andrews's brother Niall to Central America.

Mitchell was 'in the driving seat' for winning the presidential election according to another unlikely pundit a few days later in an interview with Dublin City University's student radio station, DCUfm. The man who had described Mitchell as a 'waffler' after he had clearly got under his skin and provoked a rare response in the Dáil, the former Taoiseach Bertie Ahern, described Mitchell now as a 'good friend' who would win the presidential race. 'I'd say Mitchell definitely has it,' he told the station, saying that 'his party is on 40 per cent of the vote, and if they run a good campaign there is no reason he won't hold his party vote.'

However, he blamed Fianna Fáil's unpopularity for 'snookering' his own presidential ambitions. He had considered running, he said. 'I still would have done all right. I mean, they have done some figures and I would probably sit in around 30 per cent, which you haven't a hope, as the party is on 20 per cent.' He added that 'the party popularity is the thing that snookers it, because if your party isn't winnable . . . if there was no downturn and if it wasn't all the hassle of the tribunals and everything else, then you could have had a good run at it.' Based on his experience when he was Taoiseach fourteen years earlier, he predicted that 'nobody is going to win it outright—like Mary McAleese had it won on the first count.'

On Thursday 8 September both Mitchell and Davis unveiled their posters. Davis's showed the candidate with a new hair bob and wearing a striking red dress with the slogan *Pride at home, respect abroad*. Mitchell's poster showed him in a statesmanlike pose, with a tag line TD *for 26 years*, MEP *for 7 years*— and the slogan *Pride at home, respect abroad*.

A REDC opinion poll for Paddy Power on the same day showed that Higgins remained firmly in the lead, with 36 per cent support, Mitchell in second place at 24 per cent, Gallagher at 21 per cent, and Davis moving up most, with a four-point gain, to 19 per cent.

Disturbingly for the four candidates, the poll also showed that one in three wouldn't vote for any of the candidates on offer. This was good news for two potential independent candidates who were reported to be taking soundings from TDs and senators.

'An independent President, working with like-minded TDs and senators, can be a real transforming force in Ireland,' wrote Justin Kilcullen, director of Trócaire, to parliamentarians. His letter set out his vision of 'social, economic and environmental justice'. Separately, Fianna Fáil and independent TDs were being canvassed for their support by the former presidential candidate Dana.

———

Meanwhile a two-day campaign was launched to collect thousands of signatures to have Norris re-enter the race. Acting independently of Norris, Ronan Mooney had recruited forty volunteers who would take to the streets in Dublin, Cork, Limerick, Sligo and Galway. The campaign was also run on Twitter and Facebook. It was prompted and informed by the report of an Oireachtas committee in 1998 recommending that a petition by ten thousand citizens should be sufficient for nominating a candidate.

A week earlier the *Sunday Independent*'s opinion poll had sparked a debate and campaign action to bring Norris back into the race. On the afternoon of Saturday 10 September he returned from his holiday home in Cyprus and called a meeting of his supporters for the following evening. That morning's *Sunday Independent* led with an explosive exclusive by Jerome Reilly, headed 'Senator David Norris plans to re-enter the race for president.' It reported that Norris had decided to make the announcement 'after signs of support from Fianna Fáil.' He would possibly make the formal announcement on the following week's 'Late Late Show', where he had been booked as a guest.

A compelling argument was emerging for Norris's re-emergence, a senior Fianna Fáil figure told the *Sunday Independent*:

> We haven't got our own candidate, and given the level of public support for Norris I think it would play well to nominate him. I think the party leadership would turn a blind eye if some TDs or senators signed his papers. It would probably be up to the senators. They know him. He is a colleague.

The signature campaign had also gained ground: in Dublin and Cork voters formed queues to sign the petition to bring Norris back, while seven thousand had signed the online petition.

Senator John Crown, the Socialist Party TDs Joe Higgins and Clare Daly and the independent deputies Luke 'Ming' Flanagan and Maureen O'Sullivan

confirmed their continuing support for his candidacy. Deputy Richard Boyd
Barrett of People Before Profit confirmed that he would back Norris 'in the
absence of any credible left-wing candidate emerging, which now appears very
unlikely.' His colleague Joan Collins TD was expected to give her backing too,
if asked.

But for Norris there were practical campaign problems to be addressed
when the remaining members of his campaign team met later that day. Funds
previously raised had either been spent or been returned to the donors. Key
people had resigned from the campaign, and they would have to be replaced.
And he had to win a nomination. But time was ticking away: it was Sunday 11
September, and he had only sixteen more days in which to secure the
signatures of twenty members of the Oireachtas.

As Norris was meeting his team, Fianna Fáil TDs and senators were
throwing cold water on the suggestion that he would get their support. Two
said he had been rude and dismissive of their potential support, 'and basically
thumbed his nose at us' when he thought he could pick up twenty
nominations without Fianna Fáil support. Others cited the Nawi clemency
plea as a reason for not offering him support. Senator Thomas Byrne
explained: 'I couldn't see how the party could back Senator Norris, given the
letter that came to light.'

———

At the weekend Sinn Féin held its annual ard-fheis in the Waterfront Hall in
Belfast, the first time it had been held north of the border. In his address on
Saturday evening as president of the party, Gerry Adams said there was now
an 'entirely peaceful way' to achieve national unity. 'Our duty is to develop
democratic ways and means to achieve Irish reunification and to unite behind
the leadership and the campaigns which will bring this about,' he said.

He referred to the presidential campaign, saying the Presidency was not a
trophy for the political establishment. Significantly, he added: 'Citizens from
all parts of Ireland must be able to vote in presidential elections. Irish citizens
living abroad—as is the case with many other states—should have the right to
vote also.' But he did not say whether or not the party would advance a
candidate.

The following day the *Belfast Telegraph* released an opinion poll showing
that 91 per cent of those polled were in favour of Sinn Féin running a
candidate for the Park. Paddy Power bookies had been accepting bets on
Martin McGuinness winning the office at odds of 25 to 1.

'I don't know what the party is going to decide,' McGuinness responded. 'I hadn't even considered the prospect of that, and I don't know where the bookies got my name, but we will see what happens over the next while.'

On the Monday and Tuesday a depleted Fianna Fáil parliamentary party met in Tallaght for their annual 'think-in' before the autumn Dáil session. Seán Gallagher and Mary Davis had just secured enough nominations to get on the ballot paper. But for Micheál Martin the Presidency was not a priority; the economy, unemployment, jobs and mortgage arrears would dominate the agenda. 'We have decided to take a collective approach in terms of any options that take place between now and polling day,' he said, and he confirmed that the party had received no formal approach from either of the three potential independent candidates, Dana, Norris or Kilcullen.

The *Evening Herald* columnist Anna Nolan wrote that Norris's thinking about re-entering the race

has to be one of the most ridiculous ideas I have heard, and one born, no doubt, from that characteristic that has been the common theme among the nominees—ego.

David Norris would be foolish to think that there is a change of heart. People were kind when he stood down, and there was a sense of—it could have been fun. The critics allowed him to have his final moments in peace, they even gave him a silent applause. But they will be back with a vengeance if he goes for it again. And if he uses some line like 'the people want me' or worse still 'the people have spoken' they will hang him.

Chapter 10 ✎

| LATE ENTRANTS

'Living in a big house, sleeping late and working on his golf game—what's not to like?' That's how one character summed up the Presidency; but he confessed that he was immediately sold on the idea of running for the Presidency when told that the pay was 'something in the order of €325,000 a year.' The *Irish Times* had the story exclusively on Wednesday 14 September. It also published his eleven-point manifesto, which, while Dublin-centred, had evolved from his numerous publications dealing with his views on life and living.

The only problem was that the candidate was fictitious. Ross O'Carroll-Kelly was the hugely successful creation of the journalist Paul Howard, who had a play, numerous books, a very funny Twitter account and a weekly column in the *Irish Times*. He had also been nominated for the inaugural journalism awards for his biting satirical look at modern life through the eyes of the Senior Cup medal-winner, Leinster fan and all-round archetypal rugger bugger and bad boy, Ross.

The significance of the joke was that the public too were joking, not so much about who should run for the Presidency but who *hadn't* been asked to run, such was the proliferation of would-be candidates. There was a growing cynicism and a feeling that the publicity surrounding speculation about candidates was self-serving, and this manifested itself in public discourse and chatter on radio programmes.

Some of O'Carroll-Kelly's laugh-out-loud manifesto promises included the proposal that the Superquinn shopping centre in Blackrock, Co. Dublin, the Berkeley Court Hotel, Renard's club and the corner of Croke Park where

Shane Horgan scored against England in 2007 should be preserved as part of our rich cultural heritage, similar to the Rock of Cashel and Newgrange. The new national anthem should be 'Ireland's Call', and the Presidential Salute should be replaced by a 'high five'.

His solution to the housing crisis was straightforward: people forced to trade down in the property market should be allowed to bring their postal district numbers with them, while Malahide, Howth, Clontarf and Portmarnock should be given the new code Dublin 4N, while Ringsend and Irishtown should be redesignated Dublin 4E. Or surrendered to the sea.

While Ross O'Carroll-Kelly was a fictional human character, an even more surreal character—a puppet, a talking turkey, the infamous 'fowl-mouthed' Dustin—still had his hat in the ring and was being reported in the media.

———

The uncertainty surrounding Fianna Fáil's final position was resulting in a fracturing within the party among its elected representatives. In Cork, Councillor Kenneth O'Flynn announced that he was taking over as regional campaign manager for Seán Gallagher. He was the son of a former TD, Noel O'Flynn of Cork North-Central, who had regularly won publicity and controversy by outspokenly opposing party policy. He had decided to step down at the last election, giving a party colleague, the poll-topper and former minister of state Billy Kelleher, a free run as the only Fianna Fáil candidate in the Cork North-Central constituency.

After the general election Micheál Martin issued to councillors a list of his ten favoured candidates for the Seanad, urging them to put the selected ten into the Seanad before other party candidates. He included Kenneth O'Flynn on his list for the Industrial panel. O'Flynn was unsuccessful.

Doorstepped by the media at the party's think-in, Micheál Martin said that O'Flynn's involvement with Gallagher's campaign was a matter for himself and that he was not breaking any rules 'at this stage' by his decision.

But now a new name emerged, that of Senator Labhrás Ó Murchú (72) of Cashel, Co. Tipperary (elected without featuring among the favoured ten), who was now being speculated about as a presidential candidate. He was the long-serving director-general of Comhaltas Ceoltóirí Éireann and was seen in Fianna Fáil as having the potential to attract a republican vote that would probably otherwise go to a Sinn Féin candidate. On Wednesday the 14th Ó Murchú confirmed his intention to seek a nomination as an independent candidate. He had already secured the support of seventeen Fianna Fáil and independent TDs, only three short of the number required for a nomination.

Ó Murchú's traditional Fianna Fáil image was not how Martin wanted to project a reformed and renewed party, and his confirmation would lead to questions about the authority of the leader and his ability to guide and control his own party. It would prove a damaging affair in the short term for the party.

At midday on Thursday a group of senators and nine independent TDs (of the total number of twenty-nine independent TDs and senators who had been invited) assembled in Leinster House. The meeting was arranged by Finian McGrath TD to allow Justin Kilcullen and Mary Davis (who already had a nomination secured from county councils) to address them and make a case for their support. However, Kilcullen contacted the group the previous evening and told them he was withdrawing. Supporters of David Norris now asked if he could be substituted at the meeting, sending a clear signal that he wanted to get back into the race.

'There has been a groundswell of public opinion and annoyance that David can't stand,' said the independent TD Maureen O'Sullivan, 'and they should think about giving him the opportunity, regardless of how they feel about him politically or personally.' Outside Leinster house Norris responded to waiting reporters: 'I won't be making any comment, because I made an agreement that I'm making no comment. So, there will be no comment.' Under his arm he held the 10,000 signatures gathered from the Mooney web site, wewantnorris.com, and the two-day street campaign. He had agreed to give his decision exclusively to 'The Late Late Show' the following evening.

However, when Finian McGrath met reporters outside Leinster House minutes later he was happy to answer questions. Did Senator Norris ask for their support? 'Yes, he did. David looked for the support of the members at the meeting, and the members said they'd all reflect on it.'

As McGrath finished talking to reporters, Fianna Fáil senators and TDs began assembling in their party room for their two o'clock meeting, unaware that they were about to start a new drama that would grip headline-writers over the next few days.

Senator Ó Murchú told the twenty-three members present that he had the support of six independent TDs and senators and expected to secure four more. He wanted to run as an independent candidate with the support of some of Fianna Fáil's Oireachtas members, and he asked that the meeting have a free vote on his proposal.

The declaration sparked a fierce row, variously described by participants as 'utter chaos', 'consternation', 'acrimonious' and 'bitter'.

The tense meeting ran for six hours, with a break for tea at six o'clock and a further brief adjournment as Micheál Martin took a couple of senior party members to another room—the chairperson of the parliamentary party,

John Browne TD of Wexford, and the party whip, Seán Ó Fearghail TD of Kildare South—to try to hammer out a pacifying response. He subsequently consulted two advisers separately.

One member described the meeting as 'utter f***ing chaos,' as the debate mirrored continuing resentment over the party leader's favoured ten Seanad nominees. Ó Murchú, now a four-time Seanad vote-winner, had not been included on the list.

The deputy leader, Éamon Ó Cuív, who had topped the poll in Galway West and was once tipped as a presidential candidate for the party, threatened to resign his position if Martin's proposal that the party not nominate a candidate was voted on. There were calls of 'Come back, Éamon, we love you'; and the meeting, described by another participant as a 'bitchfest', continued. Ó Cuív would subsequently deny speculation that he wanted to walk away from Fianna Fáil and set up a new party.

Senator Mark Daly, a former assistant to Brian Crowley MEP, was also to hold out hope that Crowley could be re-considered as a candidate. 'I would be hoping that if Brian Crowley is entering the race, support for him could be discussed.'

A motion by Martin that the party would not contest the presidential election or endorse a candidate was not put to the meeting, whereupon Ó Cuív said he would have to vote against such a motion if it were put.

Finally, Ó Murchú, who had threatened to press on with his candidacy, backed down and agreed to wait until a resumed meeting the following Tuesday, when the absent eight TDs and senators would be present. The party, riven with dissent, was in disarray over its policy and possible candidature for the Áras.

On the RTE radio programme 'Morning Ireland' the following day Ó Murchú disputed the tone and the accuracy of that morning's media coverage and asserted that Micheál Martin was 'a charismatic leader.'

The Fianna Fáil presidential pantomime was far from over. 'Oh no, it's not,' said the headline over Miriam Lord's Dáil Sketch in the *Irish Times*.

Independent, Continuity Fianna Fáil, provisionally speaking. That should go down well with the voters.

Micheál Martin—apparently hell-bent on bringing indecision to an art form—is showing leadership on their presidential strategy by sowing confusion. Fianna Fáil won't be nominating a candidate, but it might support somebody else, then again, it might not, maybe. All options are open and the parliamentary party is taking off in all directions. The truth is Fianna Fáil has gone feral.

At the weekend her colleague political editor Stephen Collins characterised the latest twist in the Fianna Fáil presidential debate as a sad reflection on the party's discipline.

> The fact that the party leader was unable to crush a challenge to his authority from a senator is a sad reflection on how discipline has broken down in the party, which was renowned down the decades for its discipline and unity.
>
> The threat by deputy leader Éamon Ó Cuív to resign if Martin insisted on having his way has left the party in a real mess.

He reported one TD as telling him: 'The party has been hijacked by a bunch of elderly senators who got elected by spending their time in safe Fianna Fáil houses, while we faced the wrath of the electorate. They haven't a clue about what is happening in the real world.'

After the nine o'clock news the anticipated 'Late Late Show' interview with Norris took place—but it was a damp squib, as the news was already out. Norris was going to try to win a nomination, again. 'This would be the biggest political comeback in Irish political history,' Norris told his host, Ryan Tubridy, with his usual theatrical flamboyance, confirming the earlier revelation by McGrath. However, he declined to say who would support his nomination, saying, 'This is a poker game.' But he claimed to have received three thousand email messages in support of his return to the fray and hundreds of letters. 'I'm not perfect, and I'm not pretending to be perfect. If you're waiting for a perfect President you'll be waiting for a long time.'

Explaining why he had written the Nawi letter, Norris said he hoped he would never reject an appeal for help. If he helped strangers, how could he not help someone for whom he had feelings, even if he was flawed? he asked. Further pressed, he said he was 'appalled, shocked and horrified' after he heard about his ex-partner's conviction. 'I did not condone or excuse it. I abhor the abuse of children.'

Norris was credited with giving 'The Late Late Show' an audience boost of 200,000, bringing the viewing figure up to an astonishing 744,000.

——

Speculation continued to mount over who, if anyone, Sinn Féin would nominate. The *Evening Herald*'s front page on the previous day said that the party wanted Mickey Harte, whose name had featured in media speculation. 'The party are on the verge of nominating a candidate with Harte thought to be the first choice,' it wrote. A party spokesperson couldn't confirm the story.

Harte, the most successful manager of the Tyrone Gaelic football team, leading it to three all-Ireland titles, was reported to have been approached. His family had been struck by tragedy earlier in the year when his daughter was murdered on her honeymoon. He was now the third possible candidate speculated about who had a strong GAA background—often formerly seen as a prerequisite for a career as a TD, as it provided community standing and a ready network of potential canvassers and supporters.

The following day Sinn Féin would put all the speculation to rest.

Martin McGuinness would be the party's nominee for the Presidency. McGuinness had just returned from the United States, where he was on a trade mission that included talks with movie moguls and the possibility of bringing Hollywood to Northern Ireland locations.

McGuinness's name had been floated originally by Mary Lou McDonald at a party Officer Board meeting. There had been discussion about running a TD—Adams or McDonald herself—but it was thought that they were too close to the general election and that a jump into the race for the Park would damage them politically. There was also the major consideration that significant numbers in the party felt they wouldn't win and couldn't win and that it would be a distraction instead of putting the effort into building on the successes of the general election. There was also the question of financing the campaign.

In effect, the arguments were the same ones that Fianna Fáil was having, except that the latter needed to secure the republican vote and keep Sinn Féin at bay, and to use the campaign to rebuild and rebrand the party.

While senior Sinn Féin sources would always say that Adams undertook to broach the possibility with McGuinness before the ard-fheis, the speed and efficiency shown in getting the posters, brochures and tour logistics into place showed some foresight, or an incredibly efficient machine. Commentators would argue that either was possible.

McGuinness told Adams that he would consider the offer while in the United States, 'out of respect for the work that he and I have done'. When he had made his decision he confidentially told Peter Robinson, First Minister of Northern Ireland, that he intended to step down, temporarily or permanently, from his post as Deputy First Minister while he campaigned for the Áras.

McGuinness's own progress from a Bogside rioter on the streets of Derry forty years earlier to IRA commander, then peace negotiator and Deputy First Minister, was as compelling a narrative as any that had been dreamed up in Hollywood. McGuinness said that those who had voted for him in the North would be pleased with his decision to run.

They will be very happy that I, as an Irish republican from the North, will be prepared to stand for the Irish Presidency. The whole all-Ireland nature of the agreements that we have made make it incumbent upon all of us to continue to bring about—I hope—the reunification of Ireland by purely peaceful and democratic means.

Gerry Adams said that McGuinness (61) would be 'a people's president', capable of giving hope.

He will dedicate himself to a genuine national reconciliation and the unity of our people. He will personify hope in the great genius and integrity of all the people of this island, Catholics, Protestants and Dissenters.

McGuinness is a mass of apparent contradictions, the editorial of the *Irish Independent* noted. Having been at the heart of the IRA terrorist campaign for more than two decades, he became one of the strongest supporters of the peace process within the republican movement during the 1990s. Then, following the Belfast Agreement in 1998, he took to democratic politics like a duck to water.

Will a majority of Irish voters be prepared to elect a former chief of staff of the Provisional IRA to a post which includes being commander-in-chief of the Defence Forces among its list of responsibilities?

What is certain is that Mr McGuinness's candidacy will turn what had already been a dirty campaign into an even dirtier one. Every aspect of his sometimes murky past will be dug up in search of damaging material.

His opponents will surely leave no stone unturned as they seek to derail his bid to become the next tenant of Aras an Uachtarain. However, we suspect that Mr McGuinness, as a seasoned campaigner, will be well able to give at least as good as he gets.

The good news, it also suggested, was that the 'pugnacious' Gay Mitchell would benefit from McGuinness's entry to the contest, as he would use his candidacy to tap into deep 'tribal' loyalties.

Liam Clarke wrote in the *Irish Independent*:

Suddenly Sinn Fein no longer seems the edgy or dangerous choice it once did to southern voters.

Fielding McGuinness is a master stroke. He is a polished performer, people like him and he has instant name recognition in the Republic. If he wins it will enable Sinn Fein to say that they hold high political office on both sides of the Border.

Even if he doesn't win he will, given the other candidates in the field and the absence of a Fianna Fail runner, be more or less guaranteed a creditable vote . . .

Win or lose, it is a useful exercise without any obvious downside.

The Northern editor of the *Irish Times*, Gerry Moriarty, with decades of tenure in the post, looked ahead to how the campaign would evolve.

Martin McGuinness's entry into the presidential race ensures the campaign will be as interesting and as exciting as it will be incendiary and dirty. But whether he gets elected president or not, as far as Sinn Féin is concerned it's a win-win situation.

Sinn Féin sources make two points here: one, that the party has plenty of capable personnel to replace him and—this said more quietly—while it is campaigning to win the seat, and believes it could shade the election, the emphasis is on how his running would benefit the party across the island, rather than on an actual expectation he will win . . .

There will be questions over the IRA in his native Derry. He will be asked once again, as was alleged 18 years ago, whether he encouraged alleged IRA informer Frank Hegarty to return to his home in Derry in 1986, only to be murdered by the IRA? He will be asked about the circumstances of how in 1990 the IRA in Derry turned a civilian, Patsy Gillespie, into a human bomb, and how that bomb was detonated, killing Gillespie and five British soldiers—an action the retired bishop of Derry, Edward Daly, termed as Satanic.

He will be asked many more questions, including, as was also alleged, whether he doubled as a British agent during the Troubles? McGuinness has dealt with all these matters before, but perhaps more so for a northern audience. With McGuinness running, southerners will be asked to look back on the Troubles in a manner most of them previously shied away from.

Moriarty went on to quote a party insider as saying, 'The big losers are Fianna Fáil. Once they left the field we had no choice in the matter.'

A former key member of the Bertie Ahern political machine, his former partner Celia Larkin, wrote a regular column in the *Sunday Independent* commenting on politics and political machinations, drawing on her own unique experience. She accused Micheál Martin of being burned by his solo run regarding Gay Byrne and of waffling indecisively.

Martin is more than a politician. He's a political historian. He should have foreseen problems for the party in relation to outside nominations and had the matter closed off in advance. He should have his eye firmly on the next issues that are important for the party: strategy for the upcoming Dail session and the by-election. Focus. Clarity.

As it is, Sinn Fein is whipping his ass, and looks likely to do so again having nominated Martin McGuinness for the presidency. Let's face it; with a good political candidate, as Mr McGuinness is, it will hoover up disenchanted republican Fianna Fail voters . . .

Martin needs to radically smarten up his act. There is no doubt he has an unenviable job, one few would covet. But great leaders surmount tough times.

For Fianna Fail to have any hope of keeping its head above the political parapet, he needs to shape up or ship out.

———

Another *Sunday Independent*/Millward Brown Lansdowne opinion poll showed that Fine Gael was in real trouble. In Government the party had an astounding 40 per cent poll rating—four points higher than its record-breaking general election vote—and dominated every social group and region. However, support for Gay Mitchell had fallen since the last opinion poll by four points, to 17 per cent. James MacCarthy-Morrogh on behalf of the pollsters explained that Mitchell's image had deteriorated too, and his scores for 'boring', 'conservative' and 'unknown' were all rising.

Since their previous poll, a fortnight earlier, while Higgins remained the clear front runner, at 32 per cent, support for Davis had risen significantly, by five points, to 18 per cent, only one point behind Norris. Support for Gallagher was also up, by three points, but he still trailed at 14 per cent. MacCarthy-Morrogh commented:

The presence of three strong independents in the field as well as the cross-party appeal of Higgins, has blurred the lines of party loyalty in this campaign. Gay Mitchell is the chief victim of this trend. Backed by one in three fine Gael voters, his campaign loses party supporters in all directions. The Fine Gael party chose its candidate but Mitchell is not, at this point, the one the majority of Fine Gael supporters want in the Park.

The only good news for Mitchell during the campaign came later in the week, when a Behaviour and Attitudes telephone survey of 308 members of the Irish

Creamery Milk Suppliers' Association gave him a preference of 25 per cent, six points higher than Gallagher, with Higgins polling 15 per cent and Davis 10 per cent. However, one in three said they still had to make up their minds.

———

Martin McGuinness had hit the ground running. On Sunday the 18th he was at the all-Ireland football final in Croke Park. 'I couldn't get away from people after the match coming up to me and wishing me all the best,' he said. The following day he pulled on his wellingtons and travelled to the biggest open-air festival in the country to canvass the 80th National Ploughing Championship in Athy. He had temporarily stepped down from his role as Deputy First Minister at midnight the previous day.

Only Gallagher, suffering an ear infection, did not canvass the Croke Park crowds and that evening called a meeting of his team to wonder, at just ten per cent in the polls, whether or not he should continue in the race.

At another meeting of Gallagher's core group later in the campaign, concerns were raised about how information about Gallagher's campaign was getting into the public domain, giving rise to fears they were being spied on. A private security company was contacted to check their concerns. However, a quote to 'sweep' the four-storey building for bugs was never followed through, as the €6,000 fee was deemed too expensive.

A flavour of the questions McGuinness would have to consistently face during the campaign about his IRA past was put to him in Co. Kildare.

I've never hidden my involvement in the IRA. Both the British army and the RUC murdered people in my city before the IRA fired a shot, and I was part of a young generation that decided to stand against them in the Bogside, in Free Derry, and we did stand against them, and I make no apologies for that.

But I do think that when people examine my life and my role in Irish politics they need to examine it in the round. I've been to Iraq, I've been to Baghdad, I've been to Sri Lanka, I've been to the Basque Country. I wouldn't be asked to go to these places if people didn't think I was an absolutely genuine peacemaker who has a contribution to make to outlining our vision of how we go forward in Ireland.

If people want to examine the past, then let's examine the past of everybody [in the contest]. I'm not going to get into recriminating about the past.

A few days later, interviewed on Ray D'Arcy's Today FM show, McGuinness's campaign blipped as he was unable to name the minister for the environment and the number of TDs in the Dáil—but he knew the all-Ireland hurling winners.

The entry of Sinn Féin to the race with such a well-known yet unexpected candidate was devastating for Fianna Fáil and was one of Micheál Martin's darkest hours as its new leader. It had lost the 'republican-green' vote, its role as principal opposition was now in question, and it now feared handing the centenary celebration of the Easter Rising to Sinn Féin. As dismissive media commentary piled up, Martin would spend the weekend on the phone talking to members of his parliamentary party before their meeting the following Tuesday, trying to bridge the rift in the party.

That same day, Monday the 19th, RTE issued a statement saying it had pulled Dana from the eight-part entertainment series 'Celebrity Bainisteoir', where she managed and mentored the Co. Derry club Lissan. Even though she had not officially entered the race and was still saying she was 'considering' her position, RTE said that if she did run it would have to pull the complete series, as it would be running throughout the election campaign and into the results period. 'In order to ensure RTE is unequivocally in a position to comply with our obligations for fairness and balance under broadcasting legislation, Dana has been asked to stand aside,' the statement said. Her library of hits was also suspended from the RTE playlist.

Hours later Dana confirmed that she was going to stand, on a platform of 'love and respect'. At a hurried press conference in Dublin she brushed aside questions about why she had left it so late to confirm her candidacy and refused to name the Oireachtas members who had promised her support.

There is room in Ireland for people who have values and take decisions based on a moral judgement. People must not feel unrepresented—that is not a democracy. In a diverse society like ours we need real liberalism, not intolerance that discriminates. Everyone has the right to be treated with respect and to be free to express their opinions and values.

I am calling on those members of the Oireachtas to grant me a nomination, so that the people of Ireland can decide. In the interests of equality, I ask that members of the Oireachtas make room for a second woman.

Despite instant name recognition and weeks of speculation about her entry to the race, Dana had otherwise faded from the public view. She had shot to fame as a teenager when she won the Eurovision Song Contest in 1970 with the song 'All Kinds of Everything'. Twenty-seven years later she returned from the United States, where she had a successful television career, to contest the Presidency in 1997. She was nominated by four county councils and was to win more than 175,000 first-preference votes, or 14 per cent, coming third behind Mary McAleese and Mary Banotti and ahead of the Labour Party's nominee, Adi Roche.

Dana expressed an interest in contesting for the Park again seven years later but couldn't get a nomination, and McAleese was returned without a ballot. In the 1999 election for the European Parliament, Dana was elected member for Ireland West. In 2002 she contested a Dáil seat in Éamon Ó Cuív's constituency of Galway West but was not elected. She lost her European Parliament seat in the 2004 election.

A strong campaigner against abortion, she remained suspicious of the EU project and campaigned against the Nice Treaty.

———

The following day's 'Liveline' achieved one of its highest phone-in polls, with 22,008 texts recorded within a ten-minute period, with no advance notice given, the intention being to eliminate the possibility that anyone could stuff the vote. Martin McGuinness topped the poll, with 28 per cent, one point ahead of Norris, at 27 per cent. Mitchell came in third, with 12 per cent, Davis at 10½ per cent, Higgins at 10 per cent, Dana at 6½ per cent and Gallagher at 6 per cent.

The poll was dismissed by Mitchell, who said Sinn Féin had rigged the result with 'an automatic dialling machine somewhere.' Embarrassingly, however, a couple of days later it emerged that Fine Gael head office—where Mitchell himself had his election office—had sent out a text message half an hour before the programme alerting supporters to the topic of the programme, followed by another telling them about the opinion poll, and a third advising them how to vote. A party spokesperson said that the messages seeking support had been only sent to TDs, MEPs, constituency offices and 121 members on a mailing list.

Labhrás Ó Murchú was not included in the opinion poll. The previous day he had told Pat Kenny that he was on course to win a nomination if the whip was removed from Fianna Fáil Oireachtas members, and that if elected he would not take any salary. 'I would work for nothing. I would be honoured to serve . . . I don't necessarily need the money; I lead a relatively frugal life.'

But on Tuesday he issued a statement before that day's crunch meeting of the parliamentary party.

Last week, in requesting Fianna Fáil, which will not have its own candidate, to allow a free vote to facilitate my entry into the presidential election, I suggested a moratorium of 24 hours, prior to a decision being taken, to allow for a consensus to emerge through consultation. This request could not be accommodated.

He had met Micheál Martin in Leinster House the previous afternoon for more than an hour.

> Following meetings with Fianna Fáil leader Micheál Martin and speculation in the media about his leadership, I do not wish to prolong uncertainty within Fianna Fáil. I will not, therefore, continue to seek nominations from individual Fianna Fáil Oireachtas members. In the absence of such nominations, I could not achieve the 20 nominations required. I am accordingly withdrawing my name as a prospective candidate for the office of Uachtarán na hÉireann—an office which deserves our respect and loyalty.

Éamon Ó Cuív, who had been interviewed in July by TV3 for a three-part series, 'The Rise and Fall of Fianna Fáil', clarified his statements on the programme, dismissing rumours of a potential split. Asked if Fianna Fáil was a seriously damaged brand, he replied: 'You know, the thought does enter my mind: are we going to be forever damaged by the actions of a few? If that were so, maybe we have to look at a new way forward for the very, very same ideals.'

Ó Cuív claimed subsequently that his remarks were taken out of context in reports that suggested he was about to establish a new political party. 'What I said was, we're going to be damned if we keep being seen as being associated with bankers and builders—which none of us were associated with anyway.'

The Fianna Fáil party meeting went ahead and agreed not to allow the party's thirty-three TDs and senators to back any candidate—further hampering the chances of support for a nomination for Dana or Norris.

Sinn Féin had taken the initiative. Its back-room team knew Martin McGuinness would be quizzed about his IRA membership and his past. They also knew he had gone through this process before—but in the North. In the South there hadn't been the same open examination of change and discussion; they felt that it was needed and that this was the opportunity to move Sinn Féin into a mainstream position, reflecting the role it now played in government in Northern Ireland.

Strategically, one senior member explained later that

> we knew the established media would throw everything at us, including the kitchen sink, but we were ready for that. This was the first time a Sinn Féin republican had run for the Park. Yes, it was audacious, and probably too

much for the *Sunday Independent*. Gay Mitchell—we weren't worried—he would strengthen our vote and only attract his own Blueshirt vote, and there was always the risk to Fine Gael that he'd go overboard in his comments. And Fianna Fáil were off the stage . . .

He went on to explain the crucial point for McGuinness and Sinn Féin, and why they had launched in Derry. 'Martin wasn't going to Dublin, he was bringing his people to Dublin . . .'

This was the nightmare that some people in Fianna Fáil feared. They had effectually left the field open for Sinn Féin, leaving their traditional republican vote up for grabs and, by not contesting, making themselves irrelevant to political debate and perhaps the political process. Within their own ranks, critics would say they had ceded their role as leaders of the opposition. It was a debate that would rage within the party.

Chapter 11 ∿

| THE ENCLOSURE

The blue-and-gold cloaks of the Tipperary Gospel Choir from Cashel swayed and danced in the lobby of the Royal Hibernian Academy. The choir was belting out songs as guests and the media arrived at the art gallery in Ely Place, Dublin, off St Stephen's Green, for the launch of Seán Gallagher's presidential campaign.

It was a fresh Sunday afternoon, 2 October. In the airy gallery space a small stage with a public address system faced more than a hundred seats arranged in a semi-circle for the formal launch, with a side room prepared for a press conference.

Children played and ran around the building while at the entrance three serious-looking pre-teens were pressing Gallagher stickers on everyone who arrived. The atmosphere was jolly and friendly, and everyone seemed to know each other, like an intimate village fete. This was not the sterile or impersonal managed-to-the-second event organised by large political parties, with important and self-important party members demanding a protocol of recognition. But its informality masked its earnestness.

Running fifteen minutes late, Gallagher and his wife gathered themselves around the corner from the RHA. Gallagher wore a dark suit, white shirt and bright red-and-white striped tie. They turned the corner and walked hand in hand past Labour Party head office, two doors from the RHA, into a battery of photographers and swung into the art gallery, smiling all the way.

Eventually they made their way into the room set up for the launch, having chatted and shaken hands with most of the supporters who had turned up. Even though it was a media event they seemed relaxed and not in a hurry to deliver on time.

Gallagher's Smarthomes business partner Derek Roddy introduced him. He recalled that they would often be driving home from a meeting and that Gallagher would always ring his mammy to see that she was all right. He endorsed Gallagher. 'He has a driving ambition. He's someone who focuses on achieving what he can do, not what he can't do. I believe he can make a difference.'

Gallagher then took the stage. His speech was to be repeated over the coming weeks: he spoke of his own experiences, overcoming the disability of being born with cataracts, being unemployed, and reinventing himself by harnessing his entrepreneurial spirit.

I believe the next Presidency should be about getting Ireland back to work, restoring our confidence at home and our reputation abroad. I want to set the tone, change attitudes, and have a lasting positive impact.

Electing a President with a proven track record in enterprise and job creation sends a very clear message to the country and also internationally that Ireland is open for business. We are electing a President who will be the voice and the face of Ireland. Not just of who we are but, more importantly, our ambition for what we want Ireland to become.

I have a faith and a belief that we can rebuild our country and will use my skills, life history and work experience in farming, youth and community work, public service, enterprise and job creation, to lead that change.

I've always led with my ability, not my disability. I want to raise the role of enterprise in a parallel to what Mary McAleese did with the peace process.

I met Enda Kenny. He told me he wanted to send out a flare to say that Ireland is a place to do business. I told him that I want to be that flare.

It's not just about me, it's about a message. There's one thing I know about life and Ireland is that it needs to be transformed. Why do I want to be President? I truly want to help this country. I want to bring the focus away from the problems and put it on the opportunities.

Ireland is not just an economy, it's a community. Every single one of us has a role in working together . . .

I couldn't read the blackboard at school. People thought that I was a slow learner, that I would never amount to much.

Sometimes you have to learn from others who believe in you before you believe in yourself. That young man in Cavan who couldn't read was a living example, but he became the man who last week handed in his nomination papers to stand for President of this great country.

At the end of his speech he called his second wife, of thirteen months, onto the stage, where they posed for the photographers. 'I couldn't do this without great encouragement and support from Trish,' said a beaming Gallagher to more loud applause.

There were more handshakes and chats before Gallagher made his way to a smaller room. A brief, not very attentive press conference was summed up by two of the questions put to him. He was asked by Senan Molony of the *Daily Mail*: 'Polls are showing that this race is virtually over—so why do you continue?'

'The people haven't even voted yet, people are only beginning to hear about the candidate,' he responded.

The representative of the *Examiner* suggested that his campaign was 'one-dimensional, focusing on trade and enterprise.'

On radio earlier that day Mary Davis had refused four times to say how much money she had received by serving on corporate and state boards over the previous decade. The media put out an estimate of €190,000 for state boards, which increased to 'at least €350,000' when commercial and state-sponsored companies were included.

Gallagher was asked to comment:

> I believe that anybody who has received fees or taxpayers' money for their involvement on state boards should clearly publish that. I would support that absolutely. I think it's important for transparency.

He went no further, however, maintaining his campaign creed in being positive and not straying into personal attacks. Asked about David Norris, and whether Norris should release the letters he had written, Gallagher responded:

> Everybody—I think this race needs to be transparent and open. It's the highest office in the land, and I think we need to get these issues dealt with and move on to the real issue . . . I wouldn't like to see the campaign marred or distracted by all these controversies. The office doesn't need it.

He didn't answer a throwaway question about who he'd like to give his second-preference vote to. To those who dismissed his low standing in opinion polls he said, 'This campaign is just beginning.'

There was no incisive questioning. The opinion poll showed Gallagher with little or no hope: he was at best a novelty candidate, with a few messages of positivity and a business background. Worthy perhaps but boring was the media consensus. It was difficult for him to gain traction in the media, and this, according to his advisers, was fatal: they believed independent voters would flock to one candidate with their transfers, and to be in the contest he had to be ahead of the other independent candidates.

Gallagher's media adviser, Richard Moore, cautioned him that the 'flare' analogy was one he should drop. It just didn't work, and would be interpreted in the occasional radio chat shows in the following days as a distress signal, with all its negative 'rescue me' associations. Gallagher referred to it once again in a speech, and then extinguished it. He would also joke about the 'cautions' he received from his media team—specifically chopping the air during a visit to a karate class.

The following morning's print media reflected their indifference to his candidacy.

———

Mary Davis was Gallagher's biggest threat and was polling well. She had a quasi-national network with friends and contacts made over the years through the Special Olympics network.

On the previous Sunday, Shane Ross TD in his *Sunday Independent* column had dubbed Davis a 'quango queen'. He had been searching candidates' CVs for a leader-in-waiting who might blaze a trail for Irish enterprise, but he found them all wanting. He zeroed in on Davis, who, he said, showed signs of promise. He listed her membership of the UCD Foundation, the Irish Sports Council, the Broadcasting Commission of Ireland and the Task Force on Active Citizenship and asked why she had chosen 'to omit a few rather more rewarding business achievements.' These included appointment to the board of the Irish Civil Service Building Society, a subsidiary of Bank of Ireland, whose directors were paid an annual fee of €25,000. 'As a presidential candidate—with banking experience—she could offer priceless insights into the property collapse, the current mortgage crisis and the behaviour of the Directors of the Bank of Ireland,' he wrote. She had also omitted her membership of the board of Dublin Airport Authority and of Stadium Ireland, more commonly known as the Bertie Bowl.

> Mary flourished under Bertie's Government. Not just in terms of the political appointments to the Bertie Bowl project and the DAA; she also landed the highly sensitive post on the board of the Broadcasting Commission of Ireland.
>
> A pity that she was not a bit more upfront about her business pedigree.
>
> The Queen of the quangos wants to be President of Ireland. Let us hope that she discards her halo and shares her business experience with us.

This article, linking well-paid directorships to an apparent inside track to the Government, and the snappy 'quango queen' put-down, holed the Davis campaign below the waterline.

A week later, with increasing calls for candidates to divulge business connections and board memberships and payment, both Davis and Gallagher bowed to media pressure and released details of their earnings. Over her adult life Davis said that she had worked with eighteen organisations in a voluntary capacity, and that since 2000 she had been appointed to three state boards and three private-sector boards, earning a total of €390,633. This included €58,861 from the National Sport Campus Development Authority, €86,693 from Dublin Airport Authority, €35,529 from the Broadcasting Commission of Ireland, €133,641 from ICS Building Society, €18,750 in one year (2010) from Bank of Ireland Mortgage Bank and €55,158 from the Irish Times Trust over a five-year period to 2011.

Days earlier the *Examiner* had polled the CEOs of the country's twenty-three largest charities, asking for details of their salaries, expenses, bonuses and perks, and it published the details on 26 September. The Special Olympics was one of the six charities that refused to divulge details. Of those that did provide details, Enable Ireland emerged as the top payer, offering their CEO a salary of €156,000 a year, but it also noted that the CEO had forgone a bonus payment.

Davis now revealed that she earned a salary of more than €159,000 a year as CEO of Special Olympics. No other details of the package were made available.

Gallagher gave details of his board memberships a couple of hours later. He earned €30,150 from Intertrade Ireland and also earned €11,000 from FÁS. And he trumped Davis's call to reveal details of payments funded by taxpayers, saying he had donated his FÁS fees to charity, including Down Syndrome Ireland and the Irish Cancer Society.

Martin McGuinness also requested his bank manager to provide details of his bank account, and his campaign team briefed the media that the bank statements would show that the candidate took only the average industrial wage, as he had asserted in debates.

As the North's Deputy First Minister he was entitled to an annual income of £112,000 (€131,000). His press officer, Seán Mac Brádaigh, said that the statement was expected to show that McGuinness received £1,605 (€1,874) a month and that the rest of the money went into the party's coffers.

Enda Kenny was running late for the Fine Gael presidential launch in the Science Gallery on Dublin's Pearse Street, as he was delayed after opening a primary care centre in Ballina in his home county. 'The traffic was terrible,' he explained to reporters afterwards, who wondered whether this tardiness showed a lack of enthusiasm for his candidate.

An enthusiastic group of Young Fine Gaelers, decked out in bright-yellow T-shirts with the slogan *Mitchell for President* and carrying giant posters, greeted the Taoiseach as he arrived. They had to jostle with enthusiastic backbenchers as photographers insisted that the candidate and his wife squash together for a photograph with the Taoiseach, and then all were ushered upstairs for the formal launch.

Kenny mingled easily, shaking hands with Government ministers Alan Shatter, Phil Hogan, James Reilly, Simon Coveney, Richard Bruton and Bruton's brother, the former EU ambassador and Taoiseach, John. Also mingling was Pat Cox, the defeated candidate for the Fine Gael nomination. His rival Mairead McGuinness was not present.

Backbenchers, including Olivia Mitchell, Catherine Byrne (Mitchell's successor in his constituency of Dublin South-Central), Bernard Durkan, Mary Mitchell O'Connor and Senator Paul Coghlan, swelled the crowd.

Mitchell's director of elections, and chairperson of the parliamentary party, the cheery Charlie Flanagan of Laois-Offaly, rallied the troops as the back-room number-cruncher and organiser Frank Flannery settled against a wall to watch the drama, a *Mitchell for President* sticker on his lapel.

The stage was set with an autocue and three blue-and-white pull-up displays promoting Mitchell with the slogan *Understanding our past—believes in our future.* The blue theme continued to the accessories: even the glasses and water jug were blue.

The fold-back walls of the room were thrown open to allow the crowd of about 250 to be comfortable. The top table was set for Mitchell, Flanagan, Kenny and the recently selected Fine Gael Dublin West by-election candidate, Eithne Loftus. Despite the endorsement of the country's biggest political party, of which she had been a loyal servant, the electorate would reject her in favour of a Labour Party candidate when the by-election was held on the same day as the presidential election. Flanagan called on Councillor Loftus to introduce Mitchell. She lacked Flanagan's delivery and confidence and faltered as she read from her notes.

As Mitchell rose to his feet there were a few awkward moments as Kenny's attempts at chumminess failed, underlining the awkwardness between the two men. Kenny punched Mitchell on the arm and clapped him on the back; Mitchell paused for a moment, clearly wondering what to do, before his political instinct and public relations nous kicked in and he gently punched

Kenny back. These moments showed the lack of familiarity between the two men, who had been colleagues for decades. The journalists present cringed at the telling awkward moments.

Mitchell, in a sharply cut navy suit, red tie and white shirt, spoke in an even tone, his speech delivered with the aid of an autocue. It was well crafted, covering his childhood as the youngest of nine children, his widowed mother going to work at four o'clock on dark winter mornings to support her family as an office cleaner. The repetition of the hard-times story was wearing thin with some journalists, and a party handler hissed at them to shush, saying that the story was true.

In the *Irish Times* the following day Miriam Lord sent up this story, saying he was one of a 'clatter of barefoot children, born into the notorious slum known as the Black Hole of Inchicore, but plucky Gay Mitchell rose above his lowly beginnings.' He set out his priorities for the Presidency, saying he would reflect his mother's qualities of being 'steady, reliable, honest, hard working and interested in others.'

Mitchell reminded the gathering of his experience in politics, as a TD, a minister of state and a member of the European Parliament, and of his political achievements. 'I would use my national and international know-how to work with the Government of the day,' he said.

He then went on to present his manifesto for the Presidency.

The President should be in charge of planning the 1916 centenary commemoration in five years' time.

The President should work with organisations to prevent suicide, which was claiming the lives of six hundred people a year.

As President he would set up an initiative, working with other heads of state, to reduce child mortality in the developing world, now running at a rate of 22,000 a day.

He nodded to the growing diaspora, saying he would appoint an Irish person living abroad, or one of their descendants, to the Council of State on a rotating basis, one each year for seven years.

Referring to the successful recent visit of the Queen of England, he promised to work jointly with Queen Elizabeth to 'unite hearts and respect cultures' in the North of Ireland.

His approach to the campaign and the job of President was to set out measurable and practical actions. There was less of the aspirational, emotional and nebulous talk that typified other candidates during the campaign and instead an emphasis on a job of work to be done. The practicality of his manifesto reflected his experience as a member of a large political party and of its approach to an election: launch with a fanfare, bring in the party big shots to show support, set out a manifesto, and then campaign on the streets, selling a clear set of election promises.

Kenny was questioned about how the campaign had been handled so far, specifically about whether he would condemn the attacks at the weekend on McGuinness by the Minister for the Environment and Local Government, Phil Hogan, and the Government chief whip, Paul Kehoe. These attacks would dominate the media's questions—always a sure sign of where they felt the agenda was moving—rather than the planned presentation, in this case Mitchell's set piece. Again, the media proved to be more interested in the process than the policy.

Hogan had said that the election of a 'former terrorist' to the Presidency would jeopardise foreign investment, as investors would 'not be slow to whisper about a terrorist in the Park.' His comments had made the lead story in the *Sunday Independent*, where Hogan was reported as saying: 'Putting Mr McGuinness in charge of this state would leave us looking like a banana republic . . . [which] could denude Ireland of serious levels of corporate investment within 24 months.' He also raised concerns that there could be a constitutional crisis if the former IRA leader was elected and further information about his 'murky past' emerged. 'The absence of an impeachment process within the Irish Constitution means that we could be heading for an unprecedented stand off—where both Houses of the Oireachtas would vote "no confidence" in Mr McGuinness but he would refuse to resign.'

The paper also carried the results of a telephone poll by Quantum Research in which respondents were asked if they believed that McGuinness had ceased to be involved in the IRA in 1974, as he had stated. Yes, said 25 per cent. No, said 75 per cent.

Paul Kehoe claimed that McGuinness had the proceeds of a multi-million pound bank robbery in 2004 at his disposal. 'I wouldn't trust Martin McGuinness to take my dog for a walk,' he tweeted. 'Why would you need your salary when you have the proceeds of the Northern Bank at your disposal?'

Kenny diplomatically avoided questions about the attacks but would also refuse to publicly rein in his dogs, on the grounds that he recognised the hurly-burly of elections. 'Hear my words,' he said. 'I will not comment on any candidate in this campaign except the Fine Gael candidate, Gay Mitchell. The Taoiseach of the day has to have a particular relationship with the Uachtarán, who is elected by the people.'

When it was put to him that he was dodging the issue and so had a dual strategy, he replied: 'I support the democratic process, which allows for good, vigorous and robust debate in the electoral process.' He said that in any election campaign 'things can be said; in every election campaign you're going to have comments made from people in the heat of battle. These are electoral comments. It is up to each candidate to be truthful and open in respect of the questions that are being asked of them by the people.'

He then threw the gauntlet back at the media. 'I spent most of the time yesterday in a debate with Mr McGuinness,' he told his interviewer, 'trying to establish the truthfulness of some of the claims he made, and I didn't have any success, so I wish you success with it.'

At the press conference, Charlie Flanagan had dismissed suggestions that some TDs were not campaigning for Mitchell.

Rallying the troops to support Mitchell's bid for the Park, Kenny described him as 'a good and great man. I expect and look forward, if God spares me, on Easter Sunday 2016 to have President Mitchell arrive outside the General Post Office and take the salute.'

Then it was downstairs for a photo call with his branded 2006 Kerry-registered mini-coach in Pearse Street. Kenny returned to the Science Gallery café, where he stood chatting at the coffee bar with a number of confidants, including Bruton, but not with Mitchell who moved on to the Newstalk studio to discuss his campaign launch with the presenter George Hook. Mitchell bristled when challenged by Hook that he wasn't very 'cheery', and said:

I'm sick of people telling me, 'Smile, smile, smile'. Smiles do not deliver jobs; smiles do not deliver the sort of thing that this country needs. I will smile when I need to smile, but I don't believe in the smiling business for the sake of smiling.

An hour earlier, at his campaign launch, Mitchell had referred to his party colleague Dan Neville TD and his work in suicide awareness and prevention, saying he wanted to use the Presidency to highlight the problem. 'It is a horror that stalks the land,' he said, and he pledged to work with

those people and agencies whose moral acts, done quietly and respectfully, save lives every day. A suicide counsellor told me recently that as people reach the point of no return, it's like they're in a very dark room with no door. We have to open such doors and bring light into each other's darkness.

As Hook continued to probe, suggesting he was colourless and dull, Mitchell riposted: 'If anybody says to me, "Smile," I'll jump off O'Connell Bridge.'

By coincidence, Hook had written in his autobiography about how he had contemplated drowning himself. The media seized on the remark, reminding people how the former Taoiseach Bertie Ahern was forced to apologise four years earlier when he suggested that those people talking down the economy should 'commit suicide'.

Within minutes of the programme ending, experts in the field of suicide were being canvassed by the media for their opinion of Mitchell's comments and its potential ramifications. The director of Save Our Sons and Daughters, Peter Moroney, whose own son took his life in 2003, was quoted in the *Irish Daily Mail* as saying, 'Gay Mitchell's comment was flippant and disgusting. It shows a complete lack of understanding and compassion. It was disgraceful.' On RTE the founder of the Irish Association of Suicidology, John Connolly (not the Nawi blogger), described the comment as 'unfortunate'.

However, Joan Freeman of Pieta House told the papers that had contacted her that she had not heard the interview on radio but that it was clear that the remark 'was not intended to cause hurt.'

> To be perfectly honest I am not offended at all. It was an off-the-cuff remark in a live interview and I am sure it was not intended to cause hurt or distress . . . I genuinely do not believe he meant any hurt by that comment. And I'm sure he is genuinely sick of being told to smile.

The subsequent analysis of the Mitchell interview was a clear example of how every word spoken, or misspoken, would be subjected to intense scrutiny and would act as a warning for candidates as the campaign progressed.

This examination of each candidate on behalf of the electorate fell to the media, simply because they had access and because the presidential campaigns were media events. It would be impossible to canvass the whole country; the mass media were the key to communication, and the large number of media outlets recognised this, as well as the potential for increased advertising income and credibility as a public service, by hosting and facilitating debates and other events.

———

It wasn't until the closing days of the campaign that the candidates would take control of the political agenda, and one candidate, with one political strike, would alter the course of the campaign.

The always controversial and entertaining broadcaster Eamon Dunphy was asked about his support in his column in the *Irish Daily Star* for Martin McGuinness. That support had provoked a spat on his Newstalk radio chat show the previous day, when he introduced both Mitchell and McGuinness. Mitchell declared that Dunphy's support for McGuinness was 'a disgrace'.

Dunphy defended himself. Declaring his support for McGuinness was likely to be in breach of the broadcasting code, he explained:

Declaring it as I did was the lesser of the sins; the other one would be to keep it hidden. In the end I decided that the broadcast would be fair and there would be no hidden agenda, and that it would be incumbent on me to be fair to every guest on the programme, which I endeavour to do. It is better if listeners know that your views are. It is absolutely vital to give fair and equal treatment.

Under section 42 of the Broadcasting Act (2009) all treatment of current affairs, including matters that are either of public controversy or the subject of public debate, should be fair to all interests concerned. A serious breach of the code could lead to fines of up to €250,000. By close of business that Monday evening the Broadcasting Authority had received no complaints.

––––

The following morning's *Daily Mail* gave blanket coverage to David Norris, stealing the thunder of Mitchell's launch, trumpeting on page 1 that Norris was 'facing the harrowing prospect of losing his sight' from a progressive and irreversible condition in both eyes. The most serious version of age-related macular degeneration had been diagnosed five years earlier.

Norris dismissed any concerns about his ability to run for office. 'I will be six feet under before I am blind,' he said 'This is an age-related degenerative issue; it is an issue that anyone over the age of sixty could face.' And he added that there had been no noticeable deterioration.

The report also referred to the eyesight difficulties of Seán Gallagher, who had been born with congenital cataracts, partly corrected by surgery, and to the former president Eamon de Valera's failing eyesight, which considerably deteriorated during his second term in office.

––––

The following morning, Tuesday 4 October, was an unseasonably bright, fresh October morning. Mary Davis, wearing freshly applied professional make-up and a striking two-piece suit in cherry red, now her trademark colour, walked from her car along the bank of the Grand Canal to Fitzwilliam Hall, a serviced office building at Leeson Street Bridge, with her husband. A crowd of mostly women supporters wearing branded т-shirts and carrying posters milled around awaiting her arrival. She was precisely on time, 11 a.m.—'always a plus when dealing with the media,' said one photographer approvingly, itching to get on to his next job.

The Davis campaign had taken over the same faux-Georgian offices used by Fine Gael as its headquarters for the general election a few months earlier. Davis was on first-name terms with most of the fifty or so people who insisted on shaking hands with her and wishing her well, delaying her progress up the staircase to a side room off the large three-windowed room that had been set up for the launch with a small stage, lighting and PA.

In contrast to the Mitchell launch, with its big political names, the Davis launch event was peopled almost exclusively by the media, with only a handful of her election workers present. The now retired governor of Mountjoy Prison, John Lonergan, rose from his seat among the audience and took the podium to introduce Mary Davis as a 'person of integrity and humanity'. He had forgotten to introduce himself, but later in his remarks he announced his identity.

Davis emerged from a side door and took to the podium, standing in front of the flags of the four provinces. She spoke of her experience of imagining and then bringing the Special Olympics to Ireland in 2003, her organisational skills in co-ordinating thirty thousand volunteers, and her negotiating skills as she dealt with governments and their officials in fifty-eight countries.

Setting out her priorities, she announced a work plan for the first hundred days and said she would organise conventions on mental health, the elderly, the exploitation of women, literacy and disability. She would also sponsor a Citizen's Award for people who 'give outstanding service to Irish life'—a proposal from the Citizenship Committee she had served on. She would open consultations on the 1916 centenary north and south, request the Government to extend the Freedom of Information Act to the Presidency, and publish annual accounts for the President's office. It was towards the end of the third page of her speech that media interest perked up.

> Everybody said this would be a tough, gruelling campaign—it's certainly not for the faint-hearted. Most of my rivals are professional politicians, and perhaps they thought that I would fold in the face of criticism. Let me tell them: they could not be more wrong.
>
> They are reverting to type: engaging in the type of negative campaigning that made the Irish people so cynical about politics. Paying a lot of money to polling companies to hone attack messages is not what this campaign should be about. Paying money to polling companies may serve the partisan aims of a political party but it does not serve the cause of debate about our future.
>
> But I know I can deal with negative stories for one reason: I have nothing to hide. Most of what has been written about me is already in the public domain, and I have been willing to be open and transparent in dealing with any queries that have arisen.

She was referring to nine days earlier, 25 September, when the *Sunday Business Post* published a brief article that stated that the research company Amárach Consultants, regularly used by Fine Gael, had been testing negative messages about presidential election candidates. Later that day Fine Gael would formally and succinctly dismiss her claim: 'These are surprising accusations by Ms Davis and it is hard to imagine where she got this idea.'

Davis continued:

I have provided the media with copies of my P60 and all my organisational affiliations. I now call on all other candidates to publish their P60s, equivalent documentation and tax compliance details.

After making the challenge, she went on to address one other issue in an attempt to distance herself from the charge that she was part of the establishment through her membership of politically appointed boards.

I am not a political animal in independent's clothing. I want the people to know that if they elect me they are getting a truly independent President— not only independent of any political party but independent of the political system itself.

Then she took questions.

At the weekend she had been dubbed the 'quango queen' because of a number of appointments to state boards, made, in the main, when Fianna Fáil was in power. The Independent.ie editorial said:

For a candidate who claims to be independent of any party, her ability to pick up such choice political appointments is truly remarkable . . .

Throughout her campaign, Ms Davis has stressed her lack of political affiliations. She has also emphasised her 'outsider' status, not least with the utterly daft proposal to rename Aras an Uachtarain Aras na nDaoine [made during one of the myriad television debates].

While she may not be a member of any political party, her appointment to a raft of state boards indicates that, far from being an outsider, Ms Davis is a formidable networker and consummate insider.

The following day's *Sunday Independent* published a column by Shane Ross TD that rammed home the same 'quango queen' message. The label stuck, damagingly, to her campaign.

At the official launch some journalists carried a copy of that morning's *Irish Independent*, which included an article headlined 'Davis and husband in storm over PR contract.' It was an ominous sign, and overshadowed the campaign launch. The article reported that the public relations company Fleishman-Hillard, of which Julian Davis (57)was a director, was awarded a PR contract by a charity on whose board the couple both sat. Social Entrepreneurs Ireland is funded by charitable donations, and its accounts for 2009 showed that it spent more than €40,000 in 2009 on public relations with Fleishman-Hillard and almost €30,000 on marketing and PR costs for the previous year. Julian and Mary Davis both joined the company shortly after it was set up in 2007. They were not paid fees for their role as directors.

The charity says it identifies, invests in and supports 'social entrepreneurs' and the organisations they launch. In the same way that entrepreneurs develop companies that manufacture products or services and so generate a profit, 'social entrepreneurs' create and run organisations that provide products and services to generate social and environmental return. Social Entrepreneurs Ireland holds an annual awards ceremony to present the work of Ireland's leading social entrepreneurs and to encourage others to become part of the growing social entrepreneurship movement.

The suggestion of a conflict of interest was denied by Julian Davis and the charity's chief executive, Seán Coughlan. 'The Board was happy there was no conflict of interest, in the sense that the relationship started before either Julian or Mary got on the board,' he said. The board had discussed whether there was a conflict of interest on a number of occasions, the most recent being earlier that year.

Fleishman-Hillard was awarded the contract because it had previously worked with an associated charity, the One Foundation, since 2005. Mary Davis was a director of the One Foundation from 2006 to 2008. 'It was discussed as part of the discussion on the new corporate governance code for SEI,' Coughlan explained. 'No issue was raised regarding the current contract with Fleishman-Hillard.'

Julian Davis denied there was any conflict of interest, telling the *Irish Independent* that both he and his wife had excused themselves from board meetings when the public relations contract was discussed.

It was the first question thrown from the floor. She denied it. 'There was no cronyism. I'd nothing to do with the awarding of the contract, and if there were any discussion in relation to the awarding of a contract, like a public relations contract, I was not a party to those discussions.'

There were a dozen questions from journalists. Only one referred to her speech, and that centred on her claim that she was being polled against. Who was carrying out a dirty tricks campaign? 'It would appear to me from reports in the paper that it's driven by Fine Gael,' she replied bluntly.

Questioned further, she softened her tone, but the charge remained the same. 'I would really like Fine Gael to come out and contradict that,' she said. 'Gay Mitchell would seem to me to be a very decent person, so I don't know why political groups or any candidate would use negative polling in the way that it is being used. But I do know for a fact that it is being used.'

Her advisers were beginning to wonder whether she had even delivered a speech, as every subsequent question was about her board membership as a 'quango queen'.

She denied she was an 'insider', saying she had served on three state boards for payment and on three with no pay. Asked about the policy of the ICS Bank, of which she was a member, of giving 100 per cent mortgages at the height of the property boom, she said that they had taken collective decisions and that ICS was not involved in this practice to the same degree as other banks. Questioned about the six-figure earnings of the Dublin Airport Authority's chief executive, she said that again there was a collective decision.

Ronan O'Reilly of the *Daily Mail*, who wrote the observational column 'Pres Watch', had witnessed Davis forge her way through the supportive crowd into the press launch. He wrote: 'The members of the crowd themselves were of a sort to suggest that quite a few regular coffee mornings in Dublin's leafier suburbs were somewhat short of a quorum yesterday.' But by the conclusion of the press conference he clearly had a grudging admiration for Davis.

The steely determination that got her this far was evident throughout. When she spoke of 'tough productive negotiations' with overseas governments in her Special Olympics role, she sounded like a slightly less intimidating version—slightly, mind—of Margaret Thatcher in all her pomp.

When she faced questions from the floor about cronyism—as well as the lamentable Bertie Bowl project and irresponsible mortgage lending—the brittle smile soon vanished. It was replaced instead by a disapproving frown, accompanied by an exaggerated blinking of the eyes that seemed to signal some sort of incredulity that anyone could dare to challenge her. But, as it all wrapped up, the PR tutoring kicked in and Mary Davis beamed once more. The lady's not for turning.

Later that day the chief executive of Social Entrepreneurs Ireland would tell the media that the public relations contract held by Fleishman-Hillard on a rolling basis would be put out to tender after the Social Entrepreneur Awards were held later in the month.

An avalanche of statements was issued that day, describing in detail the personal finances of a number of candidates. The most informative was a statement together with documents showing Martin McGuinness's income—and how he spent it. The Bank of Ireland's British unit released details of an account in the Strand Road Branch, Derry, jointly held by McGuinness and his wife. The manager stated that McGuinness received a monthly deposit of £1,605. The accounts, for March to September, had blanked-out references to cheques, personal debit details and balances but included details of purchases at Asda, Musgrave's, Tesco and the clothing stores TK Maxx and Foster's.

Personal finances were a continuing theme as reporters followed the money trail for stories. David Norris confirmed the same evening that he had received a disability payment for sixteen years while out of work as a lecturer in Trinity College. The payment began in 1994 and ended in July 2010, when he reached pension age. He received a pension from the college worth about €2,500 a month, the *Irish Independent* would report. He also received a senator's salary of €61,073 a year, supplemented by an unvouched Seanad allowance of €23,383.

Norris insisted that he was in perfect health and would not say what his disability was, but it would not stand in the way of his being President. In typically ebullient form he said:

> And if you look at my Seanad record you see that. I hope we're not going down the medical route of all this, but I will do any medical test you want. I just think this is getting daft. It shows how open I am: my life is an open book.

Earlier, Michael D. Higgins had conducted a sprightly canvass in Grafton Street, Dublin. He too was asked by reporters about his income. Miriam Lord reported in the *Irish Times* that Higgins maintained a statesmanlike distance from the questioning about candidates' pasts. 'It's getting ridiculous, as candidates fall over each other to account for every ha'penny they ever earned. It can only be a matter of time before they offer full details of their communion money.'

Asked about his finances, Higgins gave details of his pension and estimated the value of his house in Galway and what he earned from his literary efforts. 'The two poetry books have been declared for tax purposes,' he said. Then he added with a sigh: 'The income was minimal.'

Finances weren't the worry of his campaign team. Shaking hands with passers-by, meeting the flower-sellers on the street and the buskers, the campaign team then bumped into Stuart Gordon and his wife from the United States. They had watched 'The Late Late Show' and had spotted the Higgins entourage in the Grafton Street canvass. Surrounded by reporters, Gordon revealed that he was an orthopaedic surgeon. Minders blanched: after questions about the candidate's age, here was an expert on his damaged knee, ready to give his instant diagnosis in front of the media. The question on everyone's lips was 'Is the candidate fit?'

Higgins repeated the story he had told on 'The Late Late Show': he was on a visit with an aid agency to Bogotá, Colombia, where he slipped on tiles and damaged his knee. 'Did you have the kneecap tied with wire?' he was asked. Yes, confirmed the candidate. 'It can be taken out later, yes, I'm galloping along now.'

'He's vital and brave,' the surgeon told the media, and this was because of the wonders of modern orthopaedic surgery techniques and 'because he has a lot of heart.'

'What's the prognosis?' asked the eager reporters. Was the candidate able for the fray or already nobbled? 'He has a bit of a limp, but he seems to have a good gait, and he has a nice cadence to his gait,' the surgeon replied.

The happy exhalation of pent-up breath by the Higgins campaign team could almost be heard on radios throughout the country, covering the unplanned but, as it turned out, fortunate encounter and endorsement.

No, it wasn't a set-up, members of the Higgins team would insist later: it was just fortuitous, another positive sign for the campaign.

Chapter 12 ∾

| THE OFF

'No speeches, no talking down the clock, no pork pies,' the chairperson, Vincent Browne, warned the seven presidential candidates lined up in front of him for his live television programme on Tuesday 4 October. Mary Davis had formally launched her campaign only hours earlier.

They stood behind white lecterns, their positions drawn randomly in front of the inquisitor: McGuinness to the far left, standing beside Davis, Higgins, Gallagher, Dana, Mitchell and Norris, on the far right of the screen.

'I want a free-flowing debate,' said Browne before introducing each of the seven candidates.

'Martin McGuinness, best friend of Nelson Mandela, and, according to himself, he's been in the Oval Office more times than Monica Lewinsky.'

In the TV3 canteen, where journalists and photographers were watching on two large screens, there were hoots of laughter. 'This is going to be interesting,' one commented.

'Mary Davis, who, according to herself, has performed on more boards than Michael Flatley . . . Michael D may not be the first poet in the Áras, but he's certainly the first to write a poem about his favourite donkey.'

Browne was enjoying himself, unsettling the candidates and setting the tone for an irreverent examination of the seven. He kept up the quick-fire commentary, which drew a few nervous smiles from the candidates but nothing like the belly laughs drawn from the media entourage in the canteen next door.

'Dana is a celebrity bainisteoir, and she wants to prove that Ireland has talent . . . And David Norris was late coming to us this evening because he was writing more letters. I left out Gay Mitchell! Gay Mitchell is Gay Mitchell. I had something funny to say, but I don't want to make you smile.'

———

The TV3 studios are at the end of the Ballymount Industrial Estate, near the Red Cow, past numerous warehouses and recycling centres. Reporters who wanted to cover the debate had been assembling from seven o'clock on a cold and windy evening. A large tent, open on two sides, was the reception area for the media. Candidates would have to walk past them on their way from the car park into the building. The anonymous red-brick studio building could be mistaken for any industrial estate office and warehouse building, except for the fifteen-foot satellite dishes in their security pens. A lonely, single microphone on a stand stood in front of the tent, behind crash barriers to restrain the media and lit by four banks of floodlights. A small stage had been erected in front of it for photographers and cameramen.

As the candidates arrived, the CEO of TV3, David McRedmond, accompanied by the head of news, Andrew Hanlon, met and chatted to them, escorting them to the microphone to have a few words before the debate.

Mary Davis was the first to arrive. Gay Mitchell arrived next with his wife. An *Irish Times* photographer, Matt Kavanagh, asked Mitchell to give her a kiss. He duly obliged, and they posed hand in hand for photographs before being escorted inside to make-up and a warming cup of tea.

'My hope is this will be positive,' said Seán Gallagher. 'It's not about entertainment, it's about getting your message out.'

Martin McGuinness arrived with the largest entourage, in a jeep and a BMW. He spoke to reporters, again rehearsing his now familiar talking-points, which he had clearly prepared well. He talked about foreign investment, his visit to the New York Stock Exchange, and 'positive and constructive work' he had done to achieve the Belfast and St Andrews Agreements.

With twenty minutes to go to air time at 9 p.m., all the candidates were made up and ready to go into the studio—except Davis Norris. McRedmond and Hanlon were increasingly nervous that the programme might be in jeopardy if Norris failed to show, and staff members were making hurried phone calls for an update.

Norris, who had been in Cork on a canvass, arrived with fifteen minutes to spare, just enough time to get into make-up and go straight to studio. 'Lovely to see you. Thank you very much. See you later,' he called, waving with a big smile as he was hurried past the reporters and photographers.

Norris's adviser Paul Allen revealed after the campaign that they had stayed sitting in their car on the darkened estate until the last minute as they prepared for the debate. They wanted to avoid Norris losing focus, distracted either by reporters or by chat in the green room.

More than twenty journalists, from newspapers, radio and television, were brought into the TV3 canteen for the hotly anticipated debate. There was no room for them in the studio, and no audience; there would be a photo call with all seven candidates and the mediator in the lobby at the end of the debate. As the journalists munched on their sausages, chips and sandwiches, speculation mounted about whether Browne would show his usual dismissive impatience by skewering panellists who dodged or failed to answer questions, providing as much entertainment as information.

Browne warned the candidates that he would be as fair as possible in allocating time but advised them that they would have to fight their corner for coverage. The debate was significant, because it was the first of numerous debates and because the mercurial Browne was host.

Coverage included panning shots of the candidates' heads and shoulders. The remote control cameras didn't have to dip down to capture Higgins, as he stood on a black box behind the lectern so that all heads could be at the same approximate level. Pictures of the diminutive candidate were printed in some of the following day's papers with the box helpfully ringed.

Tony Heffernan, Higgins's media adviser, would normally check the arrangements for any studio interviews or photo calls in advance during his twenty-nine years' service as a political press officer. He had been enjoying his retirement and was reluctant to engage in the hurly-burly of a 24-hour-a-day campaign but relented in the face of constant pressure from Eamon Gilmore and the director of elections, Joe Costello.

To tempt him into taking on the role he was asked to go and see Higgins on a visit to emigrant centres in London in the second week of February. Heffernan was convinced that he had to take up the role as they met other travellers in Dublin airport. 'I'd never seen anything like it: people were coming over to him all the time, wishing him well. I was really struck by the reception he was given and later continued to receive.'

Like the photographers, however, Heffernan wasn't allowed into the studio, and as TV3 had provided the box, Higgins just stepped up onto it. There were no requests from the Labour Party team for a box for future television appearances after the media poked fun at his TV3 box. 'Look, everyone knows Michael D is small—so?' asked a team member, wondering what the fuss was all about.

The acerbic and witty television reviewer Pat Stacey in the *Evening Herald* summed up viewers' expectations of the ninety-minute programme.

There was a reason why this was called Vincent Browne's Big Presidential Debate and not Vincent Browne's Small to Medium Presidential Debate. For the average viewer this was THE BIG ONE. The one where the usual niceties could go unobserved.

Browne might be viewed by some as an eccentric presence in the TV news arena, yet television's Torquemada often makes for compelling viewing.

He was at his best here gleefully roasting all seven candidates over the spit, having first basted them in his unique concoction of spittle and venom.

Stacey went on to give the programme a rarely dispensed award of four out of five stars.

The debate got off to a slow start as Mary Davis repeated the claim made at her launch earlier in the day that Fine Gael had been paying a polling company to road-test negative messages about her. Gay Mitchell denied any knowledge of such polling. 'I know of no such thing . . . I've been the subject of negative campaigning myself; I took it on the chin.' The word was picked up by Norris, who said he would never campaign negatively; it then moved on to Dana, who talked about people watching the programme who were in negative equity. She later went on to talk about the bank guarantee scheme, until Higgins cut her off, saying, 'The President can do nothing about that now.'

Mitchell took the lead in the debate, launching an attack on McGuinness, querying him about his past as a member of the IRA and 'pretending' that he drew the average industrial wage, and claiming that he was not the Sinn Féin candidate. He said McGuinness was being disingenuous: he took a full salary, retained an industrial wage but gave the rest of the money to his party's 'propaganda machine'. 'Martin goes on with this propaganda [about his income]. Do you know how much money I gave to Trócaire last year, Martin? Why didn't you give it to Trócaire? You gave it to your propaganda machine.'

As the tensions between the candidates became more heated, Mitchell called on McGuinness to be open about his claims about where his wage was directed and said that truth was central to restoring confidence in the institutions of the state. And, he added, the voting public needed to have confidence in a candidate. McGuinness replied: 'I have made available my bank account to the media so they can look at it and see what money has been put into it by Sinn Féin. Gay will get a big shock when he sees it.'

McGuinness showed his media skills and resilience in the face of criticism. 'For some reason the people behind Gay have decided that in order to make him relevant to the campaign he has to attack me,' he said. He also claimed that 'nobody in the street' was exercised about his former membership of the IRA.

Browne now took over and asked McGuinness about his salary, about not being the Sinn Féin candidate in the election and about his membership, or not, of the IRA since 1974. Referring to his third question, Browne said, 'People have the right to know what your role was in the republican movement as [if elected] you'll be the personification of this state.' McGuinness responded that he had not been a member of the IRA since 1974 but that he had never distanced himself from the IRA and had always engaged with the IRA, which had resulted in the ceasefire.

Browne countered that everyone had heard about how Garda commissioners, the British intelligence service and ministers for justice all believed he was a member of the IRA after 1974—but, of course, McGuinness might not see them as sympathetic. He reached down below his desk and theatrically brandished a copy of *The Provisional IRA* by Patrick Bishop and Eamonn Mallie, which Browne said was sympathetic to McGuinness but whose text asserted that he was a member of the IRA after 1974.

Then he reached down again and produced another book, *Bandit Country: The IRA and South Armagh* by Toby Harnden. Then, to snorts of laughter from the media pack in the adjoining canteen, he produced book after book, like a magician pulling rabbits out of a hat, all asserting McGuinness's recent membership of the IRA. They were, in order of appearance: *Martin McGuinness: From Guns to Government* by Liam Clarke and Kathryn Johnston, *The Trouble with Guns: Republican Strategy and the Provisional IRA* by Malachi O'Doherty, *Sinn Féin: A Hundred Turbulent Years* by Brian Feency, *The Informer* by Seán O'Callaghan, *The Long War: The IRA and Sinn Féin* by Brendan O'Brien, and finally *A Secret History of the IRA* by Ed Moloney, who had extensive contacts in the IRA.

――――

Vincent Browne has been a journalist since 1968. He was Northern news editor of the Irish Press group from 1970 to 1973 and with Independent Newspapers from 1974 to 1979 and founded the investigative magazine *Magill* in 1977. He was editor of the *Sunday Tribune* from 1983 to 1994 and a broadcaster with RTE from 1996 to 2007, and while presenting 'Tonight with Vincent Browne' on TV3 was also writing columns for the *Irish Times* and the *Sunday Business Post*.

A senior and experienced journalist with substantial credentials, Browne stated that, aside from the books, which some might think were biased, 'I have reported from Northern Ireland during my time as a journalist; justice ministers have said it, authors have said it, gardaí have said it: I know you were a member of the IRA, Martin. How come that we are all so wrong?'

'Because some people jump to conclusions,' said McGuinness, who criticised some of the authors as hostile to Sinn Féin and its participation in the peace process. He singled out Liam Clarke and Kathryn Johnston's book for two factual errors about other people called McGuinness who were not even relatives.

But Browne continued, saying that he had a lot of regard for his work, his political substance and contribution to the peace process, which was a 'substantial achievement', but, he asserted, he had spoken to his contacts in the IRA and people very close to him. 'I know you were in the IRA up to three, four, five years ago,' he said. 'If people believe you are lying about this, how do they know you won't lie about lots of other things when you are elected President?'

Unlike Browne, who was passionate in delivering his argument, McGuinness's face remained unresponsive, his demeanour impassive.

> The people of Ireland are not stupid, and the people of Ireland are well capable of judging my contribution to Irish politics in the round. The media are exercised about this issue, political opponents are exercised about this issue. Nobody is exercised on the street about that at all. I am not telling lies about a substantive issue in my life. The people of Derry see me as someone who has done everything in my power to bring about an end to the vicious cycle of conflict.

He cited his role in the peace process and more recently as Northern Ireland Minister for Education and Deputy First Minister. 'I have risked my life,' he asserted, in becoming involved in the peace process. 'That's how people will judge me.'

Mitchell weighed in again. 'I also accept that Martin McGuinness contributed to the peace process—listen, we wouldn't have had the problem without them.'

The debate moved on, with regular squabbling, interruptions and cross-talking as the candidates jostled to be heard.

Browne—who is also a practising barrister—singled out Norris for a forensic examination after he spoke of the pride he would have, if elected, in reading out the Proclamation of the Irish Republic outside the GPO in 2016. 'Talking about cherishing the children . . .' said Browne, seizing his cue. He said that Norris was 'equivocal' and 'ambiguous' about sex between an older man and a boy. 'You have opposed the idea of an age of consent,' he accused.

'That's not true,' said Norris, warning Browne not to repeat untruths about him.

'People are really apprehensive that you are ambiguous on this issue,' Browne continued.

Not so, asserted Norris. 'I stand totally behind the law. I have said repeatedly, time after time, that I abhor with every fibre of my being the abuse of children—sexual, emotional and psychological.'

But Browne was relentless. 'People are further apprehensive that you refuse to release the letters—on grounds that most of us think are highly suspicious.'

'You have a suspicious nature, Vincent. I think the viewing public know that. As Martin said about another issue, the people have moved on: there is no traction out there. I challenge you to come with me to Limerick, Kilkenny. In Galway, today in Cork . . .'

'You're talking down the clock,' Browne interrupted. 'You said a few days ago that you had got legal advice that it would be improper or illegal to disclose the letters you have written. From whom did you get legal advice?'

'That is an extraordinary question for you to ask me, in my opinion,' said Norris, appearing to be taken aback. As Browne continued asking the question, he responded: 'Can I just say again, this is all bar-stool stuff, resurrected up from the past.'

'David, please answer the question. From whom did you get legal advice?'

'Is that one of these questions that you regularly produce that make very good television but seem to fly out of the top of your head?'

'From whom did you get that advice?'

Norris said he had answered the question, but no, he hadn't, Browne insisted, and he repeated it again and again as Norris stonewalled.

'I think, Vincent, that I've answered all the questions on that, and we've moved on.'

'Some people think you've made that up,' claimed Browne.

'I haven't made that up. Are you accusing me of lying?' said Norris, his voice rising.

'I wrote to people in the law faculty at Tel Aviv University, and I asked was there a plausible reason, was there a legal obstacle to your disclosing these letters, and only if you named the person who was the victim or if you revealed what happened in in-camera proceedings, there was no such disqualification or obstacle,' said Browne, pulling another rabbit out of the hat that had previously held the McGuinness library.

They continued to talk across each other, with Norris responding: 'I am not a lawyer. You have some legal training, I gather; I was an academic; but I do find it unusual that you were able to get a considered view in the space of a few hours. We all know lawyers, we all know academics. When doctors differ, patients die, when lawyers differ you're in a real quandary . . . You claim to have got advice in a matter of hours.'

'That's right, I did, yes,' said Browne, unflinching.

'Let's leave it there and move on and talk about my record. My record stands . . .'

'Is there some howler in these letters that discloses further ambiguity on your part about sex between adult males and minors?' asked Browne.

'That is quite untrue. My conscience is clear. I've been an open book all my life,' replied Norris, who again invited Browne to join him on a canvass and see at first hand what issues were important to the people he was meeting.

'And may I finally thank you. You were one of the many thousands of people who signed the petition to bring me back into the race, so thank you very much for that,' said Norris, adding that it emphasised Browne's impartiality.

———

Browne and McGuinness chatted as they left the studio to attend the photo call in the foyer. Norris left directly, and for the first time many journalists could remember on the campaign trail, or in life, he avoided the media. All the other candidates stopped for a few words with the journalists, huddled under the tent canopy after the debate, but they had nothing new to add, except to embellish their messages. The one thing they all agreed on was that the format, with seven voices competing for space, was difficult, suggesting that none were as pleased with their performance as they'd hoped.

The following morning the political media rated the performance of each of the candidates. Opinion was divided. Miriam Lord in the *Irish Times*:

> Overall, Michael D came across as the most reasoned and presidential and seemed content to let the other big hitters slug it out. Perhaps he was too low-key. Perhaps that was the plan.
>
> An intriguing debate, which threatened at times to descend into chaos but Browne managed to keep them all on the right side of civility.
>
> They all want to be inspirational. But were many inspired by what they saw? They speak of values and what they 'can bring to the role.' Ho hum.
>
> But while it was a bit fraught at times, none of them made a show of themselves. One or two quietly sank a little, others treaded water while Martin and Gay provided the turbulence.

There have been worse campaigns. This one is trundling along nicely, like a soap opera.

And it was a good night for Vincent too—savage and cuddly and daft, just the way his fans like it.

And no, we can't put him in the Áras. Ever.

The *Irish Daily Star* put Browne on page 1: 'Vincent is real debate winner.'

Of the 'Magnificent Seven' the best on the night were McGuinness, Mitchell and Michael D. Higgins. David Norris was poor as was Dana who failed to get properly involved in the debate.

Mitchell was rated 8/10. Brought entertainment to the debate. Wasn't afraid to get stuck in. The terrier of the pack.

McGuinness was rated 7/10—Hard as nails and impossible to ruffle—despite Vincent's best efforts.

Higgins—rated 6/10. Certainly the most polished of the candidates. He was well prepared and was on top of his game but again failed to get stuck in with other candidates. Davis recorded the same score—Very confident and assured. In general her arguments were well prepared but overall she failed to deliver any kind of a killer blow.

Norris rated a 4/10. Came across as shouty, had nothing great to add to the debate and his pomposity did not serve him well. Gallagher scored a similar score—Didn't add any spark to the debate. Failed to get stuck in and made too much of an issue of election literature and posters.

Dana scored just three out of ten. She was hardly at the races at all. A case of All kinds of Nothing really.

The *Herald* differed with its score card, rating Mitchell as the night's winner.

Along with Higgins, Mitchell's knowledge of the role and powers of the President as laid down in the Constitution are light years ahead of the rest of the candidates.

While his performance last night, which largely consisted of attacking McGuinness without having to dodge any bullets, was fair enough, it's unlikely to overcome the public perception of him as spiky, impatient and lacking in the sense of humour department.

Pat Stacey's score card rated McGuinness, Davis and Gallagher at only 1 out of 10. Norris scored 2 out of 10 and Higgins 8 out of 10. Dana trailed again with nil. 'Sage political analysts always claim that television debates don't decide the outcome of elections. But after Vincent Browne's cracking Big Presidential Debate on TV3 last night, the "experts" may have to rewrite the rule book.'

Another *Herald* writer commented that Dana had failed to connect with anyone and had a poor outing.

Mary Davis was rigid with tension and righteousness. She was one of the first to claim to know better than Vincent what the plain people of Ireland care about. In her case, the plain people of Ireland didn't care how many boards she served on. David Norris's plain people didn't care about whether he published the clemency letters or not. And, unless I'm wrong, Martin McGuinness's plain people didn't give a sugar about his past.

The online *Independent* (www.independent.ie) rated Higgins the winner, with a rating of 7 out of 10.

He was quickest to get his spiel across about the need for a President who can restore trust. And there was an early dig at two of his rivals. He said there was a need for someone who understood what a president could do—Mary Davis had problems here before. And he said the president was not head of Bord Tractala or the IDA—a cut at Sean Gallagher.

McGuinness, Davis and Norris scored 6 each, Gallagher and Mitchell 5 each, and Dana trailed at 4 out of 10.

Gallagher's main point was an appeal to the other candidates to have all candidate promotion letters paid for by the state and sent to each voter put into one envelope rather than have seven separate mailings. He said that Dana had responded to him, and then he challenged the other candidates to show leadership and go along with his plan. Davis said she would, but Mitchell said he wouldn't. It would save €10 million, claimed Gallagher.

But two weeks later Gallagher's individual *litir um thoghchán* began dropping through letterboxes around the country. 'Strong. Modern. Energetic. Positive. Let's put our strengths to work,' it said on the front page. His signed message on the other side read:

Ireland is a great country. We are a strong and proud people. We have an entrepreneurial spirit. We have bright and well educated young people. We are creative, loved and respected internationally. What we need now is to believe in ourselves and we can only do this by working together.

Across the top of page 1 the *Irish Daily Mail* wrote: 'Vincent threw the book at McGuinness, and Michael D stood on a box . . .' The paper's political editor, Senan Molony, delivered his verdict: 'Mr McGuinness spoke of respecting people's traditions, and said he wanted a decade of reconciliation from 1912.

Some seemed by the end to be reconciled to him. Winner: Martin McGuinness.'

Inside, the paper editorialised: 'Uninspiring debate.'

But somehow, didn't last night's debate emphasise the emptiness of much of what is said and the lack of a coherent and inspiring message among all the candidates?

Instead, we are viscerally absorbing an impression of their characters: from ponderous, earnest Seán Gallagher to wiry excitable Gay, to slick, ambitious Mary.

Perhaps this is no bad way to choose—this election is, after all, essentially about character. But the heart sinks at yet another turgid spell at those seven matching lecterns.

On the TV3 web site people were asked to vote for their favourite candidate, and 205,000 responded. McGuinness topped the poll, at 34 per cent, Norris came in second, with 19 per cent. Gallagher scored 15 per cent, Higgins 13 per cent, Mitchell 8 per cent, Dana 6 per cent and Davis 5 per cent.

Columnist James Downey, writing in the *Irish Independent*, would say that Fianna Fáil 'has effectively ceded its own position—humble enough, but enough of a base to offer some possibility of rebuilding—to Sinn Féin. And Sinn Féin is bent on completing the destruction of the party that dominated politics for so long and, ultimately, so disastrously.'

Chapter 13 ⌒

| FRONT RUNNER

'What a journey this has been so far!' said a hugely enthusiastic David Norris, waving his arms for emphasis and grinning at the relaunch of his campaign on Wednesday 5 October. 'There is another journey that begins today. The last part of the journey has twenty days to go. It will be the best part of all. Come along with me. It will be worth it. Let's change Ireland for the better.'

The relaunch was a tense affair in the Dublin Writers' Museum in Parnell Square, a short distance from Norris's home. 'Put the Message in the Bottle' by Brian Kennedy and 'Ain't No Stopping Us Now' pumped out over the PA before Norris came out to read his speech and answer questions.

The main policies enunciated by Norris for his campaign manifesto were that electing an independent would wrest the Presidency from the grip of the political establishment; that this was a referendum about change; that it was an opportunity to tear down the 'monstrous inequalities' in Irish society; and that he wanted to give priority to human rights and the inclusion of marginalised people and build a new society based on others rather than on self-interest.

The questions inevitably were about media reports about his disability pension, for hepatitis, and the legal advice he had received about why he could not release the Nawi letters. Norris said that his hepatitis had been diagnosed in 1994. It was not hepatitis A, B or C. The following year Trinity College required him to give up his job as a lecturer on the grounds of disability, and he received a disability payment, which was not funded by the exchequer. He retired from the college in 1999. In the sixteen years during which he received the payment he was a member of Seanad Éireann. He told the press conference that he was fit for the rigours of the Presidential campaign. 'Yes, I am, absolutely,' he confirmed.

Keeping a sense of proportion on the campaign, Miriam Lord in the *Irish Times* said there was a bizarre series of questions from the media about the A, B, C, D or E versions of hepatitis, and it got personal on both sides. 'One wondered if he was going to be asked to produce his liver and slap it up on the platform for general inspection.'

Norris also read out a legal statement that gave the reasons for not releasing further letters appealing for clemency for Ezra Nawi. 'Under Israeli law nothing may be published about proceedings in a closed trial without the approval of the court,' the statement from the Israeli legal firm Avitan Koronel said. This applied to letters Norris had written to lawyers acting for Nawi; and if other letters to public representatives were disclosed he could face the prospect of 'expensive litigation'.

———

On Thursday the 6th a REDC-Paddy Power opinion poll showed Higgins picking up seven points to top the poll at 25 per cent, Gallagher up ten points to 21 per cent, McGuinness holding at 16 per cent, Norris dropping back to 14 per cent, Mitchell losing three points to 10 per cent, Davis dropping three points to 9 per cent, and Dana losing one point to drop to 5 per cent.

In the cattle mart in Raphoe, Co. Donegal, Mitchell picked up the results of the poll on his iPhone as the constituency TD and minister of state Dinny McGinley introduced him to local farmers. Outside, the rain lashed down, reflecting the Mitchell camp's political mood. 'I think as the campaign goes on the Fine Gael vote will turn out,' said Mitchell in the canteen as he sipped vegetable soup. 'The highest rating anyone is getting is in the low 20s, so the Fine Gael vote alone, if it turns out, would change that. People will stop looking at this as a beauty contest and start looking at people's credentials.'

The *Irish Independent* reported the following day as it assessed the REDC poll:

Fine Gael will attempt to mount a desperate attempt to 'save face' after party insiders accepted that Mitchell's chances of becoming the next president are now 'doomed'.

Mr Mitchell's campaign lay in tatters last night as a second opinion poll in two days showed the party's candidate trailing second last out of the seven candidates in the race for the Aras. Now the poor performance is heightening divisions within the party—despite Director of Elections

Charlie Flanagan claiming that it was a 'myth' that not all its TDs and senators were canvassing for Mr Mitchell.

The *Independent*'s editorial-writer was not impressed and described Mitchell's campaign the following day as 'rapidly coming to resemble the political equivalent of a train wreck.'

The director of elections, Charlie Flanagan, would rebut the 'doomed' label applied by the *Independent*, saying that every member of Fine Gael had been 'working around the clock' for Mitchell. But the same afternoon he sent a letter to members of his parliamentary party. 'I asked earlier in the week that you would let me have details of your Facebook/Twitter operator in your office to assist in Gay's campaign. I received a mere 33 replies! This is just 30 per cent!!' Also belying the party hierarchy's confident public statements about the campaign, he added: 'I have been in contact with the FG regional organisers and I've received mixed reports on the posters, literature and canvass. In some constituencies there is little or no activity.'

Yet another opinion poll on the same day, Thursday the 6th, showed voters' intentions bunching around the three leading candidates, with Higgins at 23 per cent, Gallagher 20 per cent and McGuinness 19 per cent.

'For Mitchell and Norris the poll is little short of a disaster,' the *Independent* said, with the two candidates scoring 9 and 11 per cent, respectively. 'The big surprise of the poll is the performance of Gallagher, who is now in with a realistic chance of winning the office if he can maintain the momentum he has generated in the past few weeks.'

The magazine *Dubliner* that was inserted in that Thursday's *Evening Herald* carried a three-page polemic by Eoghan Harris that set out 'ten compelling reasons that make Martin McGuinness an unfit person to be President of Ireland.' The *Sunday Independent* columnist had moved his political affiliations across the political spectrum over the years and now offered personal reasons why he rejected McGuinness as President, 'a role that would retrospectively justify IRA murders and act as a recruiter for a new generation of gormless gunmen.' The cartoon of McGuinness with an automatic rifle and a devil's tail would be reprinted later as part of a full-page editorial in the *Herald* as the country was about to vote.

Reason number 1 was that even the remotest chance of Ireland becoming a 'Provo Cuba', with McGuinness as President, would freeze foreign investment. McGuinness's Presidency, said Harris, would be a Trojan horse. McGuinness did not understand the political culture of the Republic: he was delusional in comparing himself to Mandela—who had accepted twenty-six years of imprisonment rather than engage in reprisal murders—and his 'fight for freedom' was a futile waste.

His other reasons were that McGuinness should not be given the use of Áras an Uachtaráin as a safe house; his IRA killed seven members of the Garda Síochána and six Irish soldiers; his IRA waged war on children and on writers; his CV was a tissue of lies; and his presidential campaign was a personal therapy so that he could enjoy a sulphurous fame by presenting past criminal acts as a fight for freedom and could also be rewarded for calling off the campaign when he ran out of road.

The following Saturday afternoon a phone-caller to the *Sunday Independent* offices threatened to kill Harris. The caller said, 'Eoghan Harris should be shot for what he is writing about Martin McGuinness—and I think I am the man to do it.' The Gardaí were alerted and called to Harris's home to speak to him about the threat.

A letter-writer in the *Irish Times*, John McDwyer of Carrick-on-Shannon, asked:

> Since we seem intent on dredging through the past misdemeanours of the presidential candidates in order to diminish their candidacy, I want to know, from the other six, if any of them ever attended a Dana concert?

By coincidence, Dana was about to take centre stage as information emerged about a court case in the United States in 2008 over the ownership of some of Dana's religious recordings. The court papers provided an insight into Dana's business dealings and a bitter family row. The *Irish Times* on its front page seized on the revelation that Dana became a US citizen before putting her name forward for the 1997 presidential election. Dana's estranged sister, Susan Stein, a nurse who had moved to the United States and married a dentist, told the court that a decision was taken not to inform the Irish electorate.

> When she ran for the presidential election in Ireland, John [election adviser] and Damien [Dana's husband] and I had a meeting. She had just acquired her American citizenship at the same time she was running for president of a foreign country, and the decision was made that it wouldn't look very good if the people of Ireland knew that she was an American citizen.

Stein now barely spoke to her sister, she told the *Irish Independent*.

> If we walked past each other in the hall we would be civil to each other. But we have no personal contact any more, which is unfortunate. It is very sad.

Dana dismissed the issue, saying she hadn't sought to keep it a secret: 'Why would I? Wasn't de Valera [an American citizen]?' As she went through the citizenship process she claimed she had been assured that she could retain her Irish citizenship and that if she couldn't she wouldn't have taken up US citizenship. She added that the sides in the family dispute had reached agreement two years earlier and that part of the settlement was that they would not comment further.

The *Irish Times* described the bitter family dispute. Heartbeat was a music company established in the United States by Dana and members of her family to promote her music, and it also employed members of her family. The bulk of the company's turnover of $7.6 million between 1996 and 2005 was used to promote Dana and her music. She could earn $5,000 for a personal appearance, according to her sister. There was no written agreement over copyright. Heartbeat got into debt, Dana and her husband fell out with the company, and litigation ensued over the alleged underpayment and non-payment of royalties to Dana. The court papers included increasingly bitter correspondence between the two sisters, who had originally sung together and had won a contract with Decca Records.

Dana cut her first record in 1967, when she was a sixteen-year-old schoolgirl, Rosemary Brown. The song, appropriately called 'Sixteen', was written by her school principal and music teacher, Tony Johnston, who recognised and nurtured her talent and guided her through her school exams. Rosemary was one of seven children. Her father, Robert, played the trumpet; her mother, Sheila, played the piano. Musically gifted, she also spent time living with Johnston's family in Tamnaherin, Co. Derry, a few miles from her home but a world away from the Troubles.

In 1969 Dana entered the Irish national song contest and came second. The following year she entered and went on to win the Eurovision Song Contest and to sell two million copies of her winning song, 'All Kinds of Everything', throughout the world.

It was not until 1980 that she had another number 1 hit with 'Totus Tuus' (Latin for 'Totally yours'), a song she had jointly written with her husband and manager, Damien Scallon, in tribute to Pope John Paul II, whose motto it was. (Earlier in October 2011, Dana and Damien marked their thirty-third wedding anniversary. They had written the song on their honeymoon.) She subsequently signed a contract with World Records at the National Religious Broadcasters' Conference in Washington, and when the Pope visited New Orleans in 1987 he asked Dana to perform the song in front of an audience of 85,000 people. Four years later she moved to Birmingham, Alabama, with her husband and four children and began a career on Christian television and radio.

In Co. Kerry on Friday the 7th Dana said she had taken US citizenship because her husband went to work there and she wanted the family to remain there legally. She also said her family had no memory of comments reported in an American court that Irish voters should not be informed of her dual citizenship.

Hurt by the coverage of the divisions in her family, Dana hit out at the media, saying that every family had its disputes but that the media had 'reached a new low' and a 'very low ebb.' She said that, 'at the bottom of it all, I love my family, and we have reached agreement.'

Later in the day she was explaining herself on the RTE one o'clock news with Seán O'Rourke. She said that before she took the oath of allegiance the American official said she could not give up her Irish citizenship, and she was assured that this was not a problem, as there was a 'unique relationship' between the United States and Ireland. 'I was perfectly assured that I could take up dual citizenship, with no conflict with my Irish citizenship,' she said. She also said that she didn't take up US citizenship until 1999, not 1997, as reported in the media.

At a rally in Cork, Higgins was asked about Dana's citizenship.

It is not up to me to speculate. It would have been in the public interest if it had been made known. It is clear from what I have read that this is a matter that has a family dispute to it, and that must be very distressing. I have always drawn a distinction between the personal circumstances of my competitors and the political circumstances.

In a two-page spread in the *Irish Daily Mail*, Mitchell talked about himself, the love of his life and the Presidency. It was a revealing interview, showing the love between Gay and his wife, Norma, 'my real director of elections,' and gave him the oxygen that the campaign had not permitted so far to allow his warmth to be displayed publicly.

He told how he had organised a situation so that he could be alone with Norma and propose to her. They had been going out together, and he arranged to pick her up during her lunch break and drive her to St Anne's Park, with its beautiful rose garden.

The interviewer, Jason O'Toole, asks, 'Did he get down on bended knee?'

'No, not quite,' he laughs.

'I must get him to do that,' Norma interjects. 'It's romantic for me, so when I pass by each time I think of the fact that I was proposed to outside that gate.'

'I'm thinking of getting a plaque put up there,' Gay quips.

O'Toole writes:

It's obvious from the good-natured banter between them and their habit of finishing each other's sentences that they are a very close couple . . . 'Everybody knows that the closest person to me is Norma . . . I said when I was selected at the convention by Fine Gael: "Charlie [Flanagan], you may think you're the director of elections, but everyone knows Norma will be the director of elections."'

——

On the front page of the *Irish Daily Mail* the paper revealed that Gallagher had been a member of the Fianna Fáil National Executive until January 2011—despite claiming, as recently as that week, that he left two years ago.

The paper's political correspondent, Ferghal Blaney, said they had uncovered a 'smoking gun' letter written on 5 January in which Gallagher tells the party's general secretary, Seán Dorgan, that he is regrettably quitting. 'In it he makes none of the sharp attacks in private that he has since made in public, while campaigning for votes.' The letter of resignation was reprinted in the paper.

A campaign spokesperson countered that Gallagher had not been active in the party for the last two years, and that he had indicated his intention of resigning in September 2010 but had made it official only in January 2011.

The *Sunday Business Post*'s political editor, Pat Leahy, took an overview of the campaign, saying that it was now being directed and dominated by the media.

More than any other election in Irish history, this one is being fought out on the airwaves and on the front pages of newspapers. More than ever before, the role played by reporters, editors, radio and television producers and presenters is shaping the course of the campaign. All of the major developments of the campaign have been generated by the media's interrogation of the candidates. Increasingly the candidates are talking about the media's agenda rather than their own.

And it is having an effect. The polls published last week, a RedC poll by Paddy Power and another in the *Irish Times*, showed that media focus on stories unfavourable to candidates usually tends to damage them. The oft repeated claim—by several of the candidates—that they wouldn't dream of negative campaigning because it doesn't work is false on at least one account, and in most cases two. Negative campaigning often does work. That's why they do it. Negative publicity has destroyed David Norris and severely damaged Mary Davis.

Gay Mitchell's upfront attacks on Martin McGuinness since last weekend—egged on by influential commentators—have torpedoed his own campaign, rather than the Sinn Féin candidate's. The lesson seems to be: best leave the media to do the dirty work.

Leahy also explored some of the candidates' profiles and media exposure. Dana had largely been ignored by the media, he said.

Her supporters believe that this is because she is a representative of a conservative brand of Catholicism and Euroscepticism which is disliked by many people in the media. There is at least some truth in this, though not as much as Dana thinks. But really her lack of traction can be explained by the fact that she is at five per cent in the polls.

The candidates are presenting themselves for the highest position in the land more or less entirely on the basis of their personal character and their records. Most people would agree that voters have a right to know about their past and their character, and that's the media's job. But what is unusual by Irish standards is that the process has been led, defined and narrated by the media. It's not just part of the campaign. It *is* the campaign. For Irish politics, that is new.

The *Sunday Independent*'s editorial was strident.

Our concerns about Mr McGuinness are not confined to the lies, economic destruction, murder and repression of free speech that Sinn Fein and the IRA are so intimately linked with. The central philosophy of a peace process that has brought Mr McGuinness to a position where he can realistically contend for the Presidency was one of moral reservation where lies were presented as truth in the hope that this would serve the greater good.

Across the page the columnist Brendan O'Connor took a philosophical view of the campaign and all its utterances. He asked how the campaign had become

one of the most real, and most gripping, bouts of soul-searching this nation has had in years? . . .

Having spoken about nothing except money for years, in the last couple of weeks we have suddenly started talking about everything, about who we are, where we've been, where we'd like to go next and how we would like to see ourselves.

In the same paper, Mitchell took out quarter-page advertisements, the largest seen in the print media during the campaign.

'Why vote for Gay?' the advertisement asked. 'He understands the hardship people are going through, he would use his political experience and international contacts to support the Government in generating jobs, and has a strong record of serving the people as a public representative.' The five photographs used in the advertisements were badly lit, poorly posed and without captions, raising questions about who had an overview of the campaign.

In the *Sunday World* the outspoken columnist Paddy Murray hit out at McGuinness. He was proud of the send-off he got from Derry but made no reference to five named people who were killed in the city by the IRA when he was a member. 'McGuinness talks about "regrets" but he rarely says sorry. He wants to be our president. I'd say over my dead body, but he might take me literally.'

Mary Davis was the lead story in the *Sunday Times*, which reported that she had received funding for her campaign from the telecommunications billionaire Denis O'Brien and had voted on three decisions concerning his ownership of Irish media when she was a member of the Broadcasting Commission in 2008 and 2009. Davis had ruled herself out of votes in relation to O'Brien's companies when she joined the board in 2004, citing a conflict of interest, as O'Brien was chairperson of the Board of Special Olympics Ireland when she had been CEO. The *Times* reported that she had received legal advice in June 2008 that a potential conflict of interest no longer existed, as she had moved to Special Olympics Europe-Eurasia the previous May. Her spokesperson said that any conflicts of interest that may have arisen were made known by Davis to the board.

Speaking to reporters at Limerick Racecourse, where she was canvassing later that afternoon, Davis insisted that there was no conflict of interest between the Broadcasting Commission and its dealings with O'Brien, who has extensive holdings in commercial radio and a controlling interest in Today FM, Newstalk and a number of regional stations. 'I have acted on the board of the BCI with full integrity and taken full responsibility at all times,' Davis said.

The *Sunday Independent*'s lead story reported that Fine Gael and the Labour Party, 'in what amounts to a shift in tactics in dirty tricks,' now intended to concentrate on Gallagher and his past association with Fianna Fáil rather than on McGuinness.

> Yesterday there was a view within Fine Gael that because Mr Mitchell had failed to connect with the public it was to be expected that the Party would support the candidate of its coalition partners. As old hostilities threaten to break out again in Fine Gael, the possibility remains that the coalition

strategy will backfire, particularly if voters perceive Mr Gallagher to be a victim of unfair attention by the Government parties.

On RTE's Sunday radio programme 'This Week' Mitchell took the opportunity to swipe at Gallagher, Higgins and the media themselves. He criticised Gallagher:

> If we choose celebrity over substance I think we are making a very big mistake. I think there are people who are very good candidates but really don't have the vision and experience that I have.

Mitchell went on to say that young people should not be pushed into becoming the

> Skype emigration generation while we sip champagne in the Park, reciting poetry. In every job I have done I have brought a sense of experience and innovation. I will be the person to put jobs and the future of the country on the agenda.

He insisted that the Fine Gael organisation was totally behind his campaign.

> I'm telling you this now. The likelihood is that I'll win this election. I will let you know in three weeks' time.

He criticised the media too, saying that he favoured intense scrutiny of the candidates, particularly McGuinness on his past record.

> I think you should start asking some of them very difficult questions. When I started asking Martin McGuinness difficult questions, people say I am attacking him.

Dana was interviewed by the *Examiner*, which reported that she was willing to renounce her US citizenship 'if it was the wish of the Irish people.' She also produced her US naturalisation certificate, dated 8 October 1999, to counter the claim that she had become a US citizen when she ran for the Presidency fourteen years earlier.

———

The McGuinness campaign over the coming days was to be held to account for IRA atrocities, and in the full and embarrassing glare of the media.

Campaigners would admit later that the political dynamic in the Republic was different from that of the North. In the North the Troubles had been analysed, dissected, discussed and come to terms with; however unsatisfactorily, a conscious decision had been made to move forward rather than dwell on the past. But in the Republic legitimate grievance, loss and pain had not been addressed, and there had been no accountability.

On a brisk Monday in a shopping centre in Athlone, David Kelly stood with a framed photograph of his father, Private Patrick Kelly. His father (35) and Recruit Garda Gary Sheehan (23) were shot dead in a gun battle with members of the Provisional IRA, which had kidnapped the supermarket executive Don Tidey in December 1983 and held him in Derrada Wood, Co. Leitrim. No-one was ever convicted for their murder. Private Kelly, from Moate, Co. Westmeath, had served three tours of duty in Lebanon and was the father of four young sons, the youngest eleven weeks old when he was shot.

When McGuinness and his entourage came through the main entrance, Kelly confronted him, brandishing the picture of his murdered father. 'I want you to get your comrades who committed this crime to hand themselves in to the Gardaí,' he said. McGuinness responded: 'I don't know who was responsible for the killing of your father, but I fully and absolutely sympathise with you. This is in the past. You are heartbroken on account of it, and my sympathy is 100 per cent with you and your family.'

Kelly rejected McGuinness's words. In front of the cameras he said that McGuinness's assertion that he had left the IRA in 1974 was 'a blatant lie' and that he was 'trying to fool the Irish people.' His father was 'loyal to this Irish Republic and I'm loyal to him as a son, and I'm going to get justice for him. Before we can have reconciliation . . . there has to be truth, especially for people running for the Presidency of the country.'

The following day the brother of the murdered detective-garda Frank Hand said that there was never an apology for the IRA's actions. McGuinness's words to David Kelly were not an apology. 'They were an oblique contrition,' he said.

Frank Hand was twenty-five and married five weeks when he was shot while accompanying a cash delivery to a post office in Drumree, Co. Meath, in 1984. His brother Michael told the *Irish Independent* that the idea of McGuinness as supreme commander of the Defence Forces was 'an abhorrence'.

> I find that impossible to accept. As far as I'm concerned, he has my family's blood on his hands. Both my parents are dead now, but to my mind it resulted in their early death. It broke their hearts and caused difficulty in my family. There were seven of us. He was the middle brother. It was very traumatic.

I accept that he [McGuinness] was instrumental in bringing things about [with the peace process], but I think he has blood on his hands and he's an inappropriate candidate for the presidency of our country, of my country. And particularly for a country where my family gave blood for our country. I can't accept how someone like that can lead the army and get the loyalty of the army and the police when his colleagues were the ones who shot down my brother in cold blood.

The *Evening Herald* columnist Andrew Lynch encapsulated McGuinness's problems with his past.

The question is for how long can the Sinn Féin candidate keep running away from the truth? The voices of the IRA's many victims are finally making themselves heard—and with any justice, this could eventually become the crucial factor that keeps one of the Provos' most notorious leaders out of Áras an Uachtaráin The pressure is on McGuinness and is likely to be kept on in tonight's Primetime debate hosted by Miriam O'Callaghan. Thousands of voices will be encouraging Miriam from the grave.

——

There were two debates on Wednesday 12 October, one hosted by Barnardo's and chaired by Olivia O'Leary, but it was the later RTE 'Prime Time' debate, presented by Miriam O'Callaghan, that provided drama. Dana issued a statement:

It has come to my attention that yet further allegations, this time of a most untrue and malicious, vile nature have been levelled against a member of my family. Let it be known that lawyers have already been instructed to forensically investigate a particular communication that spread this vile false allegation which attempts to implicate me and destroy my good character.

She made the prepared statement on the programme after being approached by a newspaper. O'Callaghan, who had been given no notice of Dana's intention to read out a statement, pressed her for details. Dana declined to provide any.

We have been advised that all possible lines of inquiry regarding this communication is being pursued with prosecution authorities in the United States. I assure the Irish people that I will leave no stone unturned to expose the malicious intent at the heart of these untrue allegations.

'What are you talking about?' asked O'Callaghan, as baffled as the viewing public.

The other highlight of the programme was O'Callaghan's blunt and unrelenting questioning of McGuinness. 'How do you square, Martin McGuinness, with your God the fact that you were involved in the murder of so many people?' she asked.

'I think that's a disgraceful comment to make,' said McGuinness.

'You were in the IRA,' countered O'Callaghan.

'I was in the IRA. I joined the IRA as a result of the conflict that broke out on the streets of Derry when I was eighteen years of age . . .'

O'Callaghan went on to ask him whether he went to Confession, and about his membership of the IRA, which he said he left in 1974. She said she would 'park' what had happened in the past and asked questions about the IRA murders of members of the Defence Forces, such as Private Patrick Kelly.

'What have you done for that man, David Kelly, since you spoke to him, in terms of naming the people who killed his father?'

'Sure I don't know who killed his father,' McGuinness replied.

'But you're a republican: you know everyone in the republican movement.'

McGuinness then appeared to lose control. 'I think that's a stupid statement for you to make,' he said.

RTE said it received more than a hundred complaints about how O'Callaghan had questioned McGuinness in the debate, which attracted an average viewership of 654,000. Sinn Féin would later deny assertions that it 'orchestrated' complaints against RTE.

After the programme McGuinness confronted O'Callaghan in her dressing-room. The *Evening Herald* stated the following day: 'The IRA godfather went into a hissy fit at the RTE studios and tried to intimidate the mother-of-eight, insiders revealed today,' saying that McGuinness went 'ballistic' over her line of questioning. '"There's no doubt that he tried to intimidate her. She looked quite shaken after it but there's no way she's going to let something like that get to her," said a witness to the sinister encounter.'

———

That morning, 13 October, the *Irish Sun* revealed exclusively that Dana had phoned the police in the United States to ask them to investigate a baseless allegation of sexual abuse against a close relative sent to her by email from America. The allegation referred to a period a number of years previously, and there was never any arrest, conviction or prosecution.

On TV3 on Friday the 14th she confirmed that the allegations were about a family member and were of a sexual nature, but she declined to elaborate further.

It is of a sexual nature regarding a member of my family, and I know that it is not true—I know it is not true because the first time it was ever raised was in a court case in a family dispute—never before. It was not acted upon at that time. The second time it's raised is now in the middle of my election campaign, with the obvious desire of trying to destroy my character.

She said that the allegation came out during a court case taken against her sister, Susan Stein, and that it went back thirty-five years. 'I will not step down,' she said. 'I will not bend under this and I will not be broken under this.'

In a statement she issued after the interview she claimed that a 'despicable and malicious campaign of hatred' was being directed against her and her family.

———

The *Sunday Business Post* of 16 October reported a surge in support for Gallagher, poising him for the Áras, according to its latest REDC poll. It now seemed to be a two-horse race, with Gallagher speeding ahead with an eighteen-point jump, to give him 39 per cent of the vote, and Higgins up two per cent, to 27 per cent. 'By not putting a foot wrong and appealing to the public's desire for a non-party candidate, Seán Gallagher has pulled ahead in the latest poll,' the paper said.

McGuinness dropped three points, to 13 per cent, and Mitchell dropped two points, to 8 per cent, with Norris, Davis and Dana on 7, 4 and 2 per cent, respectively.

Commenting on the poll on RTE radio, Mitchell said:

I don't want to rubbish the people who took the poll. I'm sure they're findings they got, but you have to compare it with the same situation in the last Presidential election, when the front runner on 38 per cent ended up with less than 7 per cent. I've been speaking to friends this morning who've said they haven't made up their minds yet. In the Presidential election, 40 per cent of people made up their minds in the last week. Hand on heart, I do not believe the polls will be the same as emerges on Thursday week.

The same day a journalist, Greg Harkin, spoke to Susan Gorrell, who claimed she was molested by her uncle John Brown, Dana's brother, on a number of occasions when she was aged between five and thirteen, and claimed that Dana knew about the allegations for three decades. She told the *Irish Independent*:

> I now realise that perhaps it was a mistake not to press charges at the time, but my grandmother was still alive and my aunt was a public figure, so that led to the earlier decision not to go forward with charges. I know that keeping silent is not the answer, and perhaps by my speaking out at this time it may help other victims who find themselves in the same situation. Although I told my mother and my Aunt Rosemary more than thirty years ago, my father and other relatives did not know until recent years.

On the campaign trail in Co. Donegal, Dana refused to take questions on the issue, saying she wished to 'leave that behind now.'

The *Irish Times* reported that Susan Stein said she stood over evidence that her husband, Ronald, gave to a court in the United States in 2008. He said John Brown (Dana and Susan Stein's brother) had admitted to him in 2005 that he had sexually abused the Steins' daughter, Susan Gorrell, in the 1980s. The court heard that Brown had denied the allegation while giving evidence by way of deposition.

Meanwhile, with ten days to go, the Gallagher campaign had emailed supporters to ask them to do ten things. They included canvassing, sending text messages to their contacts, using Facebook to urge a vote, and printing a poster from his web site and displaying it. 'Keep it positive, don't be shy and don't give up,' he urged.

Mitchell had travelled from Dublin to Galway. Now, just after 6 p.m. on Tuesday 18 October, he stood outside the TG4 studios at Baile na hAbhann, near Barna, breathing in the fresh sea air. He had taken the microphone off his lapel and walked off the set as yet another candidates' debate was about to be staged. Higgins was the only Irish-speaker among the candidates, and the station he had legislated to establish was in his home constituency.

Mitchell was fuming over the format, which included an opening address in Irish, to be delivered live rather than recorded. He was cajoled back onto the set just in time for the debate to begin at 7 p.m., which would last for more than 100 minutes and be conducted in both Irish and (mostly) English.

Mitchell was the sixth to speak. He said he wanted to make Ireland a better place for the people of Ireland, and strongly believed that Ireland was on the cusp of something great. As President he wanted to guide the country to that greatness.

The debate, like many others, was a ritual the candidates had to go through, addressing different audiences but with the same now well-rehearsed messages. In the TG4 debate the importance of Irish was stressed by all the candidates; most said they would like to use it more and would address themselves to learning more if elected.

In response to the moderator, Páidí Ó Lionaird, all the candidates said they were proud of the national anthem and that it needed no changes—except Gallagher.

> I have mixed views on it. I see the traditional attachment that many older people have with it. I would be open to explore a revision of it, to make it less militaristic and celebrate our strengths. It needs to be modernised.

Although Higgins's team would say that their candidate was always positive, he referred to the involvement of his main rival, Gallagher, in the building industry during the boom years. 'There was a speculative economy that Seán might favour and a social economy that I might favour.'

The web site www.thejournal.ie carried a minute-by-minute blog of what the candidates said and the site moderator's comments on their remarks.

The final question was picked up in the following day's papers for its novelty value. 'At a social gathering, what's your party piece?' they were asked. Gallagher didn't get the switch in mood, lamenting not being able to sing or play an instrument, and said his party piece was his character, interaction and connecting with people.

Norris said he wouldn't offer any poetry or Joyce but would play the piano—Chopin or ragtime. Mitchell said he usually sang a verse of a song, while Dana admitted singing 'All Kinds of Everything'—but everyone sings it together, she said. McGuinness said he recited his own poetry. Higgins, already known for his poetry, said it wasn't his practice to read his own poems, but he hoped to release all the stories he'd collected over his life at some time in the future. Davis revealed that she loves karaoke and that she also juggles.

It had been a day of juggling for Davis, with a visit earlier in the day to the Summerhill Community Centre, where she addressed the 250 'third-agers' and had a quick waltz at their tea dance. Then it was on to a canvass in Navan and a quick return to home in Sutton, Co. Dublin, where her husband blew out candles on his birthday cake, before travelling to Connemara.

Late that Tuesday night Dana, her brother Gerald Brown, her cousin and her husband were driving back to Dublin from the Landmark Hotel in Carrick-on-Shannon. Dana was asleep in the back seat when a tyre blew out on the M4 motorway near Kilcock, Co. Kildare. Numerous punctures were visible on the outside tyre rim when the AA arrived. Dana's husband claimed that their car had been deliberately damaged in an attempt to 'injure or murder us,' and her solicitors lodged a complaint of criminal damage with the Gardaí. 'It was very, very scary to look at,' she said. 'As far as I am concerned it was a very, very lucky escape. I never start a journey without saying a little prayer, and I think we are all very lucky.'

Damien Scallon, who was driving, said, 'When you see the tyre it kind of sends home to us what they were trying to do. Injure us or murder us? Along with that they could have killed someone else.' He had wrestled with the steering-wheel to avoid a lorry in front of them and a car behind before managing to stop safely on the hard shoulder.

The Gardaí would submit the tyre to scientific examination. However, tyre experts shown photographs by reporters said they believed it had suffered a casing break-up, which is caused by the tyre being driven for a while with a puncture.

———

The following day's *Irish Independent* and *Irish Times* paid attention to Gallagher's business dealings and his exclusive claim among his fellow-candidates to be an entrepreneur. Only two of the eleven firms promised investment on television by Gallagher on 'Dragons' Den' received the agreed funds, said the *Irish Independent*. Five firms received investment from Gallagher totalling approximately €100,000, whereas on television he had offered more than €220,000. His spokesperson explained: 'It can happen that the contestant or dragon withdraws the offer when all the contractual details, obligations and financial commitments, due diligence, figures, projections and business plans are examined.'

The *Irish Times* reported that Business Expansion Scheme investors in Gallagher's company Smarthomes two years earlier were told in a letter that income would grow to €10 million in 2011 and 2012, as the company was confident that profits could be increased to 20 per cent by entering a distribution agreement with an American transnational corporation. It was indicative of the type of scrutiny Gallagher and others would come under as the pressure-cooker of a presidential election began to reach boiling point.

On Thursday the 20th the *Irish Independent* led with an explosive story that would dominate the tone and content of future debates. The headlines read: 'Gallagher linked to secret FF fundraiser' and 'Business friends paid €5,000 to dine with Cowen'. The paper's political editor, Fionnan Sheahan, reported that Gallagher personally invited donors to attend a secret Fianna Fail corporate fundraiser for former Taoiseach Brian Cowen. Mr Gallagher contacted a number of his business friends to invite them to attend the dinner, where guests were asked to donate up to €5,000 to the party.

Mr Gallagher's claims to be an independent will be damaged by the revelations.

Later that day the *Evening Herald* trumpeted the first interview with the woman behind Seán Gallagher. 'I want to have children in the Áras', said the huge front-page headline, referring to an interview inside the paper with Gallagher's wife, Trish. The 37-year-old from Kanturk, Co. Cork, who has been dubbed Gallagher's 'secret weapon', was conditioned for the gruelling campaign trail as she travelled five days a week throughout Munster, living out of a suitcase, as a sales rep for Vichy Skincare. She was a former sports instructor, and one of two girls and five boys brought up on the family farm.

> We would both love it if we were blessed with children. If it happened it would be great, no matter where—at the Áras or anywhere else—it would be just wonderful to be parents and have children.
>
> I think we definitely want to have more than one child. Maybe two. Maybe three.

Gallagher had been married before, but that marriage ended in 1999. Trish had been suggested to him as a possible date by a friend; he rang her twice to convince her to meet him; they did, and they 'clicked' as soulmates, she said. 'I think it was one of the first things that we both said to each other, that we had both found our soulmate—it was lovely,' she said.

The possible patter of tiny feet in Áras an Uachtaráin would become the source of humour in the media as the reference was facetiously transferred to the diminutive candidate Michael D. Higgins.

The *Herald*'s editorial that day put important things in perspective.

> Show a bit of sympathy for the young girls—and boys—gutted today over the news of the break up of Westlife. The massively successful band has provided the soundtrack to their teenage years. That's something that stays with a person forever. Parents and grandparents should think back to how they felt when their favourite, whether it was the Beatles or Take That, broke up.

The bookies Boylesports took a decision to pay out on the bets already placed on Higgins. 'He has it in the bag, despite it being an extremely close race,' said

their spokesperson, Leon Blanche, who said that the pay-out would cost them
€125,000.

> This is possibly the most volatile market we've seen in years, with so many
> twists and turns. The majority of punters have stuck to their guns and
> backed Michael D. Higgins. We've paid out early before and are yet to get it
> wrong, so let's hope this prediction works in our favour once more.

They still quoted odds for punters, putting Higgins as favourite at 1 to 3,
Gallagher as runner-up at 2 to 1, McGuinness at 25 to 1, Mitchell 40 to 1, Norris
66 to 1, Davis 100 to 1 and Dana at 250 to 1.

Paddy Power had also cut the odds on Higgins, making him favourite at 2
to 7, Gallagher 9 to 4 and McGuinness 25 to 1.

Gallagher meanwhile was answering questions about the Dundalk fund-
raiser. He told Michael Brennan of the *Irish Independent* that he was a 'grass-
roots' member of Fianna Fáil and had not given any personal donation at the
fund-raiser. He had not asked any of the guests for money. 'No, I didn't. I was
asked if I would let local business people know that the event as on, which I
did. But I collected no money.'

Meanwhile in Limerick, on the campaign trail with Mitchell, Enda Kenny
popped in to the Ann Summers shop in Cruise's Street, having just canvassed
Mass-goers at the city's Augustinian Church. The Fine Gael handler Vincent
Gribbin did his best to divert the Taoiseach, but Mitchell led the way, followed
by his wife and Kenny. A roar of approval went up from their supporters,
including Kieran O'Donnell TD and the former MEP John Cushnahan. There
was no-one in the shop except for one staff member, Debbie Cropper. Seán
Curtin from Press 22 got a picture of a grinning Taoiseach in the shop, and
afterwards Cropper said that they were the first politicians to canvass here and
that she would give Mitchell her vote. 'I've never seen a Taoiseach in a place
like this before,' she said.

———

The *Limerick Leader* published a brave questioning statement issued by Anne
McCabe, widow of Detective-Garda Jerry McCabe, who was shot dead by the
Provisional IRA during an armed robbery in 1996, saying that McGuinness met
her husband's killer in an IRA safe house.

> When Kevin Walsh, the ringleader of the Sinn Fein IRA volunteers
> convicted of killing my husband, Detective Garda Jerry McCabe, in Adare

on June 7, 1996, was released from Castlerea Prison our family attempted to move on as best we could with our lives.

Since that morning when the last of the murderers was freed into the waiting arms of Sinn Fein TD Martin Ferris we have refrained from any public comment concerning the political affairs of the State my husband died defending from the terror gangs of the Provisional IRA.

Now we feel we must break that silence to raise our concerns about the course of the current presidential election campaign, and specifically address matters that have arisen in the public domain regarding the knowledge and activities of Martin McGuinness in relation to those who perpetrated the murder of my husband and those individuals the Garda Siochana are still seeking to interview about that cowardly crime. In doing so we wish to endorse the courageous interventions of the Kelly, Hand, Stack and Clerkin families who still like us seek to have all of the IRA murderers involved in the killing of their loved ones brought to justice.

We know that the Garda Siochana believe that Martin McGuinness visited Kevin Walsh while he was hiding in a safe house in County Cavan. For what purpose did Mr McGuinness meet the killer of Jerry McCabe? Why did he not prevail upon Mr Walsh to hand himself in? Why did he fail to alert the Garda Siochana about the whereabouts of the man who was at the top of the most wanted list in this Republic?

The gardai believe that Mr McGuinness was a senior member of the Provisional IRA's Army Council for many years. This sinister body he regards as the legitimate government of Ireland. This loyalty to a secret illegal army presumably was more important to Mr McGuinness than helping the Garda Siochana to solve a vicious murder. It is a loyalty that we believe is incompatible with the office of President of Ireland.

As a senior IRA man Mr McGuinness is aware that two members of the IRA are still being sought for the murder of Jerry McCabe. As David Kelly said last week in Athlone: 'He knows who the killers of Recruit Garda Gary Sheehan and Private Paddy Kelly are.' We believe he also knows the current whereabouts of Paul Damery, and Gerry Roche who have been on the wanted list by An Garda Siochana since June 1996.

Mr McGuinness and his colleagues in Sinn Fein organised a vigorous campaign for the early release of the prisoners who murdered Jerry McCabe and he stated that Detective Garda McCabe's killers were 'entitled to their freedom.'

The Irish people are being asked to choose a head of state next week. A vote for Martin McGuinness is a vote for a man who refuses to assist the security forces of this Republic with its investigations into the most serious crimes committed against servants of the State. We don't believe this is an issue that can be ignored and brushed aside in the interests of 'peace'. We call on all other candidates seeking the office of president to demand from Mr McGuinness that he cooperate with the police into its ongoing inquiries into the terrorist crimes that claimed the lives of servants of this Republic.

This election is as much about the moral duties of those who seek high office as it is about their vision for the presidency and Ireland's future.

We want to move on and resume what passes for a normal life without a father and husband and brother. We can't move on if Mr McGuinness assumes he can aspire to the symbolic status of first citizen without first discharging the most basic responsibility of any citizen. If Martin McGuinness cannot or will not assist the authorities with its investigations into the murders of police officers, soldiers and prison officers how can we expect the rule of law to prevail under his Presidency?

This is a moment of truth for all of us.

Martin McGuinness owes every voter the truth and his opponents should unequivocally demand that he come clean. Otherwise we will have one law for members of Sinn Fein IRA and another law for the rest of us. In such a scenario, should Mr McGuinness prevail, the constitutional integrity of the democratic institutions of the state will be grievously undermined.

In Limerick, Enda Kenny said the McCabe family deserved to know the truth. He urged that if 'any of the candidates or anybody else who wants to stand by the profession of democratic politics' knew anything about the whereabouts of Paul Damery or Gerry Roche (who fled the country after the attack) they should contact the Gardaí.

Canvassing in Cashel, Co. Tipperary, McGuinness said there was not a 'smidgin' of truth in the charge that he met Kevin Walsh or knew the whereabouts of either Damery or Roche. Of Anne McCabe he said, 'My full sympathy goes to her. What happened to her and her family was totally unjustifiable, should never have happened. It was wrong and I unreservedly condemn it.'

On 'Liveline' the infamous interview Norris had given to Helen Lucy Burke for *Magill* in 2002 was broadcast. Norris said he had been given only thirty minutes' notice that it was about to be broadcast, 'even though RTE had the tapes for some days, I believe,' and commented that he thought 'the timing is interesting.'

Norris had challenged Burke to produce the tape during the summer, saying that his quotations had been taken out of context.

Norris said there was nothing new in the tape, and, unlike the previous storm, the 'Liveline' broadcast attracted little comment. Burke would subsequently say that she had found the tape recently but released it only in the last days of the campaign for 'impact . . . It would give people something to think about when they went to the polls. It might incite people to vote for Norris or against Norris.'

————

Mary Davis had returned to canvas her home county of Mayo and visited a local radio station before calling to Maureen Walsh's in Kiltimagh for tea and scones. Maureen had an oil painting of her son Louis in the living-room and a picture of Simon Cowell and the rest of the 'x Factor' team on the kitchen dresser. Then it was on to her old school in Kinaffe, where the children assembled to sing 'The Green and Red of Mayo' for her.

Saturday's *Irish Independent* again featured Gallagher on the front page, reporting more of his financial affairs, stating that he shared in a payment of €860,000, made up of salaries, rent owed and royalties. The Smarthomes payment was made as the company was losing money at the height of the property crash. Siobhán Creaton and Cormac McQuinn reported seeing records that showed that Smarthomes benefited from grants from state agencies totalling €830,000. A spokesperson for Smarthomes commented:

> The remuneration at the time for the directors was in line with the level of business the company was carrying out. The rent payable went to pay a mortgage on the building and was in line with rents in Co. Louth. The patents payable are in line with legal advice.

Inside the paper there was another picture of Kenny and Mitchell on the canvass trail. Having visited a sex shop, this time he was in the lingerie department of Debenham's in Patrick Street, Cork. Ralph Riegel reported:

> The sight of basques, suspenders and frilly knickers brought the entire FG entourage to an embarrassed halt—before a quick u-turn saw Mr Kenny, one MEP, two TDs, assembled councillors and bemused Young FG members rushed back to the safety of the perfume department.

In its final edition before the election the *Sunday Business Post*'s editorial said that next time we need a better campaign, and it called for reform of the nomination process.

> One by one the candidates have been subjected to intense and unmerciful scrutiny by the media; one by one they have wilted under it. Some have

been crushed by it. It has often been very harsh, but it has been necessary. This is what a campaign is: a searching job interview conducted largely by the media on the voters' behalf. Some people no doubt believe that the media scrutiny has been unfair and rather rough. All the candidates clearly believe this. But do voters really believe that they would be better served if facts about the candidates were kept hidden from them? We think not.

By Monday the 24th, with the polls to open on Thursday the 27th, the race for the Áras was a foregone conclusion according to four opinion polls published within twenty-four hours, confirming that Gallagher held a double-digit lead over Higgins. The REDC/*Sunday Business Post* poll showed Gallagher on 40 per cent to Higgins's 26 per cent. The Behaviour and Attitudes/*Sunday Times* poll put Gallagher on 38 per cent and Higgins on 26 per cent. The *Sunday Independent*/Quantum Research poll showed Gallagher at 41 per cent (up 20 per cent in a week) and Higgins at 31 per cent, a drop of five points yet still far ahead of his nearest rival, McGuinness, at 10 per cent. Other candidates failed to break into double digits.

Five hundred homes, chosen at random and telephoned by professional researchers 'using questions compiled by the editorial team at the *Sunday Independent*,' asked three other salient questions. Only 6 per cent of those questioned believed someone had tried to kill Dana. A total of 47 per cent felt that Gallagher hadn't dealt adequately with questions about his business affairs, while 51 per cent thought of Gallagher as a Fianna Fáil candidate.

That morning's *Irish Times* poll showed Gallagher at 40 per cent, with Higgins at 26 per cent. The poll was conducted among a national quota sample of 1,000 people in 100 sampling points around the country and was conducted within the guidelines laid down by the Marketing Society of Ireland and the European Society for Opinion and Market Research.

The political editor, Stephen Collins, analysed the results. The concentration on Gallagher's involvement with Fianna Fáil and his business dealings did not seem to have dented his lead, 'but these issues could still influence voters in the last few days of the campaign.' In addition, his role in Fianna Fáil had also helped him, as he was picking up a massive share of the Fianna Fáil vote—but not at the cost of votes from people who support other parties.

Reaching the target vote of 12½ per cent had to be a priority for those trailing with less than 10 per cent in the opinion polls—Norris at 8 per cent, Mitchell at 6 per cent and Dana and Davis at 3 per cent—if they wanted to recover any election expenses as a rebate from the tax payer.

The three Sunday opinion polls prompted fierce debate in the Higgins camp. Should he go 'negative' and increase the pressure on his only serious rival, Gallagher? He was advised to do so. He took the advice to heart and launched a blistering attack on Gallagher when he met journalists on a canvass in Grafton Street on a wet and windy Sunday afternoon with the Tánaiste, Eamon Gilmore. 'I am a hundred miles from the Celtic Tiger,' he said, describing himself as someone who had never had a share, who had never had a company. 'It's all in the public realm, every single aspect of what I do: what I own, what I am, what I do, my history . . . Why did I offer myself? Because I love Ireland.'

Higgins was reverting to type after a disciplined campaign of concentrating on short sound-bite answers. 'I am saying that I am more substantial and I am clearly the better candidate. We stand for a different version of Ireland.' Voters would focus on what both he and Gallagher had been doing for the past fifteen years.

Higgins said he had made the case against the excesses of the 'Celtic Tiger' and the property boom in the Dáil and had voted against the unlimited bank guarantee.

When I had the opportunity of being minister I founded a television station; I refunded the film industry; I built these canals, the Chester Beatty Library, Collins Barracks, the Folk Museum in Mayo and seventeen theatres. That's real. You don't have to go searching in the Companies Office to find that.

The following day's front page of the *Irish Daily Mail* characterised his attack as 'Higgins has meltdown'.

Chapter 14 ∾

| STEWARDS' INQUIRY

'What have you added to the knowledge of the people about the Presidency? With the questions you put to us tonight, what is that all about?' an enraged Gay Mitchell asked Pat Kenny on the live 'Frontline' television debate.

It was clear that the pressures of the campaign had prompted the tirade. Mitchell was languishing in the polls, and his own party was not delivering its national poll popularity to his campaign. He had been campaigning on serious issues, understood the role and both the limits and the requirements of the Constitution—and he was being asked what he considered an irrelevant, fatuous question.

Hundreds of thousands of voters, the biggest television debate audience, were watching, and he was arguing with the moderator—not with the other candidates—to win the hearts and minds of the viewers.

Standing behind a wooden lectern in a line with the other candidates, he prodded the air with his finger and unleashed his tirade, driven by weeks of frustration. It was Monday night, the polls would open on the following Thursday, and vital, valuable time was ticking away.

The straw that broke the camel's back was a question about the businessman Denis O'Brien, which was followed by a question to all the candidates, Would you appoint him to the Council of State? Earlier Mitchell had been asked about his own poll rating and said for the umpteenth time that he thought the opinion polls were inaccurate. He asked:

What is the relevance of that question? The President is supposed to be about leading the country, about being fair, about being inclusive. What is the relevance of that question? What is the relevance of most of these questions? What do you have to say about it, Pat? Why did you have to put most of those questions to us tonight?

Kenny was equally robust in his response.

At the very beginning we gave you the opportunity to describe your Presidency, how you might be regarded seven years from now, and you were all given ample opportunity to describe that, and then we moved on.

Then, most tellingly, Kenny went to the heart of the need for public scrutiny of the presidential candidates.

Can I just say to all, asking these questions, as diverse as they are, gives people an idea as to your temperament, your character, and it's certainly brought all those aspects out in the candidates tonight.

On the online version of the *Irish Independent* at www.independent.ie the former *Sunday Tribune* columnist Diarmuid Doyle reviewed the 'Frontline' programme.

Mitchell, the feisty no-hoper from Inchicore, finished last night's Frontline debate on RTE 1 in total meltdown, a question about Denis O'Brien's suitability to be on the Council of State having finally pushed him over the edge.

A few minutes earlier, he had announced his desire to throw excrement over somebody unnamed. While we were all trying to figure who he could possibly be talking about, he started to fire broadsides at Pat Kenny . . .

Mitchell usually looks like he's chewing on a bag of scorpions, but this was of a different order of crankiness altogether.

He'd been an irrelevance for most of the debate, and somewhere along the way—perhaps when asked whether he accepted personal responsibility for the huge gap in popularity between him, at less than 10 per cent in the polls, and his party, at close to 40 per cent—he realised that the game was up.

He had neither the charm nor the wit to recover. All that was left was a scream of despair.

———

In Killarney on the morning of Monday the 24th, Mary Davis, who was trailing in the opinion polls in joint last position with Dana, was the first out of the traps to open fire on the poll leader, Gallagher, saying the race was far from over. 'I absolutely think I can turn things around,' she said. 'I think a lot of people are undecided, and they are still waiting.'

Coverage of her membership of state boards had damaged her campaign, and some of the stories were very unfair, she contended.

There is absolutely no doubt that had an effect, and it came at a very crucial time in my campaign. It was an attack. The emphasis was on how to take me out of it. It was like demonising me for serving on three state boards, and no word at all about the eighteen voluntary organisations that I had served on. I was making a real difference in people's lives.

Asked about Gallagher, she said that all candidates had to stand on their record.

I'm not sure all of the answers have been provided at this point in time, but that is a matter for Seán Gallagher. Past records need to be investigated to ensure that everything is above board. The people of Ireland need to be happy about that.

But while Kenny had lit a fire under Mitchell, it was McGuinness who would take the central role in directing the content of the 'Frontline' debate, a riveting television production that was to shape the news agenda for the coming days and as time ran out for the candidates, with voting just over forty-eight hours away.

Earlier in the day a joint Google-Newstalk debate, hosted live from noon on the web and on the radio station, gave a clue to a new strategy that McGuinness would adopt with devastating effect later that evening.

The debate, moderated by the bookmaker and former Fine Gael Minister for Agriculture Ivan Yates, who jointly presented the morning news programme, put questions to candidates that had been posted on the internet, which included such diverse topics as religion, the Constitution, same-sex marriages and the candidate's vision for Ireland.

McGuinness waded into the debate, saying he had no doubt that the poll-topping Gallagher had strong links to Fianna Fáil.

I do think that there is no doubt whatsoever that Seán has been up to his neck in Fianna Fáil. Fianna Fáil is the party that ran the economy into the ground. Fianna Fáil was the party that was involved in the brown-envelope culture, the Galway tent, and involved in betraying the people of Ireland.

Yates, a combative and provocative interviewer on his breakfast show, was in top form for the debate. Referring to the latest opinion polls, which showed Higgins now trailing Gallagher, he thundered at Higgins: 'This was your election to lose and you've lost it,' he charged.

Slightly taken aback but retaining his calm air, Higgins responded: 'Well, that's the kind of comment that makes no sense at all. I think Thursday will decide that.'

Despite the blunt questioning, Higgins emerged as the winner in a post-debate opinion poll conducted in association with the Economic and Social Research Institute. He achieved 38 per cent of the vote; Gallagher and McGuinness both won 20 per cent, with Norris picking up 11 per cent. Mitchell achieved 6 per cent, Davis 3 per cent and Dana 2 per cent.

There was now just seven hours to prepare for the final televised debate of what had been a treadmill campaign of interviews and debates. For Higgins it would be a last chance to pull ahead in public opinion, which pundits thought might be showing a 'soft' lead for Gallagher, who would revert to his leading position and claim the keys to the Áras.

For Gallagher it was all about staying ahead, safe and sound. He would spend two hours with his advisers preparing for the debate in his four-storey head office in St Stephen's Green and in the Conrad Hotel. 'I was like a yo-yo running up and down the stairs during the campaign,' his media adviser Richard Moore would recall. 'What we really needed to co-ordinate the team was an open-plan office.'

There had been a shift in the focus of the campaign. The media were taking an increasing interest in Gallagher, who had suddenly been propelled into lead position despite little being known about him. His associations with Fianna Fáil and his business dealings would come under increased scrutiny.

A straw in the wind was that morning's editorial in the *Irish Times* and the *Evening Herald*'s front page, which bluntly asked: 'Who is he? Key questions around the presidential favourite Seán Gallagher.' Under the heading 'Mr Gallagher eyes the prize' it wrote:

> The big news from the poll is the continued surge in support for Mr Gallagher. He has doubled his level of support despite the media focus over the past week on his role in Fianna Fáil and, potentially more damaging, the controversy surrounding some of his business dealings.

The *Herald*'s lead story was more of an editorial than a hard news story.

> He's storming the polls and looks a dead cert to be our next President. But who is the real Seán Gallagher? As Ireland prepares to elect a man we know

so little about, the *Herald* today probes Seán Gallagher and the man behind the mask.

Perhaps ominously it added: 'Full story: pages 2, 3 and 12 and 13.'
The page 2 story said:

Nothing, no matter how unpalatable, can seem to stop the Seán Gallagher juggernaut from crashing into the Áras. Fresh links to Charles Haughey, €860,000 payments from one of his companies which received €830k in government funding, and today's *Herald* story that he charged €3,000 for one speech are having no effect on public opinion.   ———

Before the *Herald* hit the newsagents, voting had begun on the islands; soldiers serving overseas had already begun voting. The 760 voters on Tory, Gola, Aranmore, Inishbofin and Inishfree off the Donegal coast were the first islanders to vote that day. Ballot boxes were transported by helicopter, boat and ferry. Voting would continue on Inishbiggle, Inishturk, the Aran Islands and Clare Island the following day and on Wednesday, while islanders off the Cork coast would vote on the Thursday with mainland voters.

That evening, speaking direct to camera after the nine o'clock RTE1 news, Pat Kenny teed up his incipient drama, like an 'x Factor' promotion, with the dramatic introduction but without the show's trademark booming voice:

Seven people. One job. The final debate. What will happen here tonight will impact on voters' decisions, so there's clearly a lot at stake.

Fifteen minutes into the debate, after the candidates' opening statements, McGuinness launched his attack on Gallagher.

The grass-roots members of Fianna Fáil—in my opinion, there's absolutely nothing wrong with them. But there was something very rotten at the heart of the last administration, and as far as I'm concerned Seán was part of that.

He waited for the applause to die down before announcing that a few hours before he arrived at RTE he was contacted by a man who had been one of a group of between thirty and thirty-five people who

turned up at short notice at Dundalk's Crowne Plaza Hotel, each of them paying €5,000 to meet with the former Taoiseach Brian Cowen. This particular gentleman told me that not alone did Seán arrange it, Seán arranged for the photographs and brought the photographs to his house, and Seán also called around to his house to collect the cheque for €5,000.

Now that is indisputable. That's an absolute disgrace and clearly shows the rottenness of the system that went before in terms of the cronyism, the developers, the speculators and those who effectively destroyed the economy of this country, and Seán is up to his neck in all of that, and he can't deny it.

It was a bombshell, saying in effect that Gallagher was a senior member of the party he had distanced himself from as a junior member, and it associated him with the discredited culture of political donations that had marred political parties.

Kenny turned to Gallagher to allow him to respond, prompting: 'You're as thick as thieves with Fianna Fáil, and you're trying to deny it?'

'Can I tell you, Pat, that I've met you about as many times as I've met Brian Cowen,' responded Gallagher. Kenny cut across him to say that was just twice, so.

Gallagher went on to say that he had served on the party's Organisational Committee and went to two meetings in 2009 with the sole ambition of seeking to get support for business written into legislation.

Kenny referred to a story in that morning's *Irish Independent* that cited Gallagher's self-proclaimed association with the former Taoiseach Charlie Haughey and his experience of working in his campaign for election to the Fianna Fáil Ard-Chomhairle. Gallagher explained that he had met Haughey when he worked with Young Fianna Fáil in his early twenties, which prompted his decision to study in Maynooth to become a youth worker.

He explained that the fund-raising event in the summer of 2008 in Dundalk was set up by Fianna Fáil head office and that he had been asked, as a local businessman, to inform people about the event. 'I invited perhaps three or four,' he said.

But McGuinness repeated his charge about the fund-raising event and the cheque for €5,000.

Gallagher denied it. 'Not true,' he said.

McGuinness turned from facing front across his lectern directly to Gallagher on his left shoulder. 'He says it's not true. He's begging for someone to come forward and say that it was not true. I would caution you, Seán, at this stage, that you're in very murky waters.'

Gallagher rejected the cash-in-envelopes association. 'I have never been involved in that culture.' He then asked McGuinness to give the name and background of the man he had spoken to about the fund-raiser, before explaining:

I can tell you quite clearly I invited perhaps two to three people to that event. At the event people were asked if they'd like a photograph, as is normal at these functions, and I personally delivered—if that's the case, and I don't remember it—delivering a photograph, but I can tell you . . .

But McGuinness cut across him, saying he had called to the man's house to collect a cheque for €5,000.

'That's not correct,' said Gallagher.

'I have to say you're in deep, deep trouble,' said McGuinness, with a wide smile.

Moving the debate on, Kenny put the same question to all the candidates: would you resign if anything was to come out subsequent to your election that was concealed and that would have affected the outcome of the election? One by one they all said they would resign rather than put the country through an impeachment process.

Higgins affirmed that, yes, he would, and then, looking a little bemused, added to laughter: 'But it's a hypothetical question.'

However, Norris drew the biggest laughs to the same question when he responded with a grin: 'After exhaustive scrutiny by various sources, I'm sorry to disappoint the Irish nation, but the closet is absolutely empty.'

Norris had returned to form as a witty conversationalist and a good debater, interjecting with telling comments. The defensive fixed grin that he wore previously as he was quizzed about the clemency letters had gone; the race had moved on and he was enjoying the theatre of the 'Frontline' programme, reminding observers of his jolly persona when he entered the race.

In the same programme, when McGuinness was asked about his suitability for the role of President he spoke about how Irish he was, saying that Derry was as Irish as Cork. He began to reel off his political achievements—Minister of Education, Deputy First Minister—before Norris interrupted to ask, to much audience merriment, would those roles contrarily affect his bid for the role?

The focus was to turn to Gallagher again when a woman in the front row of the audience asked about his suitability for the job, 'given the trail of misunderstandings, accountancy errors and improper business practices that seem to have littered your career,' and suggested that his refusal to answer questions 'might bring the Presidency into disrepute at some point in the future?'

Gallagher was direct. All his business dealing were 100 per cent above board, he said.

The woman, Glenna Lynch, said that a cheque for €89,829 that had rested in his personal account should have been in a company account.

'Not so,' countered Gallagher.

'How does someone mislay a cheque for €89,000?' asked Kenny.

Lynch asked, 'Who was the client? Where did it come from?' As Gallagher tried to respond, she dismissed his explanations. 'Seán, you know that makes absolutely no sense.'

Gallagher explained that it was not a cheque from a speaking engagement but for one of his other businesses. It had been made out to the wrong account. The bookkeeper's secretary had put it into the account named on the cheque, and when his accountant's firm spotted it, in less than four weeks it was transferred to the correct account. No breach of company law took place, he asserted.

Gallagher went on to say that he was 100 per cent compliant as regards taxes and and had posted his certificate from the Revenue Commissioners online.

Kenny moved the debate on, addressing the theme of McGuinness's campaign, his IRA membership and the murderous actions of the IRA, referring to the murder of Jean McConville.

In December 1972 Jean McConville, a mother of ten young children, was abducted from her home by the IRA. She was shot in the head and her body secretly buried across the border on a beach in Co. Louth. Her children were taken into care by the local authority. The IRA claimed she had used a radio transmitter to pass information to British forces, a claim her children consistently denied. An investigation by the Police Ombudsman of Northern Ireland also rejected these claims.

Twenty years later the IRA gave information about where her body was buried. A prolonged search co-ordinated by the Garda Síochána was abandoned when no body could be found in the area specified. In August 2003 her body was accidentally found by members of the public while they were walking on Shelling Hill Beach, near Dundalk.

The *Evening Herald*'s television critic, Pat Stacey, summed up McGuinness's response to Kenny's questions, saying he simply unravelled when he found himself staring down the barrel of a direct question: Did he regard the IRA killings in Northern Ireland as murder or casualties of war?

He couldn't give a straight answer and fell back on a well-rehearsed routine which continually referred to dealing with the reality that there was 'a conflict'. There was one deeply disingenuous incident of double-speak after Kenny had asked him if he could bring himself to say he believed Jean McConville was murdered. 'I can bring myself to say the family of Jean McConville believes she was murdered,' he said.

Reintroducing the programme after the second commercial break, Kenny questioned Gallagher.

A development on the 'Martin McGuinness for President' Twitter account: Sinn Féin are saying they are going to produce the man who gave you the cheque for five grand. Do you want to change what you said, or are you still saying this simply didn't happen, or are they up to dirty tricks, or what?

Gallagher began by saying he had always tried to stay above negative campaigning and went on to start saying he understood, only for Kenny to ask him, 'You know who it is?'

Gallagher said yes, that he was a fuel-smuggler, a convicted criminal and someone with links to Sinn Féin and who had been investigated by the Criminal Assets Bureau.

'I don't want to get involved in this. I don't believe—' said Gallagher, who was interrupted and shouted down by the audience.

'Did you get a cheque from this guy or not?' asked Kenny.

'I have no recollection of getting a cheque from this guy. I can tell you—let me explain this very simply. I explained that there were two or three people that I asked. I don't know the man very well that's in question. So—'

Kenny cut across him in an incredulous tone: 'You went to a fuel-smuggler's house and invited him to a Fianna Fáil do?'

As Gallagher explained that he had been asked to contact local businessmen, McGuinness again repeated his charge.

'What I have done—I may well have delivered the photograph, if he gave me an envelope . . .' Gallagher attempted to say, before the audience interrupted him, jeering and hooting with laughter. He continued: 'If he gave me the cheque it was made out to Fianna Fáil headquarters and it was delivered, and that was that. It was nothing to do with me.'

'That's a clear admission of what I said earlier,' responded McGuinness.

Gallagher also made it clear that he was unaware of the background of the man—later named as Hugh Morgan—at the time of the fund-raiser.

Kenny did a round robin of the candidates, canvassing their views. Higgins replied that the matter needed to be clarified as a matter of urgency. Mitchell reverted to type and won audience approval: 'I already said that Seán should take the opportunity to clear this up, but I do think it's a bit much for Sinn Féin to be twittering or tweeting when Martin says he's not even a Sinn Féin candidate: we can't get that much out of Martin.' Norris was asked if he had a view. 'Not much,' he responded with deadpan humour. 'Except I think perhaps the reference to the envelope is a bit unfortunate,' to roars of laughter.

After the programme Sinn Féin denied it had issued any tweet, saying that it would produce the man who had spoken to McGuinness by phone and that it had informed him of the allegations about Gallagher's fund-raising.

The *Irish Independent* reported McGuinness as saying that the infamous Galway tent fund-raiser was now a thing of the past and that the meet-and-greet dinner event was the new method of raising funds.

What is very, very clear is that Sean is part of the Galway tent culture. The man I spoke to also told me during the course of the conversation that one explanation that was given for the meeting of thirty-odd people, a Fianna Fail fund-raiser, a meeting with the Taoiseach, which I consider to be totally inappropriate given these are builders and developers at a time when the country was going through a major crisis.

This man made it clear he was told that Fianna Fail had decided that the Galway tent operation had to fold up and this was going to be the alternative for fundraising.

In RTE's pre- and post-programme hospitality 'green' room Gallagher's media adviser recognised that his client was, in the words of McGuinness, in deep, deep trouble.

Chapter 15 ～

| THE GOING

Enda Kenny woke up on the day after the 'Frontline' debate to discover that he was still the country's favourite. The post-election honeymoon was clearly still on as his satisfaction ratings increased by one point, bringing him to a record 52 per cent.

The latest *Irish Times*/Ipsos/MRBI opinion poll would not reflect the impact of the 'Frontline' debate, as it was taken on the previous Wednesday and Thursday. Fine Gael topped the poll, with 36 per cent, up one point; the Labour Party picked up two points, to poll 19 per cent; Sinn Féin dropped three points, to 15 per cent; there was the same showing for Fianna Fáil, which had fallen one point; independents were up two points, to 14 per cent; and the Green Party dropped from 2 per cent to 1 per cent. Satisfaction with the coalition Government also nudged upwards by one point, to 37 per cent.

While the news for Kenny and his Government was good, the poll showed what could have been. The party vote was not transferring to Mitchell, the dream of the Áras was slipping away, and there were only days to go before the polling-stations opened.

The *Evening Herald*'s man on the sofa, Pat Stacey, scored the candidates in the game-changing 'Frontline' debate. Norris was the winner among the candidates, he said, awarding him 6 out of 10, saying he was witty and erudite and showed his sparkle of old—and made the point that opinion polls can become self-fulfilling prophecies.

Mary Davis was a good second at 5 out of 10. Stacey commented:

With Kenny seemingly uninterested in following up Davis's role on various state boards, she had a quiet night of it and acquitted herself well, especially when reinforcing her claim that the constitutional amendment to widen the powers of the Oireachtas inquiries could dilute the rights of citizens. If only she and some of the other candidates had been this coherent earlier in the campaign.

McGuinness was Gallagher's main tormentor, he said, and 'kept him wriggling on the hook.' But with McGuinness having fallen back on well-rehearsed routines about the 'conflict' and then saying, 'I can bring myself to say the family of Jean McConville believes she was murdered,' Stacey gave him 4 out of 10.

Gallagher looked stiff and uneasy, and questions about his association with Fianna Fáil and with Charlie Haughey, and about how he left over €80,000 resting in an account, left him 'looking rattled and unconvincing.' Gallagher dealing with the cheque allegations—saying the cheque was made out to Fianna Fáil head office and that it was delivered to them and had nothing to do with him—drew Stacey's comment 'Oops, afraid it had, Seán,' and merited him 3 out of 10.

Higgins scored 6 out of 10 for a solid performance with charm and self-deprecating quips about his age, while Mitchell scored 2 out of 10 and Dana nil.

The winner was—Pat Kenny. Awarding him 10 out of 10, Stacey said Kenny 'might be to light entertainment what Derek Mooney is to cage-fighting. But when he's in his proper setting Kenny is the best TV current affairs broadcaster we have.'

Fianna Fáil issued a statement on Tuesday confirming that it received a donation of €5,000 from Mr Morgan before the Crowne Plaza event took place. The dinner raised less than €100,000, and Mr Morgan's cheque, dated 26 June, was lodged to the party account on 30 June of that year. It refused to elaborate on who else gave donations at the fund-raiser that Gallagher helped organise. Previously, asked about the fund-raiser attended by the then Taoiseach, Brian Cowen, Micheál Martin declined to comment, stating: 'We're not involved in this presidential campaign.'

Meanwhile the bookies had been gauging the public mood, on the grounds that the public put their money where their mouth was. One punter put €6,500 on Higgins to win after the 'Frontline' debate, forcing Paddy Power to reduce their odds, from 11:10 to evens. The morning after the debate more money piled onto Higgins, tightening his odds to 8:13 and pushing the former favourite, Gallagher, from odds on to 6:5. Higgins moved to 8:13 (from 5:2) on Monday, Gallagher 6:5 (from 1:4), McGuinness 25:1 (from 50:1) and Norris 33:1 (from 66:1). Mitchell, Davis and Dana were offered at 300:1.

Since the election campaign had begun, money had moved onto different candidates in significant amounts as the political dynamic unfolded, resulting in five changes at the top of the presidential betting since the start of the year.

On the news-stands the music magazine *Hot Press* came out with a significant and expected endorsement of Higgins. He was an old friend of the magazine's founder, Niall Stokes, and had contributed a column to the magazine for years.

It also published an interview with Mitchell, who remained on message throughout, returning to the main points of his launch speech, his upbringing and his political career, and he revisited the death-penalty issue. He also denied that he had attacked McGuinness, saying he had asked three reasonable questions: when did he leave the IRA, why does he say he's not the Sinn Féin candidate and what is the status of his salary and his industrial wage. According to Mitchell, all the candidates

> are in a poll situation which is very volatile . . . The only thing you can compare it with are the polls at the last presidential election fourteen years ago. Those polls were totally wrong. They said Adi Roche would get 38 per cent and she actually got less than 7 per cent. So I wouldn't put much trust in polls right now.

It was a familiar statement that he used again and again to justify an expected surge in poll support.

'You said you wouldn't put much trust in polls, but Fine Gael conduct polls. So are any of them believable?' asked Jackie Hayden, who conducted the interview.

> I think presidential polls are very volatile. It's like a national by-election. Unlike a general election, where you have candidates in each constituency, you don't have policy debates like what are you going to do about my local school or about education generally, or about the local hospital or tax.
>
> So, the debates take place about a lot of celebrity stuff. Near the end of the campaign people look at it and say, hold on, where's our country at and who do we really need as president? Then they make a more serious decision and firm up their views.

'But you're not doing well in the poll, so what's the explanation for that?' asked Hayden.

> Well, I don't know. I suspect there may be people who feel that if they say they're not going to vote Fine Gael in the polls it might cause Fine Gael to sit up and take notice.

I'm the only candidate running on the Government side who's not retired. I'm an active member of the Fine Gael parliamentary party and an MEP. So that may be drawing some of the opprobrium. That's in the poll stages. In the final stages, people want the Government to take decisions. They want this sorted. It's in a mess and they want a future for their children. In their heart of hearts people want leadership and firm decisions made.

————

On Tuesday morning Gallagher was prepared and on his way to the RTE studios for his turn as a candidate for a scheduled interview with Pat Kenny. It was both an opportunity to clear up the questions raised on the previous evening's 'Frontline' programme and a valuable opportunity to have the last word in a one-to-one interview. It was another high-wire act, with the potential to win back lost ground or to compound a problem. Three opinion polls still showed him firm favourite, and that morning's *Irish Times* poll gave him comfort, showing that Fine Gael supporters were unwilling to transfer their support for the Government to Mitchell.

It was fight-back time. Gallagher would say he was the victim of a smear campaign, but time was running out for patching up the damage inflicted on him in the previous evening's television debate. The exchange had shown him fudging as he changed his story while under pressure from McGuinness and in response to a Sinn Féin tweet that it would produce a witness.

On air, Kenny replayed part of the previous evening's programme and asked Gallagher if he'd like to comment.

Gallagher confirmed that he had been contacted by a journalist the previous week making inquiries about the fund-raiser and went on to say that he realised as soon as he began topping the poll that he would come under political attack. Sinn Féin had set out to sabotage his campaign, he claimed.

Last night Martin McGuinness, with the help of Hugh Morgan, who loaded the gun, pulled the trigger with a different story that I allegedly went to the man's house to deliver a photograph of him with the Taoiseach.

I could have fudged the issue, but one of the things I've said in my campaign is 'never tell untruths'. I do not recall going to this man's house. I couldn't tell you or take you to his house, or even to his office, because I never met the man.

Kenny wondered how he could not have been prepared for such questions, having got advance notice the previous week of such a line of inquiry.

Gallagher said that Sinn Féin was orchestrating a hatchet job, but that any cheque he may have received would have been sent straight to Fianna Fáil head office, and he referred to the Fianna Fáil statement issued that morning. He said his lack of recollection was an honest mistake and also emphasised that the Fianna Fáil fund-raising event was legal.

Gallagher was clearly spooked by the way the campaign had turned and felt the pressure mounting. He broadened his attack to include a member of the studio audience, specifically the woman in the front row who had confronted him about his business dealings. He challenged Kenny:

> Who was the businesswoman, and what's her background, and where does she come from, and what party is she attached to? I'm tired of people being wheeled out with agendas. You put that person here in front of me, and let them tell you and me and the nation their background. You wheel a person out on a programme and they throw allegations at me without them defining who they are, what their political allegiance is, and I find that difficult.

Kenny assured him to the contrary. The woman had rung the show's office earlier in the morning to assure them that she had no political connections, he said. He then played a clip from the previous evening's programme and asked Gallagher to respond.

> The wording of that woman—I'm not casting aspersions on her, but you don't know why she was there or her political background. She's talking about 'improper', 'voter worry'. Is she in somebody else's campaign team, trying to take down my campaign to boost somebody else's campaign? Is she a member of a political party?

It was a question, with hindsight, he shouldn't have asked live on air; he should have stuck to the lawyer's adage that you never ask a question if you don't already know the answer.

Clarification came, almost instantly, when Glenna Lynch rang in to the show.

> I'm so shocked. I was driving on my way to see someone, a client in work, and I had to stop the car. It's absolutely shocking.

If jaws dropping around the country could have made a sound it would have been a deafening roar. It was to make for unmissable, unpredictable radio.

I'm a completely normal person. I have three children. I'm married, I live in Stillorgan. I am not involved in any political party. I don't know a single politician, and I think it's extraordinary that Seán believes normal people, voters, don't have the right to ask a question

She said she had emailed 'The Frontline' a list of questions, and a researcher had contacted her and asked if she'd come onto the programme and ask a question from the audience. 'I could have asked him questions for two hours,' she said.

She accused Gallagher of receiving 'extraordinary and probably unprecedented state funding' and that 'in the course of that money flowing into your company, yourself and your partner basically raided the coffers.'

'Not so,' said Gallagher, firmly denying the accusation, saying he had always acted with integrity and honesty. 'I stand over everything I have done as being impeccable with honesty and integrity. I absolutely refute any allegations that will be framed in such a way as to make me, my company or my integrity to be undermined in any way.'

He complained that his time was eaten into in dealing with the controversies and that he believed Kenny should have allowed him time to outline the vision he had for addressing the issues.

After the program Lynch explained:

I felt I just had to ring up. He just couldn't get away with that. I felt on that programme this morning that he was trying to say it was a Sinn Féin conspiracy against him. I just thought that's not fair.

She revealed that she was a former Fianna Fáil voter, until the second-last general election, when she changed her allegiance. She said she now intended voting for Higgins in the presidential election.

Does that mean that he thinks that all other women and all ordinary voters don't have an opinion and don't want answers to those questions?
I feel it's like we have somebody who is running for the Presidency and we can't ask him questions, and it's an attack on him if we do. Questions are questions, and it's reasonable to ask them.

She explained that she picked up her information from the newspapers, as she had a big interest in current affairs, and added that revelations in the media that Gallagher had charged GAA clubs in his home county of Louth as much as €5,000 to help out with applications for sports grants 'says so much about the man.'

While Lynch had brought Gallagher's record as an entrepreneur and businessman and his dealings into the glare of the television and radio spotlight, these issues had also been pursued in the print media. Colm Keena, the public affairs correspondent of the *Irish Times*, that morning published an article alleging that questions surrounding Gallagher's financial affairs remained. Gallagher's main source of income appeared to be from 'motivational speaking', he said, and his fortunes rose with the property bubble but hit a wall with the rest of the building industry as that bubble burst.

The good news for RTE was that the 'Frontline' programme was a huge success. Ratings for the station arrived that morning. They showed that the final debate in the race for the Áras had attracted a peak audience of 900,000, which would turn out to be just over half the total valid poll. The first television debate of the campaign, on TV3 with Vincent Browne, had a comparably high peak audience of 820,500 viewers.

Meanwhile that morning in Drogheda, McGuinness took a few minutes off the canvass with Gerry Adams in his constituency to talk to the press and to repeat his 'Frontline' claims about Gallagher.

> The reality is that the assertion I made that there was an event in the Crowne Plaza Hotel in Dundalk attended by something in the region of thirty people, which raised, according to Fianna Fáil, in the region of €100,000, €5,000 of which came from an individual who told me on the telephone before I went onto the 'Frontline' programme that Seán Gallagher travelled to his home and collected a cheque for €5,000. Seán effectively admitted that in the course of that discussion last night. I think that's all that needs to be said about it. The people of Ireland will judge whether that represents the rottenness at the heart of the previous administration or not.

He would also admit that there was a 'misunderstanding' about when the cheque was given.

> Due to a misunderstanding during the conversation I was under the impression the cheque was delivered after the event but it's only overnight I have learnt the cheque was delivered four days before the event took place.

That afternoon Gallagher was back to his campaign headquarters to prepare for a recorded interview with Matt Cooper of Today FM. He wrote a feature article for the following day's *Evening Herald* that would be headlined 'I'm victim of Sinn Féin ambush for connecting McGuinness to killing' and began preparing for the live 6:01 RTE news interview with Bryan Dobson.

On Today FM he was asked about his business dealings. Cooper was a former business editor of the *Irish Independent*, and he explained that the cheque for €82,829 from Beach House (which dealt with his income from speaking engagements and a Dragons' Den investment) that had first been treated as a loan to him was moved back into the correct account within four weeks when spotted by his accountants. It was an honest mistake by his bookkeeper's secretary. There was no breach of company law, he said.

Outside the shared Today FM and Newstalk offices, behind the St Stephen's Green Shopping Centre, he was doorstepped by Colm Keena of the *Irish Times*. Gallagher refused to answer his questions, referring them to his staff. Clearly angry, he said, 'I am going to clear my name from a lie and a smear campaign from Sinn Féin. I was on national TV last night and I was accused of being a liar, and I am going to deal with this first.'

The following day Keena published a half-page article, 'Gallagher: the issues', which included his business record, including the loans he had taken out of his company as a director, other draw-downs from the company, such as patent royalties, rent and director's fees, and the level of state support for his company.

He recorded Gallagher's denials, including comments by a corporate governance expert, Niamh Brennan, about a 'bad vibe' about these aspects of Gallagher's record and Glenna Lynch's accusation that he had raided the coffers of his business. He claimed that everything he had done was above board and denied weakening his company by taking too much money out of it, saying it had survived because it was prudently managed.

The three other issues were his father's farm, patent and company income and the Louth County Enterprise Board.

———

The Higgins campaign bus was doing a sweep through the south-east with a stop-over in Gaelcholáiste Cheatharlach in Carlow. Then, with his wife at his side, it was on to Dublin for a final press conference at the Alexander Hotel in Fenian Street.

The Labour Party leader, Eamon Gilmore, and its candidate were 'on message'. It was a two-horse race, and, perhaps sensing weakness in his opponent, Higgins took a second swipe at an increasingly beleaguered Gallagher. He said he had a clear policy difference with Gallagher in relation to job creation—a central plank in Gallagher's campaign. Higgins acknowledged that if he was elected he could not behave as he had when he was a minister, but he could be a source of inspiration at home while assisting in attracting foreign investment. 'Now that's very different from saying one wants to elect an entrepreneur. I believe in entrepreneurship, but social entrepreneurship,' he said.

He went on to address both issues that were damaging to Gallagher. He admitted he was not an expert in the management of companies but said there appeared to be public concern about transparency. 'The public anxiety should be fully satisfied. And that's important.' All candidates had to be 'so fully transparent as to answer any question of trust and openness which people may put to us.' Asked about the 'Frontline' programme, he admitted to being surprised about the manner in which McGuinness had raised allegations about Gallagher collecting a €5,000 cheque at a fund-raising event. 'It is true to say that as it unfolded more detail was emerging, but I really don't want to get involved in labelling . . . All the questions should be answered.'

Gilmore was more robust. It's a two-horse race, he claimed, and the contest would be close in both first preferences and transfers. He reminded voters that Higgins was attracting support throughout the political campaign and, further appealing to any 'soft' vote, he urged voters to switch their vote to the Labour Party, borrowing the Davis slogan, for a candidate who 'would command respect at home and abroad.'

Hugh Morgan, the man identified by Gallagher in all but name, issued a statement the same afternoon. His company, Morgan Fuels, a sponsor of the Armagh GAA football team since 1997, owns more than four thousand filling stations in Ireland and Britain and continental Europe, including the Netherlands, Slovenia and Italy. The company also has a heating-oil business and has offices in Newry and Dundalk.

Morgan had surfaced in February 2011 before the general election when it emerged that he owned the building in Dundalk where Gerry Adams had his constituency office in his first tilt at winning office in the Republic. Asked at the time if he had any qualms about renting an office from a convicted fuel-smuggler, Adams replied: 'It's a totally bona fide legal contract between Sinn Féin and the owner of the building. It's a short-term commercial lease. Sin é. That's it.'

A Sinn Féin spokesperson confirmed that, eight months later, Gerry Adams TD was still based in the Park Street premises and that a new lease had not yet been signed.

In 1998, aged thirty-eight, Morgan was given a suspended sentence when he pleaded guilty to charges of fuel-smuggling. The court was told he had paid £500,000 in excise duties and VAT owed on smuggled fuel. He was also ordered to pay £25,000 towards the costs of the prosecution.

In his statement, Morgan claimed that Gallagher had contacted him by phone, was invited to the dinner and asked for a donation.

> He first phoned me on 6 June 2008 and invited me to the fund-raiser. In the course of the call he requested a donation of €5,000 for Fianna Fáil. On 27 June Seán Gallagher visited my business premises at Killean, Co. Armagh. I wrote a cheque for €5,000 and gave it to him personally. In return for the €5,000 donation I was promised a private audience with the Taoiseach and I would get a photograph taken with him.

He went on to say that on the night of the fund-raiser Gallagher introduced him to Cowen and that he had his photograph taken with him. 'Approximately one week later Seán Gallagher called back to my business and gave me the photograph.' He also made the photograph available to the media.

He confirmed that he was convicted of tax evasion fourteen years previously in relation to fuel-smuggling in Northern Ireland. 'As a consequence of that I have repaid the exchequer and paid a substantial fine. I was never investigated by CAB or any other agency in the Republic.' He added that his business was successful and employed more than eighty people in Ireland, North and South.

The figure of €5,000 was significant, as, according to the law, only donations of €5,078.95 or more have to be declared to the Standards in Public Office Commission. The donation, therefore, effectually remained secret.

RTE's Six One news that evening led with the Gallagher, McGuinness and Morgan claims. Gallagher gave a recorded interview, broadcast as the lead item, claiming furiously that 'this is political assassination'.

In the second half of the programme he was interviewed live in the studio. Bryan Dobson put the Morgan statement to him: 'He said you phoned him up to invite him to attend this event and that he would then make a donation of five thousand euros to Fianna Fáil, that you visited him twice in his business premises and on one of those occasions he handed you over the cheque for five thousand euros. Is that the case?'

Gallagher replied: 'This is part of the ongoing smear campaign that I have endured for over a week from Sinn Féin, and the point is that it culminated last night live on TV on 'Frontline's' programme. Mr McGuinness made the accusation that I had visited Hugh Morgan's home after the event to deliver a photograph of the fund-raising event with the Taoiseach.'

'Did you visit him on that occasion to deliver the photograph?'

'No. What I stated last night—the accusation was that I visited his home after the event to deliver a photograph and I was given a cheque. Now, that's an absolute lie. When I challenged Mr McGuinness today he retracted that, but only following the fact that Fianna Fáil came out this morning, having checked their records, to show that the cheque was made out and lodged before the event took place.'

'This is the man directly involved, Hugh Morgan, and what he's saying is that he indeed handed over the cheque in advance of the event, and he handed it over to you.'

'And that's what he's claiming now, and this allegation arose last week as soon as I began to emerge in the poll.'

'Is this the case or not?'

'It is not the case.'

'Can you be absolutely sure of that?'

'Absolutely, because the night that Mr Morgan turned up to the event—and I didn't know Mr Morgan before the event—I was contacted by Fianna Fáil headquarters to invite some local business people. I invited possibly three or four. Mr Morgan was one of them, referenced by somebody else. He was the sponsor of the Armagh football team. I had never met the man; when he turned up on the night I didn't recognise him.'

'Sorry—if you can be so emphatic that you did not visit his business premises and collect a cheque now, why were you not in a position to give that clear answer last night when this issue arose in the first place?'

'Yes, let me clarify. This issue arose last week when I was asked did I collect a cheque before the event, which was the allegation last week. I clarified.'

'Which is this—is the same allegation as tonight. Mr Morgan has been consistent in what he has been saying on this.'

'No, what happened was, the allegation was levelled last week. The paper in question investigated and found that Mr Morgan had a criminal record and didn't go ahead with it. I clarified at that point that I had not met Mr Morgan before the event.'

'Just to clarify, he had a conviction for smuggling.'

'For fuel-smuggling, yes. He had also given his premises to Gerry Adams for his election campaign. I disputed that allegation, and it wasn't run. Last night it turned up in a different guise, where Mr McGuinness levelled these allegations after claiming that he had spoken to Mr Morgan two hours previously.'

'What you said last night was that you had no recollection of getting a cheque from this guy.'

'Correct.'

'Okay, is it that you had no recollection—it might have happened but you can't recall—or can you say emphatically that you did not receive a cheque?'

Again Gallagher replied emphatically. 'I did not receive a cheque from Mr Morgan.'

'Why didn't you say that when you were asked it the first time around? Because the truth is generally fairly simple, isn't it?'

'Well, here's the point. I made the point all along that I did not receive a cheque from this man before the event. Mr McGuinness then threw this at me last night, followed by a tweet from Sinn Féin to say that they were going to produce this man. I was shell-shocked that this was thrown in and that he was saying that I had delivered a photograph and collected a cheque, when I knew quite clearly, in my mind—'

'Why were you "shell-shocked" when a journalist came to your campaign team last week and said that these allegations had been made by Hugh Morgan in Armagh?'

'Hugh Morgan said that I had collected a cheque in advance of—and I am quite clear, and Mr Morgan said in his statement that he wrote a cheque on the 27th when I visited the premises. Fianna Fáil are saying here in their statement that the cheque was written on the 26th and was lodged.'

'It's dated on the 26th, they said. Incidentally, they don't tell us how the cheque was delivered to Fianna Fáil headquarters, whether it arrived in the post or whether it was delivered personally, or whether you went in with it as the Fianna Fáil bagman.'

'I wasn't a Fianna Fáil bagman. The organisation—headquarters—had organised this event. I let some business people know about it. I did not collect a cheque off Mr Morgan and—and Mr McGuinness's attempt last night was an absolute slur and is what I have been dealing with, Bryan, for the last week and a half, allegation after allegation in an attempt, solely because I am now leading in the polls.'

'Mr Morgan says that he never met you before, he didn't know you when you made this approach—it was a cold call, if you like, to see if he'd come along, because the cheque—'

'Somebody had given me his name.'

'Presumably when you phoned him up you did tell him there would be a donation of five thousand euros expected to attend this?'

'Well, I was asked to say that there was a level of up to five thousand euros. I have no idea—'

'That's what you told him?'

'Correct.'

'That he would pay five thousand for this?'

'Up to.'

'But previously your spokesman said you did not solicit a donation for Fianna Fáil. That's not true, is it?'

'That's not true. What I said was that there was a fund-raising event happening, and if he'd like to come along he could make a donation.'

'Right. And that doesn't count as soliciting? No?'

'I'm saying that that's what I said.'

'Is that not soliciting a donation?'

'It could be.'

'Then why did your spokesman say you did not solicit a donation?'

'Well, I'm not sure what my spokesman said, but I'm telling you now exactly what I said.'

'I'll give you the exact quote,' said Dobson. Reading the paper on his desk, he continued: 'Your spokesman said that "at no point did he actively solicit any donations. He would have been in touch with a number of people he knew, to tell them it was on", only to discover you didn't know Mr Morgan—so that's not true either.'

'Let me clarify this. I asked a number of business people in the area did they want to attend, and one of them obviously recommended Mr Morgan as somebody who might like to attend.'

'So you did ask people you didn't know, it now turns out.'

'I did ask people I did know, and if they recommended somebody else that they knew. And so—'

Dobson honed in on the admission. 'So you did invite people you didn't know, and you did solicit a donation from at least one of those people?'

'This was a fund-raising event, and I informed anybody that I rang that there was a level up to which they could nominate or donate, and that they would make that payable to Fianna Fáil headquarters.'

Dobson sat back in his seat and softened his tone. 'None of this is remarkable at all. It's what you'd expect anybody who is involved in a political party to do after an election, to try and rebuild the party coffers: ring around people who have assets and say, "Will you come along and support us?" You were doing what any other senior political Fianna Fáil figure would do?'

Gallagher wasn't relaxing. 'I wasn't a senior figure.'

'You were a campaign director for the TD at the time.'

'I had been in 2007. I was quite happy to assist in this event by inviting local business people. The allegation is made that there is something corrupt. The cheque was made out to Fianna Fáil.'

'The allegation is that you haven't been telling the truth, Mr Gallagher. That's the allegation.'

'No, not at all.'

'There is no allegation of corruption. The allegation is that you haven't been telling the truth. There is no allegation of corruption here at all.'

'I always tell the truth, and anyone who knows and has watched my campaign knows two things: that I do not get involved in negative campaigning, and I always tell the truth—always.'

There the interview ended.

It had been a forensic interrogation by a skilled interviewer, who had got his subject to admit to telling two untruths, about recruiting potential donors and then soliciting money.

————

Gallagher's attack on the motivation of Glenna Lynch made him appear bullying and unwilling to take questions from a member of the public about his financial dealings, which had been a smouldering controversy over the last days of the campaign. The crucial question now was, with a fifteen-point lead in the opinion polls, had he done enough to maintain that lead with the public—or was his campaign damaged beyond repair?

Credibility is a central characteristic required by a presidential candidate, and already political pundits were openly saying he was damaged. How much? was the question.

A broadcast moratorium was due to take effect from 2 p.m. the following day, which would end all radio and TV broadcast discussion and speculation about the election. For Gallagher the moratorium was a two-edged sword. It shut down debate and exposure on the airwaves; and that would be a positive if he had satisfactorily answered his critics and explained his case fully. The question remained: had he fudged or left questions unanswered? Only the electorate would answer those questions definitively.

Political commentators had a sense of *déjà vu* as Gallagher contradicted his own version of events. In the midst of the October 1990 presidential election campaign the Fianna Fáil nominee and front runner Brian Lenihan (senior) had denied that he had tried to contact the President eight years earlier to urge him not to dissolve the Dáil. However, a postgraduate politics student and journalist, Jim Duffy, produced a tape to the *Irish Times* that recorded Lenihan agreeing that he had phoned the Áras.

Lenihan's campaign imploded. He tried to rescue it by going on the six o'clock TV news, when he memorably said that 'on mature reflection' he recalled that he had in fact phoned the Áras. His campaign collapsed, and almost overnight his popularity plummeted by eighteen points in the opinion polls. He was subsequently sacked as a minister by the Taoiseach, Charles Haughey, and the presidential race was won by Mary Robinson.

The following morning's papers, on the eve of voting, confirmed Gallagher's worst fears. The onslaught was changing public opinion. Two opinion polls put Higgins as the favoured candidate. Boylesports carried out an opinion poll in the wake of the 'Frontline' programme that had 47 per cent saying they would trust Michael D. Higgins and 44 per cent that they would not trust Seán Gallagher as President.

A total of 28 per cent of those surveyed said the debate changed their minds on who they would vote for; 34 per cent would give Higgins their number 1, and 25 per cent would give Gallagher their number 1, and 24 per cent would prefer McGuinness.

Ballotbox.ie, which campaigns for the extension of voting rights to the Irish diaspora, published an opinion poll it had conducted over the previous six days. A total of 2,581 people took part. Higgins took 40 per cent of first preferences, Norris came second, with 24 per cent, McGuinness polled 18 per cent, while Gallagher polled 10 per cent. Mitchell and Davis scored 3 per cent each and Dana 1 per cent.

The web site required voters to provide their passport details to ensure they were eligible to participate in the real vote. Voters from the Republic were blocked with a firewall, but votes were recorded from countries as diverse as England, Australia, Canada, the United States, Nicaragua, El Salvador, Yemen and Kazakhstan. The poll was carried out with no specific reference to the 'Frontline' programme, but its result added to a growing swell of support for Higgins.

The *Irish Times* had dedicated two full pages to letters to the editor, and they ranged across the spectrum of public opinion, whether indignant, entertaining, questioning or whimsical. A serial correspondent on political matters was David Carroll, a pharmacist and political activist from Boyle, Co. Roscommon.

> The closing stage dénouement of Seán Gallagher's role as a Fianna Fáil fundraiser, collecting cheques for thousands of euros in brown envelopes, is all the worse for his initial denial that it happened, followed by his failure to recollect the specifics despite it only being a couple of years ago. Sadly, 'FF', 'cheques', 'envelopes' and 'poor recollection' are all back in the public discourse again.
>
> Mr Gallagher may well be a proxy candidate for Fianna Fáil, but he in no way represents the ideals to which the party ought to aspire if it is to survive. We have been down this road before and the time has come for us to decide what we want to stand for—populism or principles. If he wins tomorrow, it's no victory for Fianna Fáil.

The last opinion poll of the day was published shortly before the broadcasting moratorium began. Today FM's hugely popular 'Ray D'Arcy Show' opened the text lines, asking listeners: Who will you be voting for tomorrow?

The mid-morning show recorded 249,000 listeners in the most recent audience figures released shortly before the election, only 30,000 behind its competitor, Pat Kenny's 'Today Show' on RTE—figures that showed the significant reach to voting audiences. A total of 5,414 votes were cast. As it was a text vote, there could be multiple votes by supporters or even organised groups of supporters. The result, however, was instructive.

Mitchell came last, with 2½ per cent, Dana was slightly ahead with 3 per cent, while Davis scored 5 per cent and Norris 9½ per cent, which would suggest that they would not receive state funding for their election bid. Above the threshold was McGuinness, polling at 18 per cent, Higgins at 28 per cent and Gallagher topping the poll at 33½ per cent—a lead, but a much-eroded one that could see Higgins win on transfers.

Fergus Finlay, a former Labour Party contender, in his eve-of-poll *Evening Herald* column wrote that

> for many years to come, people will talk about the master stroke that catapulted Martin McGuinness into this election, and the even more powerful intervention he made on Monday night, when he fatally destroyed Seán Gallagher's credibility. The man, who had had a 'sporadic' relationship with Fianna Fáil, was suddenly revealed as a complete, and compliant, insider.

Finlay said he believed that McGuinness's intervention would not win him the election, and that

> the hand grenade McGuinness blew up under Gallagher's credibility, as devastating as it was, may still not be enough to cost Gallagher the election. But at least it crystallised the choice—and that crystal-clear choice will be what will cost Seán Gallagher this election. Good and decent people contested too, and they will lose, damaged beyond recovery by the most searching examination possible, unable to fight back against some of the most unfair accusations made.

He went on to endorse Higgins.

> Because the choice couldn't be clearer, we all know now that we're choosing between a spoofer and a statesman, an 'entrepreneur' and a man of real and transparent values.

Below the Finlay article the *Herald* published the feature Gallagher had written the previous day in the midst of the 'Frontline' storm. Gallagher's fury and bitterness breathed like a dragon's fire from the text. He raged in a vitriolic attack on Sinn Féin and a personal attack on McGuinness, rather than another attempt to explain the issues.

The programme had produced a political ambush,

> cooked up in the bowels of a party that has been such a destructive influence on this country. Sinn Féin has turned the corner in abandoning its armed struggle, but it has swapped its Armalites for the forceps for delivering a crude political hatchet job which must breed despair in any voter who believes that the discourse of elections should be above such tactics.
>
> Martin McGuinness may have proven himself to have certain qualities in helping deliver peace to this island but he is no statesman. He comes from the narrowest of confines of almost bitter party politics, a view of Ireland through a twisted prism.
>
> As I rose in the polls, the ferocity of the mud being flung in my direction intensified, almost to a frenzy. Everything seemed to be fair game, from questioning whether I had bought a farm with my late father to unwarranted intrusions into the lives of my siblings.
>
> When I dared last Sunday in the *Herald*'s sister paper the *Sunday Independent* to ask Mr McGuinness to assist the Gardaí with any information he might have regarding the murder of Detective Garda Jerry McCabe, the full wrath of Sinn Féin's muck-raking was unleashed. It may serve Sinn Féin well. Mr McGuinness may increase their vote, possibly by a sizeable margin on their showing in the recent General Election. But at what cost?
>
> I will hold my head up high that I ran a clean campaign, focused on reinventing this country through a return to community endeavour and participation. Whether the public can recover a sense of hope from a campaign mired in destructiveness and negativity is another matter.

Across the central fold of the paper the *Herald* devoted an unprecedented page to an editorial and a cartoon that excoriated McGuinness. The cartoon, published previously with an Eoghan Harris magazine article, was of McGuinness with an automatic rifle in one hand, money and a pistol poking out from his pockets, holding a Tricolour that had a clenched fist on the central panel, and displaying a devil's tail. A balaclava lay on the floor in front of him. The message was blunt.

A presidential election is completely different to any other political contest. It is not about carving up political power, deciding policies or choosing a

Government. Instead it is a moment where we make a powerful symbolic statement about what kind of country we want to be. That's why no sensible Irish person should even think about giving their number one vote to Martin McGuinness tomorrow.

The Sinn Féin candidate has certainly had a powerful impact on this race, transforming it from a bland soap opera into a struggle for the soul of the nation.

Now that the campaign is almost over, the bottom line is that there are 1,800 good reasons not to put this man in the Áras—one for every innocent victim that the IRA murdered during his time as their ruthless commander.

Over the last couple of weeks, the relatives of IRA victims have finally made their voices heard—and as far as they are concerned, the fact that he has the cheek to run at all is a slap in the face to the memory of their loved ones. From the moment he was confronted by the son of murdered soldier Patrick Kelly in an Athlone shopping centre it was clear that this was one lie he couldn't get away with. His opinion poll numbers have been dropping ever since, a clear sign that Sinn Féin's decision to bring him south was not the tactical masterstroke they thought.

Whatever Gallagher may have done for Fianna Fáil, his actions are surely in a different moral universe to what McGuinness and his armed henchmen got away with in the North for 25 blood soaked years.

Sinn Féin once boasted that they would take power in the republic 'with an Armalite in one hand and a ballot paper in the other'. Tomorrow, with a simple pencil and paper, we can make a powerful statement on behalf of the 1,800 innocent victims who can no longer speak for themselves.

It was a powerful piece of writing, unprecedented in that it didn't favour a party or individual but instead clearly and forcibly argued its view about the necessity to keep McGuinness and his party out at all costs.

The election threw up a diversity of opinion and a fierce focus of attention. In the closing week the media concentrated relentlessly on the three leading contenders—Gallagher, Higgins and McGuinness—who had moved to centre stage, ignoring the trailing candidates.

Earlier the same morning the *Herald*'s sister paper, the *Irish Independent*, published a column that argued that 'Gallagher's myth-making will bring shame on Aras.' Bruce Arnold called on Gallagher to resign from the election, because of 'sustained misleading of the public.' He went on to claim that his web site, from the start of the campaign, had been misleading about his involvement with Fianna Fáil, claiming he had invented a character for himself in his efforts to distance himself from Fianna Fáil.

Arnold also turned on the voting public.

I find all of this a deeply shocking narrative that cannot be explained, excused or exonerated. It is made worse by the gullibility of the Irish public. Their gobdaw acceptance of this man and his amazing, sustained fiction about himself has turned what many think of as a pretender into a leading contender for the highest office in the land.

——

On the campaign trail, things were not improving for either Mitchell or Davis. Davis's campaign coach, wrapped in her picture and campaign messages, broke down on the final day of the campaign in Maynooth.

In St Stephen's Green Shopping Centre, Gay Mitchell maintained that he would do better in the only poll that counted, rather than the predicted opinion polls. Fionnan Sheahan reported:

> In trademark fashion, it took him 45 seconds to get tetchy with the media and 1 minute 45 seconds to get into an argument over the questions he was being asked. 'I'm very unhappy with the number of times I have been asked about the polls and the campaign and never been asked about the Presidency or the fact that we have 437,000 people unemployed and the President can make a real difference. It's clear to me that people need to look at the media and particularly the media that you represent and ask for some sort of standards,' he said.

The *Irish Independent* printed a photograph of McGuinness in Andy Dolan's hair salon in Ballyfermot, Dublin, on the day before polling, with Adams hovering over him with a comb and scissors. Reportedly delighted with his 'Frontline' demolition of Gallagher's candidacy, McGuinness was reported as saying:

> It probably turned out to be the most important debate of all the debates that were held. I think we've seen over the last forty-eight hours the real Sean Gallagher, and I would like to think I've done a service to the people of Ireland in terms of dealing with an issue which clearly showed Sean to be absolutely at the heart of the culture of cronyism.

On the editorial page the *Irish Independent* offered its own service to the people of Ireland, urging 'Don't vote for Martin McGuinness,' saying he had failed to be honest with the electorate and did not deserve an endorsement.

From the off, Sinn Fein's Martin McGuinness has lied about his role in the IRA and has been consistently ambiguous in his condemnation of atrocities carried out by the Provisional IRA throughout the Troubles.

The families of victims of the IRA on this side of the Border have bravely spoken out against Mr McGuinness's candidacy and their voices merit being listened to.

Nobody can credibly believe Mr McGuinness's ridiculous claim he left the IRA in 1974 and played no further role—not even Sinn Fein members.

Based upon their own experiences, former garda commissioners and ministers for justice have testified that he played a leading role in the IRA throughout the organisation's campaign. The protection of the democratic institutions in a sovereign state remains paramount. Until Mr McGuinness is prepared to be open about his past, he cannot be trusted to be elected as president 'down here'.

Reminding the electorate that it was Judgement Day, the *Star*'s commentator Eamon Dunphy described Gallagher as a 'three-dollar bill', Mitchell as unwanted by his own party and Norris as carrying too much baggage. He praised McGuinness and Pat Kenny for 'exposing' Gallagher. 'Tomorrow we might be talking about President Gallagher. If we are then we will be a laughing stock and rightly so.' Dunphy also said that McGuinness had been 'savaged in the most appalling manner by official Ireland's media.'

That morning's *Star*'s front page referred to 'Hurricane Higgins' and said he was poised to win the Presidency according to the bookies, who had been correct in their predictions for the past two presidential elections. Its editorial was uncharacteristically coded in its message to readers, urging them to exercise their right to vote but to ask themselves the question, 'Which of the candidates is least likely over the next seven years to have something come back to haunt them from their past—something that could embarrass the nation and make us wish he or she was not in the Áras?'

Chapter 16 ∿

| WINNER ALL RIGHT

Members of the Defence Forces serving overseas, who were the first to vote for their new supreme commander, could watch the results unfold in real time through Irish and international news web sites. The media centre in Dublin Castle was the central studio for television and radio stations.

Within an hour of the black polling-boxes being opened it was clear that Higgins was on course for a historic victory. There had been a dramatic swing from the leader in the opinion polls, Seán Gallagher. Gallagher's campaign, as expected, had collapsed. McGuinness had polled well, boosted the party's profile and justified its decision to run a candidate.

The real loser would be Mitchell. He had failed to attract the huge popular vote for Fine Gael to his candidacy—and his director of elections would later draw up a report for presentation to the party leadership about the campaign and how the ultimate and attainable prize had slipped from their grasp.

'I'd like to send my love and congratulations to Michael D, Sabina and the rest of the family,' said a gracious David Norris. He had arrived at the count centre at 11 a.m., two hours after it had opened. RTE and other radio stations were offering regular updates and commentary as tallies poured in from count centres around the country.

Norris conceded defeat. It was a good day for Ireland, he said, adding that he'd be

happy to be an Irishman under the presidency of Michael D. Higgins. Although he is a Labour Party member, Michael D, like myself, is a little bit of a maverick, and when you have such a concentration of power in the hands of the coalition I think it's good to have somebody who will be in a position, morally and intellectually, to speak out on behalf of the marginalised. I know that Michael D will do that.

Among the commentators, pundits and experts drawn from various fields to provide comment for RTE's coverage during the count was the former presidential candidate Mary Banotti. She described her own presidential election campaign fourteen years earlier as 'completely exhausting'. From an outside broadcast unit in the gardens of Dublin Castle she told RTE's Miriam O'Callaghan:

> I hope Michael D is lying in bed with a cold compress over his eyes before he has to face the hordes tonight. I was going to say he'd make a lovely little President, but no, he'll be a great President.

Then, reflecting on her own experience, she said the 2011 campaign must have been 'horrendous' for all the candidates. 'We can all cheer for him later.'

Later, O'Callaghan, who had been speculated on as a possible presidential candidate herself, was spotted by the *Irish Examiner* drying her hair in a drab corridor of the castle complex before going live with Martin McGuinness. Shaun Connolly reported in the *Examiner*:

> It was all hugs as he bounded onto the podium, relieved he had done well enough to justify the rough and tumble of the contest—and also, no doubt secretly relieved he would not have to spend seven years in what he calls 'down here.'
>
> As his thoughts returned to Derry he quoted 'The Town I Love So Well,' musing: 'What's done is done, what's won is won.' But he did not need to deliver the next line to sum up the six contenders blown out of the race by the quiet storm of Michael D: 'And what's lost is lost and gone for ever.'

McGuinness had earlier done a tour of the count centre, a huge smile on his face, looking more like a winner than a loser. He was accompanied by Gerry Adams and Pearse Doherty, the Donegal South-West TD. There had been brief speculation that Doherty could have been the Sinn Féin nominee, until it was realised he was too young and had yet to have a thirty-fifth birthday.

The *Examiner* also noted that an 'ashen-faced' Mitchell had crept into the hall almost unnoticed. 'Mitchell, looking as miserable as his share of the vote, at least managed to keep a lid on his temper and we were spared another "Gay rage outburst",' Shaun Connolly wrote.

There was a media scrum as the candidates arrived for the declaration of the first count shortly after nine o'clock that evening, twelve hours after the first boxes were opened, from as far away as Cos. Donegal and Kerry and as near as the RDS hall across the road.

Seán Gallagher, flanked by his wife, offered his congratulations to Higgins. Shortly after 4:30 p.m. Gallagher had phoned Higgins to offer his congratulations and concede victory. In a subsequent statement he said:

> In the last hour I've called Michael D. Higgins to congratulate him on his performance and his success in this election. He will have my full support as President, and I sincerely thank him for a positive campaign. His slogan stated that he would be a President to be proud of, and I believe he will be that President.

As the first count was announced hours later he said:

> I want to wish him every success and congratulate him and indeed wish his wife, Sabina, and family every success and health and happiness for his seven years. I truly wish him well.

He also thanked his own team, which had grown from two people three months earlier to two thousand volunteers, and said he had no regrets. 'None whatsoever. It's a great thing in Ireland that anybody, an ordinary person like me, can step forward and run for President of Ireland.'

In a corner of the media centre in Dublin Castle, Greg McKevitt, Niall Glynn and Claire Brennan welcomed untold millions to the BBC blog, which ran through the day. It was a multimedia blog, including sound-bites, video and print. The following extracts give a concise account of the closing minutes.

> BBC 20.58. RTE is reporting that it's just five minutes until a first preference declaration. Cheers are resounding around Dublin castle as the president elect Michael D Higgins arrives.
>
> BBC. 21.01. Labour's Joan Burton refers to the influence of the final presidential debate on Monday night, saying that because of the floods in Dublin and other parts of the country, more people were at home watching the debate. She estimated that about three quarters of voters watched the programme.
>
> BBC 21.01. A flurry of candidates have just arrived at Dublin Castle. David Norris, Gay Mitchell and the president in waiting Michael D Higgins are here. I grab the first interview with Gay Mitchell, asking him if he's disappointed. 'I just need to gather my thoughts,' he tells me abruptly.

BBC 21.12. And it has been confirmed: Michael D Higgins tops the first preference poll with 701,101 votes.

BBC 21.12. Michael D Higgins is congratulated at the count in Dublin Castle.

BBC 21.13. Mary Davis (48,657) and Dana Rosemary Scallon (51,220) are eliminated.

BBC 21.18. And here's the rest of the vote details as we move into the second stage of counting . . . Sean Gallagher (504,964), Martin McGuinness (243,030), Gay Mitchell (113,321) and David Norris (109,469).

BBC 21.21. So with vote transfers to be reallocated from Mary Davis and Dana Rosemary Scallon, Michael D Higgins hasn't got far to go to be confirmed as president. He's on 701,101 and the quota he has to reach is 885,882.

BBC 21.24. A few more statistics for you . . . the turnout was 56.1%—1,790,438 people voted out of a potential electorate of 3,191,157.

BBC 21.32. Michael D Higgins celebrates his victory with his wife Sabina.

Mary Davis, who trailed in last, described the campaign as both dirty and challenging.

I knew going into the campaign that it was going to be difficult. I didn't go into the campaign with my eyes closed for sure. It was more challenging at times than I expected. It was a dirty campaign, there's no doubt about that, you can see that yourselves. Hopefully, I have led the way for others to be courageous enough to stand up and go forward.

The candidates lined up on the stage for the announcement of the result of the first count. Dana was the last to arrive. Would she try for the position again in seven years' time? she was asked. Prompting smiles all around, she replied:

I think I might be too old to run for President again . . . Oh, no, maybe not, because I'd still be younger than Michael D. But, however, I think it's really great to have come through a campaign . . .

The vote was adjourned to the following day.

That evening in his city-centre apartment Higgins began drafting his acceptance speech for the following day. He wanted to use postcards as prompts but couldn't find any. His family turned the apartment upside down; and then Higgins had a brainwave. He tore open the packaging of the new shirt he had bought for the following day, and pulled out the cardboard insert and cut it into postcard size for his speech.

'I will work with head and heart for the people of Ireland,' he would pledge from his makeshift prompt cards to a crowd of supporters, mostly wearing red ties or roses.

———

Both Mitchell and Davis failed to turn up for the final count and for the formal declaration by the returning officer, Ríona Ní Fhlannghaile. Davis would later apologise, saying she was unaware of the protocol and that no slight was intended.

Mitchell, who won just 6½ per cent of the vote, would tell RTE news that organisational and strategic issues lost him the election.

I lost it because people felt having a Fine Gael President and a Fine Gael Taoiseach was not ideal. There's probably other reasons: organisational reasons, strategic reasons. People want to nitpick. I was on the platform if anyone wanted to meet me. I spoke to Michael privately and publicly, and I wish him the best. He'll make a fine President. I think it's sour grapes to be asking me this. I'm tired. I've behaved honourably throughout.

Only the top three vote-catchers—Higgins, Gallagher and McGuinness—breached the 12½ per cent threshold, entitling them to recoup €200,000 each for election expenses.

Summing up the Labour Party's delight with the Higgins victory, his election agent, Kevin O'Driscoll, said their candidate had won the highest number of first-preference votes ever, and the highest number of transfers, and had received the highest number of votes ever—more than a million votes.

Shortly after 7 p.m. that evening the Defence Forces' director of administration, Col. Joe Dowling, called to the Higgins apartment in Dublin to deliver a scroll, the official notification of his election. Throughout the city similar couriers were delivering the results to the President, the Chief Justice, the Ceann Comhairle of the Dáil, the Cathaoirleach of the Seanad, and the secretary-general to the President, Adrian O'Neill.

Having delivered the scroll, Col. Dowling saluted his new supreme commander—and former university lecturer when he was a sociology student in the 1970s.

The *Irish Times* editorial of 29 October put into context the race for the Áras, centring on the emergent main candidates.

In reality, there were issues the independent candidates failed to address adequately. [Gallagher] reacted with disdain and then anger when a businesswoman legitimately questioned accounts related to one of his businesses. He repeatedly refused to respond to unanswered questions from *Irish Times* journalist Colm Keena about an €82,829 loan from one of his companies, and of his fund-raising on behalf of Fianna Fáil. Connotations associated with collecting cheques in brown envelopes resurfaced in the public consciousness. His predicament was compounded by initial denials, dissembling and poor radio interviews on subsequent days.

The *Irish Times* also noted the significance of the demise of the campaigning poster, the growth and influence of social media in stirring debate and fuelling rumour, and the dominance of negative campaigning.

For many candidates it was a brutal experience, sometimes unfairly so. The entrance of Mr McGuinness into the race broadened the debate on the new Ireland—but it is one requiring a fuller reconciliation of its past, rather than a simplistic 'let's move on'. The reward for Sinn Féin, nonetheless, is a greater foothold on the political landscape of the island of Ireland.

Stephen Collins wrote that there was some irony in the fact that, by taking Gallagher down, McGuinness contributed to the Labour Party's victory.

It seems, though, that in the battle for top dog status on the Opposition side of the Dáil scuppering a Fianna Fáil-linked candidate was the primary objective for Sinn Féin.

This time around Seán Gallagher's lack of political experience contributed to his inept handling of the McGuinness claims. His failure to come up with convincing answers to serious questions on live television about Fianna Fáil fund-raising activities raised fundamental doubts about his ability to handle the office of president.

Gallagher's business record also came under intense scrutiny in the final days of the campaign both in the print and broadcast media and ultimately it all proved too much. For all the public's desire to elect a president from outside the ranks of established politicians, it was the most experienced politician of all who showed the skills necessary to win the race.

The blame for Fine Gael's failure to win the Áras should be shared by the candidate and the party, Collins said.

The key people who masterminded the most successful general election in the history of the party last February knew that Gay Mitchell was not the best candidate for the presidency but they did not do nearly enough to let their TDs and councillors know of their concerns.

Then when Mitchell was selected against their better judgment he was largely left to his own devices . . . By the time the party leadership focused on the election, it was too late . . . The TDs, councillors and party activists who selected the candidate blithely assumed the presidency was theirs for the taking. They have suffered a rude awakening.

———

'I sent fake SF tweet,' an anonymous man confirmed to the *Irish Mail on Sunday*. The tweet Pat Kenny had read out on 'The Frontline' was a fake. It had thrown Gallagher's composure, and under pressure from McGuinness he said he may have collected an envelope from Hugh Morgan. Sinn Féin had always denied it sent the message.

Interviewed anonymously by email, the 33-year-old man described himself as not a member of any political party and at present as working in Dublin at a social media company and previously in Government departments. 'When I noticed the mainstream media were not questioning Gallagher enough, I decided to tweet during the debate. I had no plan to impact on the campaign at the start. I voted for McG, but I am not a member of SF. However, I have voted SF recently as they have policies I support.' Asked about RTE broadcasting his message, he said, 'It was a major mess up on their part. I know in other media organisations that the account is genuine and has not been hacked.' He added that he posted the bombshell tweet as 'just a bit of fun' and that he was 'just relaying a rumour'.

On 22 November, Gallagher submitted a 22-page complaint to the Broadcasting Authority of Ireland about his 'ambush' on 'The Frontline'. He was seeking an apology to be broadcast on 'The Frontline', a public hearing that RTE should be compelled to attend to explain how a fake tweet purporting to be from Sinn Féin was broadcast, and for RTE to publish and implement a policy for the treatment of material posted on the internet.

At 10:39 p.m. a tweet was posted on the account @mcguinness4pres. This was not the official McGuinness campaign account, which was @Martin4Prez2011. The tweet stated: 'The man that Gallagher took the cheque from will be at a press conference tomorrow.'

At 10:49 p.m., immediately after an advertising break, Pat Kenny addressed Gallagher. 'On the Martin McGuinness for President account, Sinn Féin are saying they are going to produce the man who gave you the cheque for five grand.'

At 11:02 p.m. a tweet from the official McGuinness campaign account stated: 'As official campaign twitter for martin we need to point out that we have made no comment on the Gallagher FF donation issue.' Gallagher said this tweet was posted to the Áras11 feed, from which RTE had taken the fake tweet earlier, but also to RTE's own feed, rtefl.

Gallagher contends that RTE knew the original tweet was a fake from that moment but made no attempt to correct it before the end of the programme at 11.28 p.m. He also alleges that RTE deliberately concealed information that would have revealed the tweet as a fake by not broadcasting corrective information released by the McGuinness campaign, and that the station made public material that it knew, or ought to have known, was false. He claims that this material distorted a crucial debate and recklessly misled him, the audience and the electorate. RTE had abandoned such journalistic norms as may be expected of it to fulfil a 'self-appointed role as a game-changer'.

Gallagher added that, notwithstanding this, RTE did not make any reference to the official tweet. It failed to draw this information to his attention, or to the attention of McGuinness, the audience, viewers or the electorate at any time during the remaining twenty-six minutes of the live broadcast.

He also accused RTE of failing to take reasonable steps to confirm the origin and contents of the fake tweet and of failing to put the tweet to McGuinness's team for corroboration during the preceding commercial break.

A spokesperson for Gallagher confirmed that a legal option of challenging the result of the election in the courts would not be pursued.

RTE confirmed that it had received the complaint and said that it would be dealing with it through the Broadcasting Authority.

———

On the same Sunday, President-elect Higgins went on RTE radio to talk about his campaign. He couldn't answer one question: it was still too painful for him, a friend explained. The question was, What would your father think of you becoming President?

It brought back painful memories of a hard childhood and a long journey to the Park. Born in Limerick, his father first rented and then bought a small pub, but it was hard to make ends meet. Five-year-old Michael and his younger brother, John, were sent to live with their unmarried aunt and uncle in Co. Clare. His twin sisters stayed with their parents. When his aunt died, his uncle convinced the Higgins family to move in with him, but, while there was great joy at the reunion, the fifties were a hungry time, with nettles growing on the holed roof and broken windows remaining unrepaired.

Michael attended St Flannan's in Ennis, cycling the round trip of twelve miles every day. He took a job in a local factory to 'pay the debts in the local shop' and later worked as a clerical officer in the ESB, after abandoning his ambition to train as a teacher in St Patrick's College, Dublin. A friend in the Legion of Mary, Redmond Corbett, would later lend him £200, which he used to go to University College, Galway, where he joined Fianna Fáil. He later studied at the Universities of Manchester and Indiana.

He switched his political affiliation to the Labour Party, inspired by Noël Browne, the former minister who was credited with eradicating TB in Ireland. He failed in his Dáil election attempts in 1969 and 1973 but won a seat in the subsequent Seanad elections. The same year he married Sabina, a joint founder of the Focus Theatre group; he had met her in 1969 at a party in the house of journalist Mary Kenny, celebrating Kenny's appointment as women's editor of the *Irish Press*. 'I was just blown over the night I met him,' recalled Sabina (69). 'I reached out and held his hand and that was that.' Sabina gave up acting but remained active in community theatre and drama education and did a masters degree in drama when she was sixty.

As a committed Irish-speaker and as Minister for Arts in two coalition Governments, between 1993 and 1997 he established TG4 and scrapped the ban under section 31 of the Broadcasting Act on broadcasting interviews with Sinn Féin.

The outgoing President, Mary McAleese, sent a final message to the country's citizens, saying she had set the theme of building bridges for her Presidency, and she hoped that she had honoured that theme.

I finish my second term as President in a very different Ireland from the one we knew in the winter of 1997. Then, both peace and prosperity seemed elusive. Peace eventually came 'dropping slow' but it was sturdily built.

Prosperity landed like a whirlwind bringing increased quality of life and a multicultural society but its foundations were weak and so, as we struggle out of recession, unemployment and indebtedness, the deep desire for a prosperous island at peace is the enterprise we are all committed to by working together in friendship and good neighbourliness. Our problems were all of human making—our solutions too are mostly in our own gift.

I have been privileged during the last fourteen years to see the fruits of the work of so many problem-solvers and so many bridge-builders. I look forward to seeing a new generation succeed in making prosperity and peace 'rhyme' at last, transforming the story of this island into something the world will talk about with respect and awe for centuries to come. As I approach the final days of my time as President of Ireland, I thank the people of Ireland who, fourteen years ago, placed their trust and faith in me.

I hope I have vindicated that faith in the intervening years when it was my joy and privilege to serve my country.

On the morning of the 11th day of the 11th month of 2011, rain fell ceaselessly, but it miraculously cleared minutes before the new President arrived at Dublin Castle for his inauguration. At 11:25 a.m., having spent the night in the renovated Farmleigh House in the Phoenix Park, President-elect Higgins and his wife travelled through the city-centre streets to the former home of the pre-independence British administration, escorted by an army motorcycle squadron.

Brought to the Connolly Room, where the workers' leader had been brought before execution, he was granted his request for a few minutes' silent reflection and then, accompanied by the Tánaiste, Eamon Gilmore, and the Minister for Education, Ruairí Quinn, he was escorted to the majestic St Patrick's Hall, with its high ceilings and splendid gilt decoration.

At noon an inter-faith celebratory ceremony began, which included Christian, Jewish and Muslim blessings and, for the first time at this ceremony, a humanist reflection. Twenty-five minutes later President-elect Higgins rose from the oak chair specially crafted for the occasion to take the oath of office, administered by the Chief Justice, Susan Denham, witnessed at close hand by his predecessors, the two Marys, who stood behind him.

A fanfare announcing that the new President had taken office was sounded and the presidential flag, with its gold harp on a blue field, was raised at Dublin Castle and Áras an Uachtaráin. Three Air Corps planes performed a fly-past overhead while simultaneously the army fired a 21-gun salute from Collins Barracks, which echoed across the city centre.

It was just before 1 p.m. when the new President gave his inaugural address, followed by the playing of the national anthem and the inspection of a guard of honour from the 5th Infantry Battalion in the Castle Yard under the command of Capt. Emmet Harney, with the colours carried by Lt Deirdre Carbery, whose father, Col. Declan Carbery, served for a period as aide-de-camp to the outgoing President, Mary McAleese.

President Higgins and his wife were then brought to Áras an Uachtaráin for lunch with ninety personal guests. They were issued with a badge to wear that allowed them onto buses to ferry them to the Áras and through security provided by military police. The new President returned to the Castle after 6 p.m. for a state reception held for 1,500 people to celebrate the inauguration.

The newly elected President's inaugural address had begun on a humble note, saying there was no greater honour than to have been elected Uachtarán na hÉireann.

I thank you, the people of Ireland, for the honour you have bestowed upon me and I accept and appreciate the great responsibilities of that office . . .

I wish to acknowledge the immense contribution of those who have previously served in this office, particularly the two great women who have immediately preceded me.

They have made contributions that developed our consciousness of human rights, inclusion, and the important task of deepening and sustaining peace within and between communities in every part of our Island. It is work I will endeavour to continue and build upon.

As your President, I am grateful for the extent of the support, the strong mandate, you have given me. I also realise the challenges that I face, that we face together, in closing a chapter that has left us fragile as an economy but most of all wounded as a society, with unacceptable levels of unemployment, mortgage insecurity, collapsing property values and many broken expectations.

During my campaign for the Presidency, I encountered that pain particularly among the most vulnerable of our people. However, I also recognise the will of all of our people to move beyond anger, frustration or cynicism and to draw on our shared strengths. To close the chapter on that which has failed, that which was not the best version of ourselves as a people, and open a new chapter based on a different version of our Irishness—will require a transition in our political thinking, in our view of the public world, in our institutions, and, most difficult of all, in our consciousness . . .

We must seek to build together an active, inclusive citizenship, based on participation, equality, respect for all and the flowering of creativity in all its forms. A confident people is our hope, a people at ease with itself, a people that grasps the deep meaning of the proverb 'Ní neart go cur le chéile'—our strength lies in our common weal—our social solidarity . . .

My Presidency will be a Presidency of transformation, recognising and building on the many positive initiatives already under way in communities, in the economy, and in individual and collective efforts throughout our land. It will be a Presidency that celebrates all of our possibilities. It will seek to be of assistance and encouragement to investment and job creation, to innovation and original thinking—a Presidency of ideas—recognising and open to new paradigms of thought and action. It will aspire to turn the best of ideas into living realities for all of our people, realising our limitless possibilities—ár bhféidearthachtaí gan teorainn . . .

In preparing for my Presidency, I recognise that our long struggle for freedom has produced a people who believe in the right of the individual mind to see the world in its own way and indeed that individual innovation and independence of mind has given Ireland many distinguished contributors in culture and science, often insufficiently celebrated.

However, in more recent years, we saw the rise of a different kind of individualism—closer to an egotism based on purely material considerations—that tended to value the worth of a person in terms of the accumulation of wealth rather then their fundamental dignity. That was our loss, the source in part, of our present difficulties. Now it is time to turn to an older wisdom that, while respecting material comfort and security as a basic right of all, also recognises that many of the most valuable things in life cannot be measured . . .

Our arts celebrate the people talking, singing, dancing and ultimately communing with each other. This is what James Connolly meant when he said that 'Ireland without her people means nothing to me.' Connolly took pride in the past but, of course, felt that those who excessively worshipped that past were sometimes seeking to escape from the struggle and challenge of the present. He believed that Ireland was a work in progress, a country still to be fully imagined and invented—and that the future was exhilarating precisely in the sense that it was not fully knowable, measurable.

The demands and the rewards of building a real and inclusive Republic in its fullest sense remain as a challenge for us all, but it is one we should embrace together.

So concluded the ninth President of the Republic of Ireland, Michael D. Higgins.

APPENDIX:

Presidential election count, 2011

Michael D. Higgins was declared President-elect after reaching the quota on the fourth and final count. He secured more than one million votes. The total poll was 1,771,762; the quota was 885,882. The turn-out was 56 per cent.

The count took longer than expected and resumed at 9 a.m. following an adjournment after the second count at 1:30 a.m.

First count
Higgins, Michael D.: 701,101 (39.6 per cent)
Gallagher, Seán: 504,964 (28.5 per cent)
McGuinness, Martin: 243,030 (13.7 per cent)
Mitchell, Gay: 113,321 (6.4 per cent)
Norris, David: 109,469 (6.2 per cent)
Scallon, Dana Rosemary: 51,220 (2.9 per cent)
Davis, Mary: 48,657 (2.7 per cent)

Second count
Davis and Scallon were eliminated after the first count was announced, and their transfers were subsequently distributed.

Higgins, Michael D.: + 29,379 (730,480)
Gallagher, Seán: + 24,437 (529,401)
McGuinness, Martin: + 9,581 (252,611)
Mitchell, Gay: + 14,036 (127,357)
Norris, David: + 7,057 (116,526)

Third count
No-one reached the quota following the second count. The count was adjourned following the elimination of Norris.

Higgins, Michael D.: + 62,648 (793,128)
Gallagher, Seán: + 18,972 (548,373)
McGuinness, Martin: + 12,585 (265,196)
Mitchell, Gay: + 8,952 (136,309)

Fourth count

Mitchell and McGuinness were eliminated at the end of the third count. They were excluded together, as the total of their votes was lower than that of the next-highest candidate, Gallagher.

Higgins, Michael D.: + 213,976 (1,007,104)
Gallagher, Seán: + 79,741 (628,114)